When Words Deny the World

Other Books by Stephen Henighan

Other Americas, 1990, Novel

Nights in the Yungas, 1992, Stories

The Places Where Names Vanish, 1998, Novel

North of Tourism, 1999, Stories

Assuming the Light:
The Parisian Literary Apprenticeship of Miguel Angel Asturias,
1999, Criticism

Lost Province: Adventures in a Moldovan Family,
2002, Travel

When Words Deny the World

THE RESHAPING
OF CANADIAN WRITING

STEPHEN HENIGHAN

The Porcupine's Quill

NATIONAL LIBRARY OF CANADA CATALOGUING IN PUBLICATION DATA

Henighan, Stephen, 1960–

When words deny the world : the reshaping of Canadian writing

ISBN 0-88984-240-X

1. Canadian fiction (English)-History and Criticism.
2. Globalization-Social aspects.   I. Title.

PS8199.H46 2002   C813'.5409
C2002-900541-8
PR9192.5.H46 2002

2   3   •   04   03   02

Published by The Porcupine's Quill
68 Main Street, Erin, Ontario NOB 1TO
www.sentex.net/˜pql

Readied for the press by John Metcalf; copy edited by Doris Cowan.
Typeset in Minion, printed on Zephyr Antique laid,
and bound at The Porcupine's Quill Inc.

Represented in Canada by the Literary Press Group.
Trade orders are available from General Distribution Services.

We acknowledge the support of the Ontario Arts Council,
and the Canada Council for the Arts for our publishing program.
The financial support of the Government of Canada
through the Book Publishing Industry Development Program
is also gratefully acknowledged.

ONTARIO ARTS COUNCIL
CONSEIL DES ARTS DE L'ONTARIO

Canada

The Canada Council | Le Conseil des Arts
for the Arts | du Canada

The writer's very reason for being
is protest, contradiction and criticism.

            – Mario Vargas Llosa, 'Literature is Fire'

Table of Contents

Introduction
One Writer Reads...

Every writer is first a reader. The impulse to write may spring out of the soil of experience, but the seeds of an author's work lie in the stories he has read, the tones of the language resounding in her memory. Literature passes its genetic code from generation to generation; in each era, like a hardy crop, the strain mutates to cope with environmental conditions.

But, unlike that of the berry or the grain, the writer's adaptation is a contradictory, personal affair. Rather than developing into a variant species better suited to a warmer or cooler climate, the writer – the writer who grips us and forces us to *see* – evolves in opposition to his environment. The writer emerges as an antagonist to or subtle dissenter from the surrounding society; she wants to write the books that are missing from the catalogue of literature.

In this sense fiction – and particularly the novel – takes root at the meeting point of the writer's critical engagement with literature and his critique of society. Haphazard, omnivorous adolescent reading – nearly always a prerequisite for later writing – becomes more focused as time passes. We pursue those works most useful to us, most illuminating of the problems we are struggling to dramatize. From the vast annals of world literature, we choose our ancestors. While fiction, overtly or covertly, almost always keeps one foot in the past – in the era in which we were raised, in the unsolved mysteries of our childhoods, in distorted reflections of patterns that the passage of time has etched on our psyches – we write, publish and make our careers in the present.

I began to write as an adolescent in rural eastern Ontario in the 1970s. My fiction writing was interrupted by my university education in the United States, where I wrote little more than the standard undergraduate quotient of strained poems. My career began to develop with greater seriousness during the eight years I lived in Montreal in the 1980s and early 1990s. I spent most of the middle and later 1990s exiled to England, searching for a financially viable way to move back to Canada. I have now settled – for the moment, at least – in southern Ontario.

The essays that follow chart my attempt to define my literary environment: to work out what it means to engage with literature as a Canadian fiction writer of my generation; to respond with both intellect and emotion to the books, writers and writing institutions of my time and place. My approach to this problem is personal, arguably atypical, possibly even eccentric; my hope is that the idiosyncrasies of my outlook will provoke thought in others.

The essays in this book trace the evolution of my reactions to the changing Canadian literary world from my late twenties to the brink of my fortieth birthday – from 1988 to the turn of the millennium. Future historians are likely to look back on these years as a watershed between an era distinguished by the clash of ideologies and an era ruled by massive, homogenizing trade blocks; between a culture governed by beliefs and a society in which every impulse or idea undergoes an instantaneous conversion into merchandise. Though this book makes only occasional reference to the larger picture, it does offer a half-askew literary record of one writer's path through some of the alterations in the texture and focus of literary debate in Canada between the late 1980s and the present. I believe that my generation of Canadian writers – those born around 1960 – has a responsibility to leave some record of these changes. We were the only literary generation to complete our professional coming of age under the 'CanLit' umbrella of proliferating literary journals, small publishers, subsidized readings and independent bookstores. Much of this apparatus has now been sluiced away by budget cuts, or corporatized by commercial pressures. Older writers, who helped to build the 'CanLit' edifice in response to the impoverished state of Canadian literary culture in the 1950s, may wish to reflect on the type of sensibility nurtured by this set of arrangements; younger writers – today's twentysomethings and those who follow them – may express a passing curiosity about what Canadian literary culture used to be like. Or they may not.

My view is necessarily partial. Like most writers, I am a peculiar blend of insider and outsider. Having arrived in Canada at the age of five, I am an immigrant writer – yet no one thinks of me in that way. I am the quintessential rural Canadian with a farm in his upbringing – but I have been nourished on emotional and intellectual links to far-away places and foreign-language traditions. I think that history is important. History shapes us; it often shapes us most decisively in eras such as the present one, when it has become fashionable to deny history's claims, depicting the individual as infinitely capable of painless self-reinvention. We *can* reinvent ourselves, but at a price. An important part of literature's role is to assess that price: to dramatize the making of our individuality within the context of our history, to express the emotional and psychological stresses induced by this process. Literature – again, perhaps especially the novel – narrates our interaction with our history through the forms offered by present commercial conduits.

If this is a book about one writer's attempt to define his literary posture within the changing contexts of the Canadian writing universe, then the tally of preconceptions I bring to bear includes not only assumptions about history and genre, but also about literary form. The form that has gripped me since childhood is the novel. The novel creates an alternative life in its totality; at the same time, merely by narrating a full life, the novel engages with history and presents, at least implicitly, a critique of society. Literature helps us to understand who we are; the novel, more than other literary forms, helps us to understand who we are *within a context*. For that reason, essays about novels, and the problems raised by writing and publishing novels, predominate here. I have much less to say about poetry, which I no longer write, or even short fiction, a form with which I do continue to grapple.

My approach to literature coalesced out of the blur of my frantic adolescent reading. After one's late teens or early twenties, the capacity for absolute, unthinking immersion in a work of fiction diminishes. More mundane concerns – the job, the rent, the family – become harder to shake off when one opens a book. Concentration turns into a question of effort, a willed act. The teenager or young adult's susceptibility to the swamping of life by fiction, to a yielding of self before an enchanted merging with people of other times and places, may never return in its full youthful resilience, but it does bequeath a vivid legacy to the perpetually distracted adult. In the peculiar, individual contours of this legacy lie the outlines – the themes, literary sensibility, cherished characters and images, ideals and modes of engagement with a narrative universe – of the books that the mesmerized adolescent reader may one day write. As I have always kept lists of my reading, I am able to dip back into the feverish world of the teenager I used to be. I can see, for example, that between July 11 and August 16, 1977 – the summer of my seventeenth birthday – I read *The Antiquary* by Sir Walter Scott, *Humboldt's Gift* by Saul Bellow, *La Chute* by Albert Camus, *The Good Soldier Schweik* by Jaroslav Hašek, *The House of the Dead* by Fyodor Dostoyevsky, *Buddenbrooks* by Thomas Mann, *The History of the Conquest of Peru* by William H. Prescott, *Mysteries* by Knut Hamsun, *The Iliad* by Homer, and *La Condition humaine* by André Malraux. All in a month and five days! Today that list would represent at least three months' reading – if I managed to finish these books at all. I question whether any seventeen-year-old today could secure enough peace and quiet to plough through these books. My farm, with its long, isolating laneway and its single portable television set receiving three local channels, seems like an oasis of benign neglect by comparison with today's satellite dishes, video games and World Wide Web connections.

Looking back from the perspective of incipient middle age being lived out in a nondescript suburb on the farthest fringes of the Greater Toronto sprawl, I find my adolescent self terrifying. I prefer to keep my distance from his overheated voraciousness. This teenager is clearly in desperate need of *something*, and, whatever it may be, I fear his adult self has failed to provide him with it. But a few points need to be made. Much of my reading consisted of European literature in translation. In tune with my immigrant background, the books written in English tended to be from Great Britain. The Enid Blyton and Arthur Ransome of my early childhood gave way around the age of eleven or twelve to C.S. Forester, then to Ian Fleming, Agatha Christie and Alistair MacLean and, shortly thereafter, to Joseph Conrad and volumes from the leatherbound complete works of Charles Dickens, Sir Walter Scott and Robert Louis Stevenson lining the shelves in the living room of our red brick farmhouse. As a child of the Trudeau era, growing up within reach of Ottawa, I adopted the then-common notion that a Canadian was someone who had inherited equally from the English-language and

French-language traditions. Attempting, like any other immigrant, to make myself into a full-fledged Canadian, I internalized the Trudeau axiom, considering Marie-Claire Blais and Anne Hébert to be as much mine as Margaret Laurence and Hugh MacLennan (the English-Canadian writers I was reading at that time), and taking Flaubert and Stendhal to be as central to my extended tradition as Dickens and Scott. I learned French well enough to read French-language literature in the original from the age of fifteen; by nineteen or twenty, my self-taught Spanish supplemented by a few months of university study, I began to read Spanish American literature in the original. My exposure to these literatures – Russian, French, Québécois, Latin American – led me to conclude, somewhere around the age of twenty, that the English-Canadian novel's prospects for development – a development to which I ardently planned to contribute – were hamstrung by a central 'problem'.

The 'problem' of the Canadian novel, for me, was that Canada – as I was painfully aware, sitting in the Ottawa Valley reading my stepfather's copies of the *Manchester Guardian Weekly*, with its inserts from the *Washington Post* and *Le Monde* – was a nation marginal to the epicentres of global culture and global power, yet endowed by history, as if as a joke, with the literary language of the world's two most powerful empires, the nineteenth-century United Kingdom and the twentieth-century United States. The language did not fit the experience. When I looked around me I saw a marginalized world of faltering family farms, regional customs and accents, a certain tenacious allegiance to a distinct history on the brink of being overwhelmed by a mass culture both alien in its origins and irresistible in its comfortable assumptions. The novels of Mann, Turgenev, Tolstoy, Stendhal and Balzac seemed to offer viable models for approaching this world, yet each attempt I made to express my vision of my surroundings was thwarted by the traitorous inheritance of the Anglo-American literary idiom, which converted any effort to dramatize ideas or portray the individual as an outcropping of his history into bad sociological fiction. The Anglo-American tradition, unlike the continental European or Latin American traditions, was drenched in the imperial hatred of theorizing – for the empire, seeing its own ascendancy as natural, can only scorn theories of why power is distributed in one way rather than another. The art of empires snuffs out the possibility of dramatizing from within life in peripheral societies; it kills the novel of ideas and the novel as the emanation of history. The dominant English-language literary traditions, I concluded, debased any serious attempt to describe the world I saw around me. In my early twenties I came to perceive this inheritance as the central obstacle to the development not only of my fiction, but of the Canadian novel in general. (A later formulation of some of these ideas appears in the essay 'Writing in Canadian: The Problem of the Novel'). I took to saying that I wished I could write in French or Spanish, because then I might be able to dramatize life as I had experienced it.

The English-language tradition, though, was more diverse than I was giving it credit for. The bathos of the early Dickens, the sentimentality of John Steinbeck, the naturalism of Jack London or Theodore Dreiser were not the only approaches to dramatizing the individual in a social and historical context. A number of writers could have shown me a way out of this cul-de-sac. As it happened, my liberator was George Eliot, the most European of the great English novelists. One afternoon I lay curled on a hillside amid tall grass and opened an ancient paperback copy of *Adam Bede* from which the pages were coming unstuck. In an instant I was transfixed; the spell lasted for days. Here was a rural, marginal world I recognized as a distant cousin of my Ottawa Valley surroundings, described in the English language yet with an integrated understanding of character, history and culture I had discovered previously only in novels written in languages other than English. (Doris Lessing, who in her introduction to *The Golden Notebook* expresses some of the same frustrations with the traditions of the Anglo-American novel that I am outlining here, is correct when she writes that 'the book which bores you when you are twenty will open doors for you when you are forty or fifty – and vice versa': years later, in graduate school, *Adam Bede* popped up as required reading on a course. I could not, in spite of my most determined efforts, finish it. I had already learned what it had to teach me.)

George Eliot offered an intellectual way out; William Faulkner showed me how the perceptions of George Eliot could remake the twentieth-century novel. Attending university in the United States confirmed my self-definition as a Canadian. The more I learned about the society of the United States, the more the superficial similarities between Canadian and U.S. life shrank before the cavernous psychological and historical differences. Among the benefits of my U.S. experience was being obliged, in two different courses, to study the work of William Faulkner. The marginalized world of Faulkner's novels was a world I recognized; in fact, it was the opposite wing of the world I knew. Faulkner's South was one of the paths not taken by the United States: an agrarian society defeated by the U.S. industrial heartland in the Civil War. The loyalist, royalist exiles who had brought their traditions to eastern Ontario, dispatched into a foreign land by the new republic's first flexing of its muscle during the American Revolution, represented another path not taken: that of evolution away from the European past, rather than violent revolt against it. Canada, like the U.S. South, endured reproof for its economic backwardness and lack of entrepreneurial savvy, its vestigial investment in vaguely European-style hierarchies; both worlds were deemed inferior to the ever more economically powerful northern and western United States that would go on to impose its commodities and cultural precepts on the planet. It was not a coincidence, I asserted, in an essay written for one of my undergraduate courses, that Quentin's roommate in *The Sound and the Fury* was a Canadian!

Faulkner's Gongoresque inflation of English prose, his contorting of the conventions of syntax, his deliberate creation of myths to express a marginalized reality, his incessant delving into remote history, his denial of linear chronology, showed me that it was possible to rewrite the Anglo-American novel from the edges of the English-speaking world. At this point, the doors of literature opened wider and wider to me. My reading in Spanish exposed me to a multiplicity of literarily innovative means to dramatize Western hemisphere lives that did not conform to the patterns established by the hemisphere's dominant culture. Spanish American writers took Faulkner's arsenal and recast it to mythologize their own off-centre realities. The relationship was obvious in the similarities between Faulkner's *The Wild Palms* and Mario Vargas Llosa's *The Green House,* between *Absalom, Absalom!* and García Márquez's *One Hundred Years of Solitude,* between the genealogy of Yoknapatawpha County and that of Juan Carlos Onetti's fictional town of Santa María. Through Salman Rushdie's *Midnight's Children,* with its homages to and borrowings from García Márquez, I found my way back into the English-language novel. I felt that I was beginning to identify my tradition; to engender my literary ancestors. It was at this point, around the age of twenty-five, that I started to write my first published novel, portraying Canadian experience as one variant of the multiple, marginalized, non-imperial societies of the Western Hemisphere. My reading having outrun my life experience, the novel was less successful than it might have been. But it did enable me to conceive of myself as a Canadian writer, to develop a personal critical perspective on Canadian writing and, around the time of this novel's publication, to begin to express my critical outlook on Canadian writers and Canadian writing institutions through book reviews, articles and essays that I began to contribute to a variety of publications.

This is where the present book begins: with the author of a first novel taking a stand. Only one of these articles – the opening piece on Josef Škvorecký – dips back to before the great chasm of 1989. I have included this article for two reasons: because it represented my initiation into the world of Canadian literary debate, and as a reminder of the rigorous bipolarity of the pre-1989 world; that world's Manichaean patterns of expression, it seems to me, continue to govern in a furtive way a great deal of the public thinking and arguing we undertake amid the supposedly easygoing, diverse multiplicity of our millennial present.

The positions I take in the essays at the end of this collection, inevitably, are somewhat different from those proposed at the outset. As a result, internal contradictions abound. Since the purpose of this book is to narrate one writer's developing relationship with his tradition, I have let most of the contradictions stand.

The majority of these articles and reviews appear here as they were first published. I have eliminated a few particularly egregious idiocies, tightened sloppy sentences and suppressed the odd adjective or dated reference. Each article is followed by the details of its publication. In a few cases, articles have been expanded or merged with others. Contrary to normal practice in collections such as this one, I have appended commentaries on how some of these articles were received: the reactions provoked by these pieces also form an indispensable part of this story.

Guelph 1999–2000

Part One
Writers and Words

Josef Škvorecký
and Canadian Cultural Cringe

Few Canadian writers have received such generous treatment from the press and media as Josef Škvorecký. Since his immigration to Canada in 1968, Škvorecký has been the subject of countless magazine articles and television interviews. This exposure has permitted him to express his political views to an unusually wide audience, including many people who have never read his books. His prestige accrues in part from his romantic status as an exile from a country languishing under Soviet oppression. During the last five years Škvorecký's visibility has increased markedly, his reputation enhanced both by the translation of work previously unavailable in English and by a swing to the right in the public mood. In a climate of reactionary chic, Škvorecký's pronouncements on the evils of Eastern communism and the naïve duplicity of Western liberalism, both in interviews and in his humorous, sometimes bawdy, fiction, have found a receptive audience: he is Solzhenitsyn with sex-appeal, as in tune with the fashionable wisdom of the 1980s as Allen Ginsberg (whose work Škvorecký has translated into Czech) was with that of the 1960s.

One of the dangers of a writer's being a representative of the dominant ideology of his time is the latitude he is allowed to indulge in statements that in retrospect appear ludicrous. Ginsberg has stated that he now regards his pro-communist rhetorical excesses of the 1960s as a public embarrassment. Unfortunately, the Canadian critical milieu appears to be too tepid to call Škvorecký to account for his excesses. One of the rare attempts to challenge Škvorecký's declarations was 'Political Judgments', Terry Goldie's review of Škvorecký's Governor General's Award-winning novel *The Engineer of Human Souls* (*Canadian Literature*, Spring 1985). Prying beneath the protective armour of anti-communism, Goldie found a novel that was sexist, racist and 'also anti-union, anti-Vietnam war draft dodgers and generally anti-anything which smells of leftism'. He predicted that most critics would be too seduced by the novel's fashionable commie-bashing to question Škvorecký's vision: 'I can hear a thousand cheers for the anti-communism but at best a few muted rejections of the anti-feminism, the racism, and the general anti-social character of the novel.'

Unfortunately, Goldie's prediction proved correct. Few Canadian critics appear willing to criticize the U.S. media orthodoxy that while all writers are equal, anti-communist writers are more equal than others. Goldie's review earned him a barbed response from Škvorecký himself (of which, more later) in addition to a singling out for special opprobrium in Marketa Goetz-Stankiewicz's survey of some of Škvorecký's reviews (*Canadian Literature*, Fall 1986). The fact that Goldie's position is such an isolated one serves as a damning comment on the timidity of Canadian criticism, especially when addressing European-born writers. The Australians refer to this habit of self-abasement before the wisdom of the metropolitan centres as 'cultural cringe'. Škvorecký, as a European-born writer promoting an ideology made fashionable by the government of Ronald Reagan, evokes the two centres to which Canadians habitually pay obeisance, bringing out a particularly ferocious strain of Canadian cultural cringe.

The British reviews of *The Engineer of Human Souls* provide an instructive contrast to the Canadian reaction. Goetz-Stankiewicz omits the U.K. critics from her survey, noting only that these reviews 'have a rather different tenor'. Indeed they do! Unlike those by both U.S. and Canadian critics, the British reviews do not reflect an assumption that support for Škvorecký's anti-Sovietism need necessarily translate into *carte blanche* approval of his politics on all fronts. Even the neo-conservative magazine *Encounter*, while granting Škvorecký full marks for anti-communist orthodoxy, worried about 'questionable attitudes smuggled through in the diplomatic bag of dissident status' (July/August 1985). Reviewer James Lasdun noted that the novel 'casts the dissenting reader into the role of a brainwashed ideologue ... despite his affable manner, [Škvorecký] seems fundamentally short on tolerance and magnanimity; one would not relish having him in a position of power.' Ironically, this conservative critic echoes many of the concerns of the 'leftist' Terry Goldie. Like Goldie, Lasdun is disturbed by the narrator's sexism; he remarks that 'his gleeful relish of the sexual opportunities his position as teacher affords him ... becomes somewhat objectionable.' And where Goldie, to the apparent consternation of Marketa Goetz-Stankiewicz, speaks of a 'failure of humanity', Lasdun concludes his review by criticizing Škvorecký for 'a defect of the soul'. One need not be a leftist dupe to be disturbed by Škvorecký's vision in *The Engineer*.

The assumptions underlying this vision have repercussions in the spheres of gender relations, race relations and international relations. Goldie remarks on Škvorecký's sexism, observing that his female characters tend to conform to stereotyped portrayals of women as either virgins or whores. Škvorecký responds by accusing Goldie of falling into the trap of the 'ideological critic', who 'asks the writer not to recreate reality, but to create ideals, or to criticize reality if it does not comply with the ideal.' He defends his portrait of the virginal Nadia by observing that, 'in 1944, in the Czech mountain villages of northeastern Bohemia, there were no feminists.' Fair enough – but Škvorecký's fictional alter ego, Danny Smiricky, continues to portray women according to these stereotypes in the scenes set in 1970s Toronto, where there were feminists in abundance. Three of the four women characters upon whom Goldie bases his remarks appear in the Toronto scenes, yet Škvorecký concentrates his retort on the one who does not. Why does he not attempt to defend his portraits of women in the Toronto sequences? The introductory description of Margitka suggests that his position is well-nigh indefensible: 'I usher her in, admiring her ... well-proportioned little bottom as she slips past. Progress does exist after all. In my parents' generation, forty-year-old women were usually three times that wide.'

Both Škvorecký and Goetz-Stankiewicz, in their respective essays, lash out against 'ideological' feminism. Goetz-Stankiewicz excoriates *Globe and Mail* reviewer 'Claude Corbeil' (by whom I assume she means Carole Corbeil) who, she says 'is too angry to notice that the professor-student seduction scene ... is purposely couched in the vocabulary of the plastic values of contemporary Western society.' The contrast between the language of the seduction and that of the similar scene involving the village girl Nadia is interesting, as Goetz-Stankiewicz suggests. Her next leap, however, defies all logic. 'To speak here of anti-feminism,' she writes, 'is to miss the point.' In drawing this conclusion,

Goetz-Stankiewicz falls into the same trap (although in this case it may be a ploy) as those reviewers who, beguiled by Škvorecký's anti-communism, turn a blind eye to his sexism, racism and historical distortions. The fact that Škvorecký counterpoints two sexist descriptions to create an interesting literary effect does not, as Goetz-Stankiewicz contends, make his sexism disappear. The French novelist Louis-Ferdinand Céline turned spite, and even anti-Semitism, to literary advantage. Yet few, if any, critics would argue that Céline was not an anti-Semite simply because he used his anti-Semitism creatively. It is intellectually dishonest to try to whitewash Škvorecký's sexism on similar grounds.

Škvorecký attempts to extract himself from the mire of racism by invoking E.M. Forster's distinction between flat and round characters. Yet, if the characters belonging to visible minorities are to be 'furniture', identified by one or two salient traits, why does the narrator choose traits that conform to racist stereotypes? 'Mispronunciation of English, I guess, is part of the Indian stereotype,' Škvorecký comments sarcastically. Unfortunately, one of the most common slurs against Canada's East Indian community does consist of mockery of Indian pronunciation; whether or not he is aware of it, Škvorecký is buying into the standard racist line. His response to Goldie also contains some fast backtracking on the subject of Bellissimo, the Italian student. While the novel predicts for him a future spent 'disentangling more than one Mafioso from legal embroilment', Škvorecký's reply to Goldie waxes lyrical on the intelligence of this young man, who 'will make a first-class lawyer and become the joy of his working-class father's declining years.' The reply hastily revises the language and message of the novel.

Only on the subject of Larry Hakim, the radical Arab and Vietnam draft dodger, does Škvorecký remain unrepentant. Arabs, he reaffirms, are inseparable from 'wild, barbaric actions, hijackings, internecine wars, senseless bloodshed presented as something "healthy" for the people; to pre-adolescent boys being sent to the front in a senseless, unending medieval war.' The final clause of this catalogue of horrors would seem to be a reference to Iran's assault tactics on Iraq during the Iran-Iraq war. This is puzzling, since most Iranians are not Arabs: they are Persian – at least as different from Arabs as Czechs are from Germans. At the beginning of *The Engineer* Škvorecký quotes William Blake on generalizers being idiots. His fictional alter ego admonishes his ideological foes (Hakim among them) for employing generalizations that 'cannot stand up to microscopic examination'. But Škvorecký scores many of his own ideological points by means of broad (and often inaccurate) generalizations.

Škvorecký's other favourite strategy is precisely that which he accuses Goldie and his ilk of using: 'that universal malaise of the Western leftist ... "selective indignation."' *The Engineer* contains a discussion of events during the 1970s in the Angolan civil war; Škvorecký returns to this topic in his reply to Goldie. In both instances, he focuses obsessively on Cuba's intervention in the war, portraying the arrival of Cuban troops as analogous to the 1968 Soviet invasion of Czechoslovakia. In Škvorecký's Ministry-of-Truth account of the war, crucial details vanish. While the Cuban intervention is condemned, the South African invasion of Angola, which prompted the governing MPLA to call for Cuban help, is never mentioned. (For an eyewitness account of this sequence of events, see Ryszard Kapuściński's *Another Day of Life*.) Škvorecký portrays the Cubans as Soviet lackeys, ignoring the Cuban role in crushing the pro-Moscow faction of the MPLA, allowing a more Third World–oriented faction to retain power. And if Škvorecký really holds the MPLA government entirely responsible for Angola's current misery (absolving the South African–backed UNITA insurgents, whose sabotage has destroyed the country's infrastructure, from all blame), why does he focus his anger on Moscow to the exclusion of the U.S. oil companies which, by remaining in Angola, furnish the regime with the hard currency that allows it to survive? Granted, these points are details; but, as Blake reminds us, there is rarely much merit to the writer who flees details for grandiose generalizations such as 'the Cubans ... with their ... Soviet-supplied war technology ... subjected the ... population to foreign supervision.'

Perhaps the most ludicrous of Škvorecký's outbursts comes towards the end of his reply to Goldie, where he attempts to fashion a causal chain linking Marx and Engels's recommendations for the liquidation of 'reactionary nations' to Stalin's oppression of ethnic minorities. Extending this chain into the present, Škvorecký writes, 'The present ruler of Abyssinia follows that recommendation and – in a milder way, because Uncle Sam is dangerously near – the Sandinistas are trying something similar with the Miskito Indians.'

23

The passage on which Škvorecký bases this polemical conceit is not necessarily a definitive statement of the Marx-Engels position. While Marx and Engels shared the racial and rationalist biases of other nineteenth-century Europeans, they were also capable of transcending these limitations. Witness, for example, Marx's 1850 speculation that defeated European reactionaries fleeing across Asia might reach the Great Wall of China to find 'the very stronghold of arch-reaction' transformed into a democratic republic. In any event, it is highly dubious to contend that Soviet imperialism against surrounding nations stems from a direct attempt to implement Marxist principles. As any student of politics knows, institutional momentum often supersedes ideology in determining policy; it was not Karl Marx but the Red Army that marched into Prague and deported the Tatars from their homeland. In one of the British reviews ignored by Marketa Goetz-Stankiewicz, Ernest Gellner distinguishes Škvorecký from an earlier generation of writers on Soviet repression: 'Škvorecký, by contrast [to Koestler, Orwell, etc.], belongs to a later generation whose involvement was no longer with a genuine creed, but rather with the doctrinal superstructure of the Red Army' (*Times Literary Supplement*, March 8, 1985). Škvorecký has repeatedly voiced his impatience with those 'who have not had my life experience'. While respecting his hardships and insights, Canadian readers should not collapse into cultural cringe and submissively take his experience to be more inclusive than it actually is. Škvorecký is a valuable witness to the imperialism of the Nazis and the Red Army. However, his lifetime does not span the entire period from *Das Kapital* to the Gulag; the answer to the question of whether the Gulag represents the inevitable consequence of trying to implement Marx's analyses remains outside Škvorecký's 'life experience'. His views on this subject are not necessarily any more privileged than those of other thoughtful observers.

Moving past Škvorecký's dubious contention that the Ethiopian dictatorship's repression of the Eritreans stems from its nominal Marxism rather than from long-standing racial animosities, one arrives at the assertion that the Sandinistas' policies regarding the Miskito Indians amount to 'something similar' to 'liquidation'. This, to put it bluntly, is disinformation. In 1981 tensions between Nicaragua's mestizo government and its isolated native minority (aggravated by Sandinista ineptitude on one side and a U.S. propaganda blitz wooing the Miskitos to join the contras on the other) culminated in the Sandinistas' decision to relocate the Miskitos away from their homes facing the contra front along the Coco River. Clashes between Miskito rebels and Sandinista troops during 1982 resulted in the deaths of between thirty and ninety-five Miskitos and the jailing of several hundred others. By 1985, however, despite an intensification of the contra war, the Sandinistas had financed the Miskitos' return to the Coco River, sacked officers who had committed human rights abuses and offered the Miskitos a semi-autonomous homeland – including the right to keep both their language and their guns (see John A. Booth in *Current History,* December 1986; Scott Wallace in *Newsweek,* 15 December 1986; and Dennis Gilbert in Blachman, LeoGrande and Sharpe [eds.], *Confronting Revolution*). Rather than some sort of ideologically inspired extermination campaign, the details of the case reveal a pattern of ethnic strife and gradual reconciliation. If, as Škvorecký implies, Uncle Sam truly lay awake at night fretting about the destruction of Central American Indian communities, he would turn his attention not to Nicaragua, but to Guatemala, where a genocide is in progress. (But Škvorecký, with his right-winger's selective indignation, never mentions Guatemala.) Guatemala's Indians, who make up more than half of the country's population, have suffered a systematic government assault so severe that even a report sympathetic to the Guatemalan regime was forced to concede 'a count of over 100,000 Indian children orphaned by the death of at least one parent in the years 1980 to 1984' (see Robert Trudeau and Lars Schoultz in Blachman, LeoGrande and Sharpe). Meanwhile, the Canadian media, which Škvorecký portrays as naïve conduits for Soviet propaganda (see his 'Are Canadians Politically Naïve?' in *Canadian Literature,* Spring 1984), obediently churn out a dozen articles on the hardships of the Miskitos for every one on the wholesale slaughter of the Quiché and the other peoples of Guatemala. In light of this ordering of priorities, Goldie's judgement that Škvorecký's engineer 'perpetuates injustice and inequality in the world', seems not far-fetched but rather mild.

Guatemala also raises the thorny question of Škvorecký's unblinking admiration of Israel. The Israelis built Central America's first munitions plant in Guatemala in 1979; the soldiers who carry out the genocide of the Quiché are trained by Israeli military advisers, armed with Israeli Galil rifles and wear Israeli uniforms (see Trudeau and Schoultz; also 'Forged in Action', [Montreal] *Gazette*, December 20, 1986). Refusing to criticize a nation responsible for the indiscriminate aerial bombardment of Beirut, massacres of refugees and the subjugation of a million and a half people in a worse-than-apartheid-like political limbo requires a selective sense of indignation indeed. Škvorecký is quick to criticize the violent retaliations of the oppressed; but he has only sympathy for their oppressors. He argues that his autobiographical persona, Danny, became 'pro-Jewish' because he 'happened to be an eye witness of the holocaust.' This equation of 'pro-Jewish' with 'pro-Israeli' is at best outdated and at worst a tired right-wing device. However true it may have been in 1948, it can no longer be axiomatic at a time when Israel is increasingly dominated by non-European Jews who do not share the democratic ideals of most of the holocaust survivors and most Jewish North Americans. Surely, condemnation of the European holocaust does not preclude condemnation of the bombardment of Lebanese children and supervision of the holocaust in Guatemala?

All of which leads one to ask why Terry Goldie's review is such an anomaly. Why do Canadian critics so seldom challenge Škvorecký's erroneous declarations? It seems we still react with a cringe of inferiority to the statements of writers hailing from more 'cosmopolitan' climes – a tendency bolstered in the case of Škvorecký by the current popularity of many of the right-wing clichés he evokes. In such a context, the imperative to distinguish a writer's literary strengths from his or her moral failings becomes doubly compelling. As is so often the case, one may find good counsel in the works of George Orwell. In an essay on Salvador Dalí, Orwell lamented that the critical debate over the painter appeared to be divided between those who, impressed by his art, whitewashed his personal life, and others who, finding his personality repellent, insisted that Dalí's art was worthless. Why, Orwell asked, could one not recognize that Dalí was both a remarkable artist and 'a disgusting human being'? Substituting 'political extremist' for 'disgusting human being', one could apply this statement to Céline, Ezra Pound, Knut Hamsun – or Josef Škvorecký. That is the challenge Škvorecký poses to the Canadian milieu: to recognize the wonders of his writing – especially of the early novels like *The Cowards, The Miracle Game* and

Miss Silver's Past – while casting a cold, critical eye on the moral implications of the alien ideology he would try to foist upon us. In retrospect 1984 may be seen as the high-water mark of the right-wing fad in Canada: the year the middle class voted for Brian Mulroney and the literary establishment accorded its highest award to *The Engineer of Human Souls*. But what matters more in the long run is that we learn to value the best of Škvorecký's writing without lumbering ourselves with the worst of his ideological baggage.

'Josef Škvorecký and Canadian Cultural Cringe' was published in *Canadian Literature*, no. 116, Spring 1988.

* * *

The steamrolling of the rules that enabled the 1984 Governor General's Award for fiction in English to be given to a book that was not written in English remains one of the low points of Canadian literary life. At the very least, Škvorecký should have shared the award with his able translator, Paul Wilson. The deeper point is that the rules were never twisted to provide access to the Governor General's Awards to refugee writers fleeing dictatorships from the opposite side of the ideological divide. Gonzalo Millán's book-length poem *La ciudad* (*The City*), written and published in Spanish in Montreal in the early 1980s, is a major work of Chilean exile literature, which later won Chile's National Poetry Prize. In 1991, when Split Quotation published the full text of the *The City,* together with a selection of other work written by Millán during his Canadian exile, under the title *Strange Houses,* no one proposed nominating the book for the Governor General's Award for poetry. In fact, almost no one noticed. Ideology may have been only part of the reason for this particular case of selective indignation. There has been a tendency for writers fleeing nominally left-wing dictatorships (Czechoslovakia, Hungary, China) to settle in Toronto, while those fleeing implicitly or explicitly right-wing dictatorships have tended to settle elsewhere in the country: the Haitians in Montreal, the Chileans in Montreal and Ottawa, many of the Salvadoreans and Guatemalans in Vancouver. This has given the anti-leftists access to the national media to an extent not available to the anti-rightists. But a cynic might claim that the media were already leaning in that direction.

This article was an important learning experience for me. In its aftermath, I began to grasp the aversion to debate slumbering at the core of Canadian literary culture. 'Cultural Cringe' was accepted for *Canadian Literature* by the editor, W.H. New, at a time when the prolific George Woodcock, who had founded *Canadian Literature* in 1959, continued to play an active role in the journal. A few weeks after I had received New's letter of acceptance, a second letter arrived. In this letter, New expressed his fear that the language of the article was too strong, its attacks too *'ad hominem'*. Could I tone the piece down? I refused, in very strong terms, to touch a word. New did not insist. But I did wonder what had happened. An acquaintance familiar with *Canadian Literature* suggested that probably what had happened was that George Woodcock had read the article and objected to it. This suspicion grew stronger when, a few weeks after 'Cultural Cringe' was published, Woodcock took to the nationally syndicated review column he was then writing to denounce 'those who would criticize' Škvorecký. Needless to say, he did not mention my name, or address in concrete terms the issues raised by my criticisms of *The Engineer of Human Souls*. That might have sparked a debate, and debate is anathema to Canada's neo-colonial literary culture, where the imposition of fashionable opinion suffices to prove any point.

A second example of the use of the authority of fashion occurred two years later, when an academic named Sam Solecki published a book on Škvorecký's writing, entitled *Prague Blues*. Solecki devoted a footnote to denouncing Carole Corbeil, Terry Goldie and me. When I spotted the reference to my name in the index, I opened the book, eager to see how Solecki would respond to the litter of factual errors and selective uses of evidence I had identified. But Solecki chose to retreat into dogma, writing:

The only good novel, from their [i.e. Corbeil's, Goldie's and my] standpoint, will be one that is pro-feminist, pro-communist, pro-whatever is deemed progressive.

There is a not particularly funny joke somewhere in all this: in 1959 the Czech official Stalinist 'left' found Škvorecký to be too far to the right; in the late 1980s a segment of the Canadian left condemns him of the same sin. Each wants him to write a fiction that is ideologically correct. Each, in other words, wants him to produce socialist realism.

I see. Is that what I meant when I praised the 'wonders' of Škvorecký's writing and suggested that even those, such as myself, who did not agree with his politics, should be able to enjoy his fiction?

Solecki's cynicism flabbergasted me. I was young and naïve and not long out of a rigorous undergraduate education in the United States, where statements of position had been met with hard-nosed, empirically based rebuttals. I could not believe that a writer could consider such an offhand, inaccurate dismissal to be an adequate response to a point-by-point refutation of his position. Slowly, I began to realize that in the Canadian milieu – or at least the Toronto milieu – Solecki did not need to marshal arguments to support his case; in fact, it would have been against his interest to do so. The authority of fashion was on his side. He had only to drop a sideways accusation of 'Stalinism', make a passing allusion to 'socialist realism' and, no matter how liberal my article was in its assumption that one could revile a writer's politics and still enjoy his work, a Stalinist I would become.

Josef Škvorecký, of course, has continued to write – even to write well, though rereading him today I find his outlook essentially adolescent. Here is a writer who rarely writes of intimate relationships; in whose work family life appears as a moronic impediment to the seduction of wives and daughters; a writer who can describe school and lust and young soldiers, but whose vision of adult experience is not so much comic in the grand tradition as reductive in its snickering disdain. He *is* funny, but he is not as deep as even his critics once thought him to be. In recent years, Škvorecký's public profile has shrivelled. The reasons for this, sadly, are extra-literary. In the aftermath of 1989, Škvorecký's form of right-wingism lost its usefulness. The media found other cultural champions to wage the combats of the 1990s.

Writing in Canadian
The Problem of the Novel

A few years ago, when I was living in South America, people on buses used to stare at me and ask what country I came from. On hearing that I was Canadian, their stares would change to perplexed frowns. I learned to recognize this frown, which indicated that a question was on the way. And the question, when it came, was always the same: 'What language do you speak in your country?'

Last year, at a conference in Montreal, I was introduced to a Costa Rican novelist who was visiting Canada for the first time. Having met in the space of a few minutes five or six Canadian writers, some of them English-speaking and others French-speaking, she looked bewildered. Glancing around her, amid loud conversation in both languages, she asked me: 'What language do Canadians write in?'

I faltered. I realized that this was a question to which I did not know the answer. I have been thinking about it ever since. The simple answer to the question is that most Canadian writers write in English, some Canadian writers – mainly those living in the province of Quebec – write in French, and that a few write in other languages. The complicated answer to the question, which I did not attempt to give at the time, is that Canadian writers, and particularly Canadian novelists, may not yet have discovered their language.

A Swedish writer writes in Swedish, and a Dutch writer writes in Dutch. The moment such a writer sets pen to paper in his native tongue, he assumes a Swedish or Dutch outlook on the world, shoulders – implicitly or explicitly – the burdens of Swedish or Dutch history, and usually describes people, places and sensations that most Swedish or Dutch readers will recognize. Likewise, a writer who writes in French in Quebec enjoys the privilege of being defined by her language. The peculiarities of Québécois idiom and experience, differing markedly from

31

those of both English-speaking Canada and those of French-speaking societies elsewhere in the world, create a pact between writer and reader similar to those enjoyed in Swedish or Dutch writing. The Québécois writer writes in Québécois: in the language of the surrounding community.

But what of the English-speaking Canadian writer? Unlike the Québécois or the Swede, we do not write in a language imbued in shared historical experience. One of our prime ministers remarked that Canada had too much geography and not enough history: what could a few million people scattered over an area the size of all of Europe possibly have in common? To make matters worse, we write in English: the Latin of the high-tech world; the language of computer programs, rock videos, air-traffic controllers and robots. English is everyone's second language. Can we, who speak it as our mother tongue, use it to express the peculiarities of our private and public lives? Canadians have inherited the English language from arguably the two most powerful empires the world has known: nineteenth-century Great Britain and the twentieth-century United States. The British empire gave us our government institutions and our laws; the United States has given us television programs, blue jeans, big cars and much of the rest of our popular culture. Yet both these nations were empires; the language we have acquired from them is laden with the assumptions of global power. We have adopted the syntax and vocabulary of two empires without being able to make the same imperial assumptions. This is not to say that the world does not contain other small or medium-sized countries whose language is English. But where Australia or Jamaica, for example, have developed their own distinctive varieties of English, adapting the language to the peculiarities of Australian or Jamaican experience, Canadian English actually seems to be losing its distinctive features. Since the 1970s, when the advent of cable television began to bombard us with programming from the United States, the old Canadian accents and usages have begun to erode. Linguistic surveys show that most adolescents growing up in downtown Toronto and Vancouver no longer use the 'ou' sound typical of a Canadian accent; in cases where Canadian and U.S. usage differ – for example, 'chesterfield' instead of 'couch', 'grade one' instead of 'first grade', 'Mum' rather than 'Mom' – an increasing number of Canadians now prefer U.S. usage. It may prove to be one of the ironies of Canadian cultural development that we lost our idiom at the moment when we were finally ready to begin creating a distinctive literary voice.

Like the literature of other colonial societies, Canadian writing began with sketches and travelogues: with people describing what they saw around them. Most Canadian writing of the nineteenth and early twentieth centuries is now largely of historical interest. In these early works, sociological accuracy is still at least as important to the author as quality of language, imagery or emotion. In the absence of a shared history or a cohesive society, the development of the novel was stunted. The dominant literary form remained the sketch. Our literature was more concerned with documenting Canadian customs than with expressing our humanity in a Canadian voice.

The problem persisted into the middle of the twentieth century. The tendency to value documentation more highly than creativity was reinforced by the fact that, with one or two valiant exceptions, there were almost no Canadian publishing houses. The Canadian writer sat down to work in the knowledge that his book would be published, in all likelihood, in New York or London. Under these conditions, it is not surprising that writers devoted themselves to artificial 'explanations' of the reality around them, rather than exploiting this reality as an imaginative point of departure. A reader in London, possessing no experience of small-town Canada, had to be told everything. Unfortunately, ignorance of Canadian reality was not confined to foreigners. Due to the poor distribution of books and other sources of information within the country, few Canadians knew very much about their vast, disconnected homeland. When Hugh MacLennan was writing his novel *Two Solitudes*, he deliberately stuffed its pages with documentary-style explanations of the political and religious affiliations, habits and prejudices, of various segments of Canadian society. To a certain extent, MacLennan seems to have been trying to explain his country to his wife, a journalist from the United States. *Two Solitudes* used to be described as the beginning of the modern Canadian novel. From today's perspective it looks more like the end of the colonial documentary tradition: it is one of the last works of Canadian fiction to address itself to an imaginary foreign reader.

During the 1950s, the old colonial ties with Great Britain began to wither and new ties with the United States were forged. U.S.

corporations began to buy up large sectors of the Canadian economy. Middle-class Canadians became wealthy on the proceeds, but cultural life remained bleak. There were still few publishing houses; the audience for literary fiction was practically nonexistent. Almost all the promising young Canadian writers of the 1950s – Margaret Laurence, Mordecai Richler, Mavis Gallant, Norman Levine – left Canada and settled in Europe. It was only in the 1960s that Canadian writers of fiction began to discover a language capable of imaginatively expressing reality.

This spirit of self-confidence took root for a variety of reasons. Continued prosperity, and the expansion of the university system, enlarged the audience for Canadian fiction. The 1960s was also marked by a buoyant Canadian nationalism, which peaked with the celebration of the hundredth anniversary of Canadian nationhood at Expo 67 in Montreal. The combination of economic good times and nationalist fervour resulted in the foundation or expansion of publishing houses committed to promoting Canadian writing, and the extension, through the Canada Council, of increased government support for the arts.

All of these developments were reinforced by United States intervention in the Vietnam War. It is one of the peculiarities of this vital period that virtually all the best Canadian fiction of the time – all the works that writers of the 1980s and 1990s look back upon as the beginning of modern Canadian writing – were published between 1965, when the United States first committed combat troops to Vietnam, and 1975, when the North Vietnamese Army captured Saigon. Without falling into complete historical determinism, I think one may suggest that U.S. military involvement in Vietnam made Canadians stop and think. At the time of the U.S. intervention in the war, Canada, under the leadership of Lester Pearson, was pursuing a policy of integration into the U.S. economy and, through the formation of NORAD, into the U.S. military hierarchy. The widespread unpopularity of U.S. involvement in the war, the fact that Americans were fighting in Vietnam and Canadians were not, and Canada's eventual transformation into a refuge for U.S. draft dodgers brought into sharp contrast the differences between the two societies. The novel, traditionally Canada's weakest literary form, began to show signs of development. In reflecting upon the unique trajectory of Canadian experience, the writers of those years gave us most of the best novels that have been written in English-speaking Canada.

34

The years between 1965 and 1975 saw the publication of Margaret Laurence's entire Manawaka cycle (except the first volume, *The Stone Angel,* which was published in 1964), Robertson Davies's *Fifth Business,* Alice Munro's *Lives of Girls and Women,* Margaret Atwood's *Surfacing,* Mordecai Richler's *St. Urbain's Horseman* and a handful of interesting lesser works. All of these novels and stories are reflections upon the past; they attempt to dramatize a history that lacks definition. Yet History with a capital H – wars, political crises and so on – does not appear in most of these books. These are stories of individuals: biography-like accounts of representative Canadian lives. The tales told in some of these books, such as Richler's *St. Urbain's Horseman* and Munro's *Lives of Girls and Women,* are completely personal (and to some extent autobiographical). In others the personal story serves as an allegory, a dramatization of the experience of the larger society. This is the case of Davies's *Fifth Business,* where the life of Dunstan Ramsay, the man forever on the margins of great events, parallels Canadian history in the twentieth century. In Atwood's *Surfacing,* with its opening image of 'disease ... spreading up from the south', the allegory is less grounded in history and more directly anti-American. Nonetheless, even *Surfacing* – centring on the heroine's search for her lost father – remains a quest for origins. Perhaps Margaret Laurence succeeds most gracefully in combining the personal story with the dramatization of a common history. Morag Gunn in *The Diviners* moves from Western Canada to Central Canada to England and back again, in a personal quest that evokes, without directly dramatizing, the eternal Canadian search for identity.

All of these works fall somewhere between realism and modernism in terms of literary technique. The urge to document remains strong, producing the customary avalanche of remembered physical and verbal detail. Memory is subordinated both to aesthetic criteria and to the desire to reclaim ancestry. One description must stand for many, but Margaret Laurence's rendering of the Manawaka town dump in *The Stone Angel* typifies much Canadian writing of this period:

Above Manawaka and only a short way from the peonies drooping sullenly over the graves, was the town dump. Here were crates and cartons, tea chests with torn tin stripping, the unrecognizable effluvia of our lives, burned and blackened by the fire that seasonally cauterized the festering place. Here were the wrecks of cutters and buggies, the rusty springs and gashed seats, the skeletons of conveyances purchased in fine fettle by the town fathers and grown as racked and ruined as the old gents, but not afforded a decent concealment in earth. Here were the leavings from tables, gnawed bones, rot-softened rinds of pumpkin and marrow, peelings and cores, pits of plums, broken jars of preserves that had fermented....

Not all this detail is essential to Laurence's evocation of the dump. At one level the description recalls earlier writers who flung in detail indiscriminately in order to convince themselves of the authenticity of their fledgling postcolonial world, or in order to tell others what their region of Canada looked like. Part of Laurence's purpose in this description is simply to document the kind of objects one might expect to find in a town dump in rural Western Canada. But the aim coexists with another goal, one typical of the novelists of the 1960s and early 1970s. Laurence chooses detail that conveys a sense of her community's history. The parallel between 'the wrecks of cutters and buggies' and 'the town fathers' breathes life into the litter, making it speak of a pioneering existence that was passing from living memory at the time Laurence was writing.

The predominant tone of the fiction of these years remains realistic. But here and there one can see the beginning of a transition to full-blown modernism. Margaret Atwood's carefully developed imagery, Alice Munro's rigorous selection of detail, and the ambitious structures of novels such as Laurence's *The Diviners* and Mordecai Richler's *St. Urbain's Horseman,* suggestively mingling past and present experience, all seem to presage a leap to the sort of modernist or even postmodernist epics of cultural identity to which other peripheral and postcolonial societies have given birth during the last thirty years.

Yet this transition has not occurred. Since 1975 Canadian writing has made enormous gains in commercial viability and international recognition. Toronto literary agents now routinely make deals to sell foreign rights to new Canadian works of fiction. Yet the writing itself, it seems to me, has lost much of its intensity, its sense of engagement with vital questions. Margaret Atwood and Robertson Davies, and to a lesser extent Mordecai Richler and Alice Munro, have become international literary successes, but they have done so at the price of being packaged as veritable brand names. Each new book must resemble its predecessors in order to satisfy the mass market. The new novelists who have emerged during the last ten or twelve years – Timothy Findley, Janette Turner Hospital, Matt Cohen, W. P. Kinsella, Katherine Govier – are less ambitious than the novelists who made their marks during the 1960s and early 1970s. Findley, Hospital, Cohen, Kinsella, Govier and others are consummate professionals. But the search for new forms, for a language capable of dramatizing our lives in our own voices, has lost its urgency. A desire to give voice to a nation's humanity has declined into mere professionalism. Halfway along the road of its development, the Canadian novel has stalled.

It is difficult to say why this should have occurred. Some would blame the decline in nationalist sentiment within Canada, the renewed and increasing cosiness with the United States, and the consequent slackening of interest in our own historical distinctiveness. Others blame the decline in literary ambitiousness (though not in literary ambition) on the internationalization of the publishing industry. Books, in order to be published, must now be deemed to show 'international potential'; a novel that interests readers in only one country does not interest many publishers at all. In response to the demands of the new international market, many Canadian writers are discarding their Canadian subject matter. The mid-1980s has witnessed a rash of Canadian novels set in Boston and Iowa and London and Paris. Such works are easier to sell in the international marketplace, but all too often they are superficial because the writer lacks an intimate knowledge of the world he is describing. Of course no one can remain bottled up in a single country these days. The world is growing smaller by the week: the shape of our lives depends more and more on events in other nations. But it is not this dynamic of interdependence that is being investigated in these Canadian novels with foreign settings; rather, we are witnessing the spread of a fashionable false consciousness. The writer, inspired by an event that occurred in Toronto or Vancouver, sets her novel in New York or Los Angeles. The resulting work is slick and professional, yet feels strangely hollow. The setting refuses to snap into focus, important characters lack conviction, the reader who knows New York or Los Angeles notes an error of detail. Where the Canadian writer of the last century addressed a foreign reader, the contemporary Canadian writer often pretends to be a foreigner. We have arrived at the brink of a new form of alienation.

There is an alternative response to the conditions of the contemporary world. And it is here, I believe, that the Canadian novel may find its way out of its present impasse. The novelists and short story writers of the 1960s began the long process of excavating our history and mythology, of developing a language in which to express ourselves. In so doing, they snapped the yoke of regionalism and naturalism that had weighed down so much earlier Canadian writing. They pushed the Canadian novel into realism and to the verge of modernism *because their subject matter made such techniques necessary.* The unambitious commercial fiction favoured by many contemporary Canadian writers has abandoned this quest: books that are too intensely Canadian, it is feared, will not receive a warm reception in the international marketplace. But what if we turn this proposition on its head? What if we resolve to push the work of the writers of the 1960s and 1970s one step further? What if we write novels that are obsessively Canadian? The results, I believe, would prove fascinating.

As I remarked at the outset, one of the difficulties confronting anyone writing English-language novels in Canada is that, although we are a medium-sized country that has remained on the margins of most of the world's great events, we have inherited the vocabulary and syntax of two empires. Part of the literary baggage of those empires is an assumption that there exists an unbridgeable gap between writing that is aesthetically challenging and writing that is historically engaged. This is an imperial assumption; it should not and cannot be ours. The nineteenth-century British writer could be either Jane Austen or Sir Walter Scott – either the novelist of style or the historical chronicler. Similarly, the twentieth-century United States novelist can be either John Updike or Gore Vidal. But the worldwide development of the novel during the last thirty years has demonstrated that if you are an Australian or an Indian, a Peruvian or a Mexican, a woman or a minority, then historical engagement and artistic innovation are inseparable from one another. In a world in which first empires and now a global mass culture have dictated an immutable, linear conception of progress, on a planet that is becoming more and more uniform, the history of anyone on the edge of events is bound to force narrative into new shapes; fragmentation, circularity, wordplay and rebel mythologies undermine the rhetoric of linear progress. The paradox that conventional outlooks cannot explain is that among writers from marginal societies, the most politically and historically engaged novels of the past two or three decades have also been, in many cases, the most challenging from a purely literary standpoint. Peter Carey in *Illywhacker* and *Oscar and Lucinda*, Salman Rushdie in *Midnight's Children* and *Shame*, Nadine Gordimer in *Burger's Daughter* and *A Sport of Nature*, Günter Grass in *The Tin Drum*, Mario Vargas Llosa in *The Green House* and *Conversation in The Cathedral*, Gabriel García Márquez in *One Hundred Years of Solitude* and *The Autumn of the Patriarch*, Carlos Fuentes in *The Death of Artemio Cruz* and *Christopher Unborn*, and many, many others, have explored the histories of homelands pushed to the edge of events and emerged with vital, challenging art.

One step beyond the Canadian novel of the 1960s and 1970s lies the modernist (or, sometimes, postmodernist) epic of cultural identity. It is here, rather than in light, entertaining tales set in Iowa or Boston, that the Canadian novel – indeed the novel of any non-imperial society – may hope to find room to develop and grow. The paradox that appears to be blocking us at the moment is that in order to reach the world with a deeper, more resonant voice we must turn away from the international mass market and focus on our own myths and peculiarities. It is flattering that Canadian books are being read in other countries; but too many of us are setting forth, in the phrase of the Australian novelist Peter Carey, pretending to be 'imaginary Englishmen'. Only by acknowledging our own existence in its full historical richness and complexity will we be able to create a distinctive literary language – and by this I do not necessarily mean a particular dialect of the English language, but a mythology that expresses our historical experience, expresses the kinds of people we have been and are becoming. This is what the Dutch or Swedish writer does, consciously or unconsciously, when sitting down to write in Dutch or Swedish. It is the work of the novelist who writes in Australian English or Colombian Spanish; it may become the work of writers who strive to give the English-Canadian novel more range and depth, and more international relevance, by writing in Canadian.

What language do you speak in your country? What language do you write in? These questions will never cease to be crucial. We are always in the process of discovering our language; and our language, forever evolving, wriggles out of our grasp just when we think we have defined it. To understand ourselves, to engage our own histories and realities, is the essential point. Our eccentricities and our myths are certain to strike a chord among readers in other parts of the world, for more people live in marginal societies than central ones; more and more people see their identities as peripheral, in one way or another, to the central thrust of global entertainment culture. Even many of those living in the hearts of empires need not share imperial conceptions of progress: how else to explain the work of Emily Brontë; or William Faulkner? Ultimately, the best writers are usually on the margins and for the marginalized, since only by engaging with the history of our own place on the planet can we be sure of sharing our humanity with the world.

'Writing in Canadian: The Problem of the Novel' was delivered as a lecture at Kossuth University in Debrecen, Hungary in April 1989 and was published, in somewhat different form, in *Hungarian Studies in English* xxi, 1990.

Layton and the Feminist

A few years ago a friend of mine announced her intention of writing her master's thesis on the poems of Irving Layton. Her father, who had been taught by Layton in high school, recoiled. 'You're not going to interview him alone!' he said. 'Irving Layton was a dirty old man even when he was a young man.'

Layton owns up to this charge, in his irrepressible way, on the opening page of his collected love poems, *Dance with Desire*. In 'To the Girls of My Graduating Class', first published in 1953, he confesses to feeling 'fierce and ridiculous' as he slavers over the 'saintly breasts' of his female students.

To readers better acquainted with Layton's bombastic public stance as Canada's leading lecher than with his verse, that 'ridiculous' may come as a surprise. As Layton has aged, he has displayed little sensitivity to the absurdity of an old man ogling women several decades his junior. The Layton of the 1950s and 1960s, as represented by the first third of this book, was a subtler, more perceptive man. He was also an exceptionally fine poet. This was the period when Layton was writing such enduring works as 'The Birth of Tragedy' and 'A Tall Man Executes a Jig'. His best love poems of the time are highly accomplished. By dressing up his romanticism in appropriately lavish language, replete with classical allusions and risky inverted syntax, Layton succeeded in wringing genuine feeling from his fleshly obsessions.

His downfall lay in his penchant for satire. A poem like 'The Day Aviva Came to Paris', in which Layton imagines the French capital struck dumb by his wife's arrival, succeeds wonderfully both as a statement of devotion and a vehicle to lampoon Parisian-style stuffiness. Layton's satire, though, eventually fused with his titanic ego, creating the bloated self-parody all too familiar from his poems and interviews of the past twenty-five years. *Dance with Desire* is top-heavy with poems in which

Layton's rambunctious public persona bludgeons any visible glimmer of insight or feeling.

'Am I mad to see soft breasts everywhere?' he writes in one poem. Mad, no; infantile, yes. Layton's women seem to consist of little more than pairs of surging breasts. They scarcely have arms or legs – let alone hearts, heads or brains. Layton may love women, but like most philanderers, he doesn't seem to like them very much. Lines such as 'I plug the void with my phallus' suggest a fear of female sexuality; a poem detailing his inability to come to terms with his wife's menstruation reinforces this theme.

These days, Layton's posture as a sexual rebel seems merely foolish. Like any aging revolutionary, he has lost touch with forces he himself helped to unleash. His explicit praise of female body parts made him a literary outlaw in the 1950s and an icon of the hip in the late 1960s, but subsequent generations, for whom the pursuit of desire has become both highly politicized and potentially lethal, have regarded him as either boorish or outmoded.

Curiously, the love poems that made Layton notorious now appear to be a fragile part of his poetic legacy. *Dance with Desire* may prove to contain a portion of the Layton oeuvre destined to slip into obscurity.

. . .

'Half the men you've ever met / will rape you / if they think they can / get away with it,' writes Montreal poet Sharon H. Nelson in the opening sequence of her collection, *The Work of Our Hands*. Turning to Nelson's gritty analysis of sexual politics after being immersed in Layton's odes to seduction is a bracing experience. In Nelson's work, desire becomes merely one more tool of a controlling patriarchy.

Nelson's direct, unadorned phrasing works best in poems focusing on everyday tasks such as household labour. A tension arises, though, between her efforts to evoke the workaday world and her need to elaborate a theory of how language alienates us from this world. Her plain style becomes flat when propounding theoretical verities which, while sometimes persuasive, are not startlingly original. A happy exception crops up in the long, free-form poem 'Making Waves', where Nelson develops a richer, more untrammelled language capable of embodying her search for a poetics rooted in physical experience.

Even when she overstates her points, Nelson's voice, alternately genial and caustic, remains engaging. Irving Layton should read this book.

Originally entitled 'Are Old Men Absurd If They Ogle Women?', this essay was published in the *Montreal Gazette*, 13 June 1992.

* * *

No article I have written has elicited as much response as this one.

Letters of protest streamed into the *Gazette* for weeks after the publication of this piece. The Layton media persona, I learned, was sustained by a core of devoted readers to whom he had given an elegant vocabulary for longings they had scarcely dared to voice.

The best letter was from Irving Layton himself. Demonstrating that his ego had not smothered his sense of humour, Layton wrote: 'Young fogeys afflicted by mediocrity and the itch to write ... have never hesitated to reveal their animus against high spirits, wit, irrepressible creativity and my fame both here and abroad. I sympathize with them, for their suffering and deeply felt humiliation must be intolerable.... Clearly, Stephen Henighan lacks both common sense and common decency.'

Layton's riposte was a natural response to a sour review. Sharon H. Nelson, who turned out to be the founder of the Feminist Caucus of the League of Canadian Poets, confounded expectations by rushing to Layton's defence. In a three-page single-spaced letter that she faxed to more than thirty prominent cultural figures, Nelson denounced my dastardly attack on a sexual liberator. She went on to threaten various libel actions. The *Gazette's* managing editor issued a formal rebuttal to Nelson's threats. *Maclean's* magazine got wind of the tempest and ran a short article on Layton's 'new alliances' and my lack of repentance for my cultural sins.

Yet the Layton-Nelson axis was no new alliance. Why did the founder of the Feminist Caucus side with the self-proclaimed slaverer? I later learned that, early in her writing career, Sharon H. Nelson had been a Layton protégée. The incident underlines the prime law of Canadian

WHEN WORDS DENY THE WORLD

literary debate: differences of opinion, aesthetic creed or ideology are overruled by personal allegiances. Unlike the United Kingdom or the United States, where friends and acquaintances may cordially and vigorously disagree in print, Canada remains a colonial society; here friends must think alike and unanimity among the Family Compact of the chattering classes is still the hallowed aim of public utterances. In Canadian literary circles, the opinions you express continue to be a function of who you know rather than what you think.

In the Heart of
Toronto's Darkness

Nearly a century after its publication, Joseph Conrad's *Heart of Darkness* remains one of the most fertile works in English literature. Conrad's tale of Marlow's journey up the Congo in search of the deranged Kurtz has attracted interpretations of every critical stripe. Artists from V.S. Naipaul in *A Bend in the River* to Francis Ford Coppola in *Apocalypse Now* have paid homage to the enduring resonance of Conrad's imagery. In evoking *Heart of Darkness* in his novel *Headhunter,* Timothy Findley has provided himself with a storehouse of potential allusions.

Headhunter begins and ends as a Torontonian retelling of the tale of Kurtz and Marlow. The Toronto of the near future in which the story unfolds is both strange and familiar. Sturnusemia, a lethal epidemic spread by pigeons and starlings, is ravaging the population. Gangs known as Moonmen and Leatherheads lurk in the city's parks. Into this dystopian environment, a wayward spiritualist inadvertently releases Kurtz from page 92 of her copy of *Heart of Darkness.*

Kurtz enters Toronto fully formed, fitted out with a personal history and a powerful position as director of the Queen Street Mental Health Centre. Findley's futuristic Toronto merges with a vision of the city that is familiar to the point of seeming outmoded. Kurtz's wealthy patients inhabit the Anglophile milieu of a past era. With the exception of some domestic servants and a couple of minor Jewish characters, Findley's entire cast is of British extraction. His Torontonians mimic English customs, referring to German shepherd dogs as 'Alsatians', and using expressions such as 'I haven't the foggiest notion.'

Findley offers no resolution to the contradiction between his futuristic setting and his anachronistic portrait of Toronto society. What rivets his narrative attention, delaying the emergence of the duel between Kurtz and his questing subordinate Dr Marlow, are the dissolute lives of their patients. All of Rosedale seems to be undergoing treatment at the Queen Street Mental Health Centre. Schizophrenia, alcoholism and sex clubs dominate their lives. Most of the patients are acquainted with or related to one another; as their vices intertwine, the reader witnesses the decadence of an entire social class.

This is a powerful theme. Findley's rendering of it is most successful when he keeps his distance and writes in detached, ironic narrative summary: 'Warren's mother, Freda Manley, never gave up her own name. Eddie Ellis, Warren's father, was not the first of her husbands, nor her last. He was, however, Freda's most ardent and devoted lover – and the father of her only child. That Freda Manley, in her race to the top, had paused long enough to produce a son had left those who knew her stunned with amazement.'

Headhunter would have benefited from more of this sort of narrative summary. Findley's dramatizations of individual scenes – his predominant mode in this novel – are notably weak. His imagination, capable of roaming with mythologizing force over the First World War battlefields of *The Wars* or the storm-tossed seas of *Not Wanted on the Voyage*, becomes constricted in the drawing room and the psychologist's office. The broad strokes Findley used to paint his allegories in the earlier novels grow clumsy when turned on the subtleties of social interaction. Findley's narrator coaches the reader incessantly, breaking in to explain – often in self-conscious italics – the significance of each revelation or hypocritical phrase. It may seem churlish to raise the writer's-workshop distinction between showing and telling in reference to a novelist of Findley's experience, but without a masterful grasp of this opposition, domestic fiction rarely achieves memorable effects. In *Headhunter*, Findley tells obsessively. Every idiosyncrasy of upper-crust decadence is so thoroughly explicated as to leave little place for the reader's imagination.

The story picks up steam in its final pages, as Kurtz and Marlow, whose rivalry has occupied a secondary role for much of the novel, battle for control of the Mental Health Centre's potentially explosive files. Their struggle, though, amounts to little more than an uncomplicated contest of good and evil. In Findley's view, every Marlow needs a Kurtz to lead him into the darkness where he can 'find new light' and know that he 'has penetrated just a little farther than his counterparts before him.'

Headhunter ends on an optimistic note. The detailed Conradian parallels – in both books the statement left behind by Kurtz after his death is seventeen pages long – highlight the gulf dividing Findley's conventional, patriarchal, progress-centred conclusion (focused on the virtues of 'penetrating' farther into 'the unknown') from the multifaceted scepticism rippling through the final section of Conrad's work. Unlike Naipaul's or Coppola's complex, allusive creations, Findley's novel squanders its Conradian inheritance. While *Headhunter* does offer a few bright moments, reading this novel ultimately resembles a hard upriver journey through crudely mapped territory to a disappointingly predictable destination.

'In the Heart of Toronto's Darkness' was published in the *Globe and Mail*, 10 April 1993.

* * *

This review represents two milestones: the end of Timothy Findley's status as an 'untouchable' in the world of Canadian, and particularly Toronto, reviewing; and the conclusion of my early association with the *Globe and Mail*.

When the *Globe* phoned me in England – where I had moved to begin a doctorate, having despaired of surviving as a freelance writer in Montreal – the young sub-editor assigning the review said: 'We've got to get this one out of Toronto.' Misconstruing this yearning for the appearance of impartiality as a desire for a truly impartial review, I accepted the assignment. I had been reviewing for the *Globe* for three years at this point, and this was the first Canadian book I had been offered. I had enjoyed Findley's *The Wars* and substantial sections of *Not Wanted on the Voyage,* but felt that the rest of his fiction was clumsy and sentimental. His enshrinement in the Canadian literary canon seemed to be less the consequence of solid achievement than of the authority Findley, as an upper-class Rosedale WASP possessing an actor's media-friendly suavity, exercised over the middle-class Torontonians working at the CBC, *Maclean's,* etc. On reading *Headhunter,* I realized that it was Findley's clumsiest novel in years. Still, in the climate of the early 1990s,

47

where a negative review of Findley in a major Toronto newspaper was unthinkable, I realized that I had to be careful to leave my critical conclusions for the end of the review. I'm a little embarrassed today when I reread the paragraph summarizing Warren's mother's character, that I quoted as being 'successful'. The writing here is coy and superficial; but at least it is less disastrous than Findley's mawkish attempts to create fully dramatized scenes.

After I had submitted my review, the young sub-editor called me, transatlantic. 'When I read your review, I went and got a copy of the book. I've read the book now and … and I just want you to know that I agree with everything you say!'

I should have sensed trouble. To its credit, the *Globe* published my review without changing a word. But, as I soon became aware, I had uttered the unutterable. A newly appointed professor of Canadian literature at an Ontario university told me: 'I got halfway through the review, then looked to see who had written it – who was saying these things about Timothy Findley? You just can't say that about him!'

The Family Compact closed ranks. The University of Toronto professor Rosemary Sullivan wrote a letter to the *Globe* dismissing me as an upper-class Oxford twit – a tactic I found disingenuous given that Sullivan and I had met and spoken at length not long before on the decidedly non-upper-class campus of Concordia University in Montreal. Linda Spalding and Michael Ondaatje's magazine *Brick,* notorious for routinely taking one to two years to respond to submissions – let alone publish them – rushed into print in its next issue a lengthy essay by Sullivan providing the 'correct' (i.e., adulatory) response to *Headhunter.* For its part, the *Globe* did penance by running a flattering profile of Findley containing quotes that could be used – and were used – on the paperback edition of *Headhunter.* My invitations to review for the *Globe* dried up. When I phoned to ask about doing more reviews I was told that other writers wrote 'accurate articles'; the name Findley kept cropping up. Only in 1999, a number of editorial teams later, was I again invited to review for the *Globe.*

Yet the dam had burst. Other reviewers, notably Philip Marchand of the *Toronto Star,* also began saying the unsayable. The fate of Findley's latest novel *Pilgrim,* the object of what *Quill and Quire* reported to be possibly the most expensive promotional campaign in Canadian literary history, has been that of pesky criticism making inroads into a wall of glossy hype.

The purpose of criticism is to clarify what has been achieved in a literature. Good criticism points readers towards books that will challenge them, and helps writers to face the work of creating vital new fiction out of an awareness of what has come before. Even making allowances for the usual subjective factors – differing points of view, the shift of perspectives over time – a winnowing-out process occurs in each generation. Some neglected writers are resurrected by readers of later eras; and many writers highly successful in their own times prove to have been popular entertainers rather than artists of lasting significance. In Canada, where mass popularity and literary significance are often confused, the need to refine these distinctions is arguably more pressing than in other literary cultures. If we are lucky, the adjustment of Findley's reputation that has begun in recent years will be the first of many literary reappraisals.

Behind the Best-Seller List

Every author longs to write a best-seller. It's only human, after all, to want to be famous. The same egotism that is required to complete a book – a capacity for remaining convinced over a period of years that others will be intrigued by what you have to say – also dictates that yours must be a book whose advent the world is awaiting with breathless anticipation. I knew that my first novel, published in 1990, would be a best-seller. No other outcome was possible. When the novel sank, more or less without a ripple, I spent most of 1991 adjusting to this fact. I stitched together the conventional patchwork of part-time jobs – a little teaching, a little reviewing – and kept plugging away at my next novel, for which I nourished the usual vain hopes. Then one day the telephone rang.

'Stephen, how much do you figure your time is worth?' The experienced freelancer learns to lapse into cunning silence upon hearing words such as these, especially when the speaker is the books editor of a major newspaper. I managed not to reply. Bryan Demchinsky of the Montreal *Gazette* explained that he was planning to overhaul the paper's best-seller list. He was looking for someone to run his new list. An article by another *Gazette* journalist recently having drawn to Bryan's attention the picturesque poverty in which I was living, he wondered whether I might be interested in the job. He could pay me $75 a week.

I accepted. The prospect of one steady source of income, however small, to anchor my various erratically fluctuating odd jobs, was irresistible. And – who knew? – by working on best-sellers I might unravel the secret of how to write one.

Until mid-1991, the *Gazette* reprinted its best-seller list from *Maclean's* magazine. The decision to stop using the *Maclean's* list was based on its perceived failure to reflect the reading habits of Montreal book buyers. The two books whose sales careers exposed the gaps in the *Maclean's* approach were a curious pair: V.S. Naipaul's *India: A Million Mutinies Now* and Reed Scowen's *A Different Vision: The English in*

Quebec. In its hardcover edition, Naipaul's book lacked a Canadian distributor. Despite being effectively barred from most of the retail outlets in the country, *India: A Million Mutinies Now* popped up week after week on the best-seller list the *Gazette* received from *Maclean's*. All of the booksellers the *Gazette* consulted agreed that the national sales figures implied by the *Maclean's* listing were virtually unattainable for a book lacking a Canadian distributor.

National anomalies were matched by regional omissions. As I went about setting up the list by establishing contacts at English- and French-language Montreal bookstores, my preliminary inquiries confirmed a widespread impression that the former Quebec Liberal politician Reed Scowen's *A Different Vision: The English in Quebec* was selling at a briskly best-sellerish pace. The fact that Scowen's book appeared on no national best-seller list provided more support for Demchinsky's arguments in favour of a 'made-in-Montreal' list. The policy might in some ways seem insular, but as I was discovering in my exploration of other publications' lists, all of these rankings – supposedly the ultimate 'objective' measure of the literary marketplace – were subject to their own peculiarities. Sometimes, as in the presence of Naipaul's undistributed book on the *Maclean's* list, these wrinkles defied logic; other trends, such as the sometimes disproportionate success enjoyed by Toronto writers on the 'national' list of the *Globe and Mail,* appeared all too predictable. The most desirable course seemed to be that adopted by the *Village Voice Literary Supplement,* which compiles a list of 'Our Kind of Best-Sellers' from information provided by the sort of stores where *Voice* readers are likely to shop. Taking into account the differences between our respective readerships, I decided to try to make the *Gazette* list a similar 'Our Kind of Best-Sellers'.

A couple of weeks before I was due to compile my first list, Amy Tan's *The Kitchen God's Wife* leapt onto the *Globe and Mail's* national best-seller list. I made a quick tour of downtown bookstores to see how Tan's novel was selling locally. *The Kitchen God's Wife* was nowhere to be found. Had it already sold out? No, I was told, it hadn't arrived. A metaphysical conundrum reared its head: how could a novel not yet on the market have become a 'best-seller'? Richard King of Paragraphe Books provided me with an answer. 'A best-seller,' he said, 'is a book that is meant to be a best-seller.'

The *Globe and Mail* list was, and to some extent still is, dependent on chain stores. The legend at the head of the *Globe* list states that 500 bookstores across Canada contribute each week to its compilation. Two or three independent stores are mentioned as being 'among bookstores participating in this week's survey'. Ruth Noble, who puts together the *Globe* list, estimates that 40 per cent of the input comes from chain stores. According to Noble, the *Globe* is working to increase the proportion of independents among its contributors in order to give the list 'a more national feel of what people are buying in little shops across Canada'. She points to Timothy Findley's *Headhunter* and Jane Urquhart's *Away*, both of which made the *Globe* list at times when they weren't being stocked by Smithbooks or Coles, as evidence of the *Globe*'s success in building up a solid base among the independents. At the same time, Noble concedes that the *Globe*'s reliance on chain stores was more pronounced a couple of years ago, when *The Kitchen God's Wife* appeared. And the *Globe* list still has its detractors. Some booksellers complain that the *Globe*'s contributor's form, which lists twenty potentially best-selling titles (while also allowing space for write-in votes), predisposes them to mention a given cluster of highly promoted books. Others continue to doubt the *Globe*'s commitment to the independents. One Ontario independent bookseller whose store has been included in the *Globe*'s list of 'bookstores participating in this week's survey' told me: 'Given the frequency with which they've cited us in the last year, they're sure as hell not polling many independents.' Ruth Noble, however, states that *Globe* policy is to continue to shift the list 'more strongly towards the independents'.

It is tempting for best-seller lists to rely on chain stores: chains are easy to poll and can supply centralized statistics. Their operations are so tightly coordinated, in fact, that one of the problems I encountered in setting up the *Gazette* list was that the Smithbooks store at the Fairview-Pointe Claire shopping mall didn't know what its own best-sellers were. Until a diligent and helpful assistant manager agreed to perform a weekly tabulation on the *Gazette*'s behalf, the store relied on a monthly listing of national best-sellers sent from head office. National fashion, rather than local book-buying preferences, determined the books the store stocked and the quantities in which it ordered them. Coles has become even more notorious for huge, blind orders of highly promoted books. The result of this kind of homogenized bookselling is that any best-seller list heavily dependent on chain stores measures orders rather than sales.

There are two theories about why this occurs. The cynical theory dictates that having ordered tens of thousands of hardcover copies of the latest blockbuster, the chains are angling hard to sell the book even if it turns out to be a dud. They include it on their best-seller list in the hope of creating a self-fulfilling prophecy. The charitable theory focuses on the individual Coles or Smith's manager. Receiving a phone call from a newspaper best-seller list, the harried manager glances across the store, spots stacks of unsold copies of the latest Robert Ludlum or Danielle Steel doorstop and blurts out the title of the book that is piled highest as being at the top of the list.

The cynical theory has more adherents than the charitable theory. A newspaper editor with whom I broached the subject of Coles's contributions to various best-seller lists, interrupted me in mid-sentence: 'They lie.' The manager of one of the stores contributing to the *Gazette* list – an independent with a strong commercial slant – warned me that she would not supply me with more than three titles each in fiction and non-fiction. She went on to explain, in a spirit of back-to-basics fervour, that she had begun her career at Coles. She had been so disheartened by being obliged, she claimed, to report 'untrue' rankings that she had promised herself in future, if she contributed to a best-seller list, only to mention titles which she was certain were selling well in her store that week.

The Kitchen God's Wife became a best-seller before arriving in the bookstores because it received big advance orders from the chains. The chain stores' assumption of a homogeneous national market made their outlook inimical to our attempt to compile a local, 'Our Kind of Best-Sellers' item. Bryan Demchinsky and I agreed that we would weigh all stores we surveyed equally, regardless of their sales volume. In part this was a response to our suspicion that the chains' listings might not be reliable and in part, in *Village Voice* fashion, we had decided that such a policy represented the best way to cater to readers of the *Gazette* books section. The consumers of Ludlum and Steel did not make purchasing decisions on the basis of reviews; the people who read the *Gazette*'s Saturday review section to keep abreast of new books were more likely to shop at the independents.

For the next fifteen months of my life Tuesday became best-seller day. Calling on Tuesday gave the stores time to tally up their weekend sales, while ensuring that the list was ready for the Saturday books section's Wednesday evening lay-out. Every Tuesday afternoon from 1:30 to 3:30, or as long as it took, I dialled frantically to reach every store on our list. Each week there would be at least a couple of stores where something had gone wrong, requiring me to plead, cajole or call back several times. Most weeks, though, we managed to get our full complement of contributing stores. Once I had finished, I would perform my calculations, copy out the three lists – Fiction, Non-Fiction, and Books in French (which mixed fiction and non-fiction) – and jump on the Métro to deliver the list to the *Gazette*'s front desk by five p.m.

My afternoons on the phone ushered me into a world of diverse enthusiasms. The Smithbooks assistant manager raved over the phone about Robert Jordan fantasy novels. A manager at one of the more refined independent bookstores, utterly scrupulous about the figures he submitted, also took advantage of my calls to offer judicious literary criticism of each of the titles he cited. Some stores would use my call as an opportunity to complain if a book they were promoting had received a bad review in the previous weekend's *Gazette*. Most stores ended up knowing my home phone number which, since it ended in '-oo', they mistook for a *Gazette* office number. I began to receive calls at odd hours from stores attempting to answer customers' queries about titles, authors and literary prize-winners. I developed a network of collaborative telephone relationships with a number of people whom I had never met. This proved especially true at the French stores, where menacingly formal voices, which for the first few weeks addressed me as *vous* and *Monsieur,* soon melted into confidante-like intimacy, making me the repository of problems with bosses and boyfriends in pauses between reading out the week's best-sellers.

An unbridgeable gulf divided the English and French reading publics. Compiling the list heightened my awareness of the extent to which mainstream writers from France, such as Sébastien Japrisot, Annie Ernaux, Régine Desforges and Alexandre Jardin, dominated the Quebec bookselling scene. I discovered that in addition to the literary Québécois writers with whom I was familiar, there existed a vigorous strand of Québécois popular fiction represented by genre writers such as

Chrystine Brouillet. The manic Québécois passion, largely imported from France, for translations of U.S. writers such as Paul Auster, David Leavitt and John Irving, also came as a surprise. Less surprising, though more discouraging, was the mutual lack of interest displayed by English-Canadian and Québécois readers in one another's fiction. The only Québécois novel to appear on my English fiction list was Roch Carrier's *Prayers of a Very Wise Child* (which also appeared on the *Globe* list, suggesting that Anglo-Quebec readers take no greater interest in Québécois fiction than English-Canadian readers elsewhere in the country). The only English-Canadian novel to make my French list was Nino Ricci's *Le Serpent et les yeux bleus,* the translation of *Lives of the Saints.* Part of the reason for the translation's success was that it originated in France and arrived in Quebec supported by the clout of a major Paris publisher. Ricci also did two things right in his dealings with the Quebec media: he spoke French, and he spoke it with an Italian accent rather than an English accent, circumventing the resistance to English-Canadian culture often evinced by Québécois journalists.

The disparity between English and French outlooks came to a head with the publication of Mordecai Richler's polemic *Oh Canada! Oh Quebec!* The week after the book came out, one English store gleefully reported having sold 362 copies in less than three hours at a Richler signing. A few minutes later I phoned Coles. Due to a mix-up, the manager of the store's French section was assigned to read the English list to me over the phone. When he reached Richler's name, he became nearly inarticulate with rage. 'This book is not fiction, it is not non-fiction – it is science fiction!' It took nearly ten minutes to extract the remainder of the list from him.

Looking back, I realize that our success in putting together a significantly different kind of best-seller list was limited. A few political books sold better in Montreal than elsewhere. Students of the McGill philosopher Charles Taylor bought enough copies of *The Malaise of Modernity* to hoist it onto the non-fiction list for a couple of weeks. Barry Lazar and Tamsin Douglas's *The Guide to Ethnic Montreal* also did well. British literary fiction by writers such as Margaret Drabble and Martin Amis sold somewhat better in Montreal than it did nationally; some Toronto writers prominent on the *Globe* list either didn't do as well in Montreal (Daniel Richler) or failed to show entirely (Douglas Cooper). During the fifteen months that I compiled the *Gazette* list, no English Montreal fiction writer appeared on it – though Edward O. Phillips and David Homel each just missed on one or two occasions. The only hardcover English-Canadian first novel to crack my top ten was Carole Corbeil's *Voice-Over*. ('There really aren't that many copies out there,' Corbeil murmured during her Montreal tour, when I told her that her novel had placed second on the coming Saturday's best-seller list.)

A best-seller remains, as Richard King told me, a book which is meant to be a best-seller. We were able to avoid listing books before they appeared in the stores, but we couldn't escape the structure of mass book-marketing. Most best-sellers are predetermined, though the scope of a particular book's success may vary according to timing, review space or the author's performance with the media. What I learned about writing a best-seller, in short, was that best-sellerdom has little to do with writing. Book marketing is increasingly international in scope. The result, as a recent article in *The Economist* noted, is that the same small group of books comes to dominate the best-seller lists in country after country. Back in Montreal, Bryan Demchinsky remains, 'absolutely committed to a local list despite all the problems'. One negative consequence of mass marketing, he points out, is that booksellers rarely respond quickly enough to promote local books which show best-seller potential: 'In your own backyard, with as much publicity as you could wish for, your chances are still pretty slim.' A list devoted to regional tastes has become a quixotic notion in an era of global markets – but that may be all the more reason to keep such specimens alive.

———

'Behind the Best-Seller List' was published in *Books in Canada*, September 1994.

'Appropriation of Voice'
An Open Letter

A short novel of mine recently made it to the brink of the 1995 list of a Canadian publisher significantly larger than those I've worked with in the past. I was told that as long as the external reader's report was positive, my chances of receiving a contract were good. The reader's report arrived: it recommended publication. The reader's only misgiving concerned possible accusations of 'appropriation of voice'. The novel's central character was Ecuadorean, dark-skinned and female; I am Canadian, light-skinned and male.

The reader's report prompted a swift re-evaluation of my manuscript. The novel was rejected. A senior editor at the company said: 'I would rather publish an inferior novel by a real Ecuadorean woman than this novel.'

This phrase, it seems to me, lays bare the two most negative tendencies induced by the 'appropriation of voice' fallacy. First, 'appropriation of voice' bullies editors and reviewers into glorifying inferior literature *as inferior literature* in order to prove their sympathy for the disadvantaged. Second, 'appropriation of voice' substitutes 'real' experience for persuasive depictions of experience – an amateur-night confusion. In no way does this debasement of literary standards assist talented minority writers who are closed out of the literary circuit.

I have never been an advocate of the libertarian position on freedom of speech. I would rather not hear from Ernst Zundel. I have seen how the 'free speech' of fanatics and media monopolies can pervert debate or, at an extreme, contribute to plunging nations into strife. But I do think we should credit that sliver of the population constituting the market for literary fiction with sufficient critical acumen to distinguish between the insulting caricature of, say, W.P. Kinsella's Hobbema stories and the honourable homage (though a woman would certainly have written it differently) of the Molly Bloom monologues in *Ulysses*. Nor will the distinctions always be so readily apparent: the process of debating who is a Kinsella and who a Joyce forms a vital component of a healthy literary culture. Evading this debate by suppressing or sidelining books which raise difficult issues of representation will have – arguably already has had – a crippling effect on Canadian literature and criticism.

Whatever one thinks of the Writing Thru 'Race' conference, it plainly demonstrates that writers of colour are taking the initiative on this subject themselves. They don't need, and won't benefit from, the guilty, unproductive paternalism of complacent white writers competing for trendiness points by accusing each other of cultural appropriation every time one of them dramatizes a non-white character. Most people resident in large cities have access to a many-cultured existence; to stifle the literary byproducts of this experience is a form of self-distortion. The Zhdanovite crudity of the 'appropriation of voice' slogan beggars the complex provenance of most literary prose, thwarting our imaginations while casting our readers as parrots awaiting lines to mimic. It's a truism that we are all both language's makers and its prisoners, but for the writing community, who disseminated this unfortunate term and now find our imaginations shackled by it (or our careers curtailed, if we have the temerity to imagine more than fashion dictates that we are allowed to imagine), the joke has worn thin. Nearly every writer in Canada ridicules 'appropriation of voice' in private; in public, good little toadies to a man and woman, we pay obeisance to its petty dictates. At the risk of fighting one piece of cultural intolerance with another measure equally draconian, the time has surely come to purge the words 'appropriation of voice' from our vocabularies.

'"Appropriation of Voice": An Open Letter' was published in *The Writers' Union of Canada Newsletter*, vol. 22, no. 4, October 1994.

* * *

This blast appeared in the 'Members' Words Unedited' section of *The Writers' Union of Canada Newsletter*. At the time, 'Members' Words Unedited' was the primary forum for ongoing Union debate. If you published a piece here, you usually got a few responses. (Members' Words Unedited has dwindled in recent years, as discussion of the issues of the day has migrated to the Union's e-mail list-serve.) A number of writers who read my letter told me privately that they agreed with my position. But no one committed words to paper, either to agree or disagree. Was 'appropriation of voice' an issue too dangerous to discuss in print? The publishers who changed their minds about bringing out my novel *The Places Where Names Vanish* certainly thought so. Commenting on the external reader's report in an internal memo that I was not supposed to see, one editor stated to another editor that he was 'concerned about the appropriation of voice question [the external reader] raises at the end, not just because of the debate "per se" but also because of the practicalities of marketing the book for university courses. My sense of professors' proclivities is that they tend to prefer authentic voices even if the writing isn't as good.'

This is a dazzling example of how academic fads – or industry perceptions of these fads – skew decision-making in literary publishing. The withering-away of a general readership has converted the captive readers of university literature courses into an important market. Yet, like other markets, the university bookstore is prey to the volatile swings of fashion. Both on the campus and in the larger world, the craze of the moment ('authentic voices', for example) becomes the benchmark by which publishers make acquisition decisions. Within a few months or years, this fashion is supplanted by another. The result is a literature of up-to-the-moment triviality, whose prospects of achieving enduring resonance are limited.

The Places Where Names Vanish was finally published by Thistledown Press in 1998. Reviews were generally favourable. Not a single reviewer mentioned the issue of voice appropriation.

The Terrible Truth About 'Appropriation of Voice'

In November 1994 *The Writers' Union of Canada Newsletter* published the final report and recommendations of the Writing Thru 'Race' conference. The conference had been organized to allow Canadian writers of non-European descent the opportunity to discuss common concerns. Chief among these, Cyril Dabydeen had reported in the September 1994 issue of *Books in Canada,* was the perception that writers of colour were not 'on a par with their white colleagues in having access to all aspects of periodical and book publishing'. But the recommendation heading the list of resolutions published in the *Newsletter* by conference organizer Roy Miki did not address this issue. The most vital imperative facing Canadian writers of colour, the conference report stated, was to 'lobby to get copyright protection for oral storytellers, particularly from First Nations communities, whose stories have been appropriated by non-Native writers and then published as a written text.'

Did 180 writers of colour, after a weekend of intense debate, decide that this was the most pressing issue before them? It seems unlikely. Precious few contemporary white writers have intruded upon Natives, thrust tape recorders in front of a traditional storyteller, then scurried back to the city to publish the tales and rake in the profits. Even W.P. Kinsella's condescending, commercially successful fiction about Frank Fencepost and his friends has been accused of appropriating people's names, not their ancestral stories.

In the Canadian literary scene, 'appropriation of voice' – henceforth I will adopt quotation marks for this construct – has become an ideological credibility marker. Miki places it at the head of his list in the same spirit in which the Orange Lodge hangs a portrait of the Queen in its meeting hall. The invocation of 'appropriation of voice' tells the reader what Miki stands for; it signals that he is on the side of the progressives.

The problem is that, like the Queen, 'appropriation of voice' has become an opaque symbol mediating a host of meanings. Interpreted literally, it would be best suited to contest the activities of white anthropologists of two or three generations ago. Applied to the cultural snarl of present-day Canada, 'appropriation of voice' serves to conceal, rather than lay bare, the sources of literary authority.

Appealing in its simplicity, the 'appropriation of voice' fallacy has been swiftly assimilated into our collective literary consciousness. The extent to which this catchphrase has silted down into the sediment of literary life is obvious to anyone who has dealt with a Canadian publisher in recent years. The climate, if not precisely one of fear, reflects a large measure of anxiety and apprehension. 'Appropriation of voice,' in its vaguest, most menacingly nebulous incarnation, is seen as the dictate one must not disobey. The climate of intimidation is accentuated by the fact that few publishers are confident of being able to identify precisely what 'appropriation of voice' does and does not allow. The editor-in-chief of the press that published my last book worried constantly that he would be accused of 'appropriation of voice' for bringing out my stories about young white Canadians travelling in Latin America. The fact that I was a white writer writing almost exclusively about white characters did not suffice to allay his fears. More recently, a press which had expressed a strong interest in a novel of mine changed its mind when an otherwise favourable reader's report suggested, in its final sentence, that the manuscript might be subject to accusations of 'appropriation of voice'.

Publishers fear the opprobrium they may attract by breaking rank with fashion. But their worries are also financial. An internal memo issued by one major Canadian publisher stated that the potential cost of losing the school and university markets rendered impossible the consideration of manuscripts which might be perceived to violate the credos of 'appropriation of voice'.

Faced with the task of weeding out such manuscripts, publishers are working to codify what Canadian writers may and may not say. Take, for example, the instructions Orca Books issued to prospective children's authors in the Summer 1993 issue of *CANSCAIP News:*

The subject of voice appropriation is still a very sticky issue in Canada and one we'd prefer to avoid on our list. We are too small a publisher to invite this kind of controversy. We will not, for instance, consider a native Indian myth told by a non-native. But we will look at carefully researched tales of Chinese, Japanese, Egyptian, British Isles and Northern European origins without insisting on seeing the writer's family tree!

The nervous wish not to offend, culminating in that beseeching final exclamation point, epitomizes the well-meaning way in which the creative imagination is stifled in contemporary Canada. Any writer who undertakes a work of the imagination accepting that she is permitted to write about Japan but not, say, about the Philippines, has already surrendered her artistic integrity. I once heard the Spanish novelist Juan Goytisolo describe his efforts, during the Franco era, to slip a book past official censorship. Goytisolo mastered the regulations of the censor's office, revised his controversial manuscript in such a way as to conceal its transgressions and saw the book receive the stamp of approval. When he read the published edition, Goytisolo realized that he had written a servile, anodyne work. By following the rules, he had become his own censor.

This is precisely what 'appropriation of voice' invites Canadian writers to do. Orca Books even offers authors tips on self-censorship: 'One rule of thumb a writer might consider in choosing a story from a culture other than their [sic] own – is the culture a fragile one?' The assumption behind this statement is that one can repair inequalities of access to publishing opportunities and media attention by restricting the subject-matter of writers seen to be occupying positions of relative privilege. Yet such a policy would do nothing to right wrongs or correct systemic imbalances; its only real effect would be to encourage a tepid, half-articulated literature.

The notion of 'appropriation of voice' has been accorded the imprimatur of authority through the advocacy of publishers, successful writers and the media: all members of the predominantly white establishment. These forces have leapt upon 'appropriation of voice' as a tool with which both to salve their own consciences and to mollify the rising ranks of new, largely non-white cultural figures. Broadcasting concern for minority issues to the point of promising sanctions against 'appropriators', while actually diverting attention from their own positions of authority, established cultural figures have found in 'appropriation of voice' the ideal mechanism of co-optation.

Establishment liberals' promotion of 'appropriation of voice' breeds curious paradoxes and zealously authoritarian prescriptions. In the final section of Timothy Findley's novel *Headhunter*, for example, the servant Orley Hawkins, the token African-Canadian character in a novel dominated by upper-class Rosedale Wasps, suddenly discovers the truth of 'appropriation'. In a cheer-leading five-page interior monologue, Hawkins champions Whoopi Goldberg, Alice Walker and Toni Morrison to the detriment of Carson McCullers and William Faulkner. The former are complimented: 'Because they are themselves. Entirely.' Faulkner's depiction of Dilsey in *The Sound and the Fury* is dismissed as 'a white hand hovering over the page'. Findley disparages Faulkner's work not through a critique of its literary merits, or even an assessment of its depiction of African-American characters, but because of who wrote it. The author's identity, rather than the quality of the work, becomes the pivotal factor in determining its worth. The chapter ends: '*From now on,* Orley decided, *I will write myself.*' In promoting this view, Findley nullifies his own right to create the scene we have just read – though this may be his way of bidding farewell to the vice of 'appropriation' and communicating to his readers that he will never again write about anyone other than Rosedale-reared Wasps like himself.

The rampant essentialism embodied in Findley's advocacy of 'appropriation of voice' underlines the central contradiction implicit in the notion's adoption by the literary establishment. In terms of literary history, 'appropriation of voice' is a concept properly belonging to the 1830s. In order to believe in such an anachronistic dictum as 'being yourself entirely', it would be necessary to toss overboard most modern philosophy and literary theory – particularly that of the last forty years – in order to return to the tenets of Romanticism. 'Appropriation of voice' depends for its legitimacy on the assumption that there exists an undiluted, 'authentic' core to each culture, reflected in its traditional art. Yet most of this century's literary criticism, from Bakhtinian polyglossia to New Criticism to Derridean deconstructionism to Cixous's efforts to 'write the body' to Bloom's descriptions of the 'anxiety of influence' to Marxist and Lacanian approaches, has developed, in different ways, from the notion that literary language is a hybrid, impure conglomeration of coded assumptions and shadows of half-absorbed past systems of writing. One of the most bizarre spectacles induced by the 'appropriation of voice' carnival has been the sight of trendy fellow-travellers of literary fashion simultaneously proclaiming their allegiance to the mutually exclusive assumptions of contemporary literary theory and 'appropriation of voice'.

The Romantic roots of contemporary white liberal injunctions to Natives and other racial minorities that they should 'be themselves entirely' are brilliantly dramatized by the U.S. Sioux writer Susan Power in her novel *The Grass Dancer*. Set mainly on a North Dakota reservation, the novel includes, as a kind of running gag, a meddlesome white liberal named Jeanette McVay. As a teacher in a Native school, McVay tries to instill in her charges an appreciation of their cultural wealth by reading aloud passages from James Fenimore Cooper's *The Prairie*. When the students express their boredom with Cooper, McVay shifts gears from nineteenth-century Romanticism to its contemporary equivalent: 'We're going to tell our extraordinary stories and confirm our way of looking at the world. Your voices are valid.' By having McVay tell her students that each of them is 'the receptacle of ancient wisdom', Power makes explicit the linkage between Romantic fiction's exoticization of the Native and the continuation of this process in the present by 'voice' rhetoric. The students, Power makes clear – the novel ends with a call to 'tell two stories' – are the products of a hybrid culture. The assumptions underlying notions such as 'valid voices' would disenfranchise them from one half of their cultural heritage.

The hybrid and the migrant, Salman Rushdie argues in *Imaginary Homelands*, are the pivotal figures of our age. Their endowments are often richest when, like Rushdie in *East, West*, they 'refuse to choose' between their ancestral and host cultures. The neo-Romanticism of 'appropriation of voice' dogma sometimes blinds us to the fact that the voices we hear in the writing of a Thomas King or an Austin Clarke are impure, mongrelized. In mastering the conventions of English literature, writers from colonized or minority backgrounds deliberately absorb an even larger dose of Western or mainstream culture than others in their respective communities. The writers may avenge themselves on the dominant culture by hybridizing its speech and writing – witness the changes wrought in U.S. literary language over the last fifty years by Jewish, African-American and more recently, Hispanic writers – but the price they pay is that, like nearly all writers, they become outsiders within their own communities: archetypal alienated modern artists. 'Appropriation of voice' dogma suppresses this complexity by equating writers of the level of sophistication of Toni Morrison with 'receptacles of ancient wisdom' whose task is to edify and entertain the white mainstream by, as Timothy Findley would have it, 'being themselves entirely'.

The dynamics of literary authority in Canada cannot be captured in a slogan. No senior editor at a major Canadian publishing house comes from a racial minority background; on the other hand, four of our most popular, successful male novelists are named Mistry, Vassanji, Bissoondath and Selvadurai. One might venture that novels by men of South Asian ancestry receive prominent billing while poetry collections by women of Native Canadian or Afro-Caribbean heritage do not. But most poetry collections by white men are also granted scant attention. In addition to ignoring distinctions of form and genre, the one-dimensional focus on race elides questions of gender, class and region. Is a writer of colour possessed of a good education, a professional position and a Toronto base – a lawyer like M. Nourbese Philip, a successful journalist like Cecil Foster – axiomatically at a disadvantage, in the battle for publication rights and media attention, to a white male writer from Prince Edward Island, a working class Manitoban – or even a white writer from the hinterland of Ontario itself? Talking about 'appropriation of voice' is an excellent way to avoid having to deal with many intricate yet crucial issues of literary authority.

Toronto, the site of far too many national cultural institutions and vested literary interests, has also been the source from which the 'appropriation of voice' slogan has radiated through the land. Without the Toronto media's aggressive popularization of this phrase, it would be difficult to imagine the Writing Thru 'Race' conference taking place, let alone perching the talisman of 'appropriation of voice' at the top of its report. It can be easy to forget, in the jangle of our postmodern lives, that Canada is not only a multicultural society but also a postcolonial one. Little more than a generation ago Toronto, in cultural terms, was still a compliant colonial outpost. While Alberta, Quebec and Newfoundland have all developed their own distinct traditions of dissent, Toronto the Good evolved into Toronto the Trendy. The line dividing the two is as thin as rice-paper: both worship the authority of fashion, both use disapproval and exclusion to enforce a constipated conformity with fashion, both fear challenges to and even discussion of recognized norms and hierarchies. It has become a commonplace among Toronto-based cultural outlets (and increasingly among those based elsewhere), to speak of 'the "appropriation of voice" debate'. This media sham has hoodwinked us. No such debate has occurred; there has been only a sucking-away of creative breathing space before the inexorable advance of a slogan which purports to foster change while it in fact reinforces the status quo.

'The Terrible Truth About "Appropriation of Voice"' was published in *Matrix* no. 47, Summer 1996.

A Language for the Americas

Midway through Francisco Goldman's first novel, *The Long Night of White Chickens,* the fast-talking Guatemalan-American narrator retreats to New York from the turmoil spawned by the murder of his foster sister in Guatemala City. Attempting to get in touch with his Central American roots, he reads every book he can find on Guatemala. Many of these books are written from a left-wing point of view. 'Guatemala,' he notes, 'has not tended to attract intellectual defenders of the right.'

With its violently enforced racial chasm dividing the rich white minority from the poor Indian majority, Guatemala has always been the left-winger's favourite police state. Few journalists have interpreted Guatemala's agony with as much skill and passion as Francisco Goldman. During the early 1980s, when Central America was constantly in the news, Goldman became something of a cult figure to my generation of politically committed U.S. university students. Suspicious of the mainstream media in the United States, we marvelled at Goldman's ability to infiltrate the glossy pages of *Harper's* magazine with analyses compatible with our own left-wing outlook.

When Central America dropped off the front page, Goldman, too, slipped from view. His reappearance as a novelist represents less a metamorphosis than a change of strategy. Goldman's subject in this elliptical novel, woven from a tissue of obsessive digressions, is once again Guatemalan misery.

Roger Graetz, half Guatemalan and half Jewish-American, is quietly assimilating into life in suburban Massachusetts until his Guatemalan grandmother sends his parents an Indian girl to work as a domestic servant. Roger's father decides to treat the girl as a daughter and give her a good education. To Roger, Flor de Mayo Puac becomes both an intriguingly exotic older sister and a reminder of his own Central American ancestry. After her graduation from an élite New England college, Flor de Mayo defies everyone's expectations by returning to her homeland to run an orphanage. Her murder sends Roger scurrying back to Guatemala to find out what happened.

As Roger plunges into the vortex of Guatemalan society, encountering everyone from oligarchs to street children, it's difficult to escape the feeling that Goldman is cramming in every fact and anecdote omitted from his 1980s magazine articles. Many of the characters are barely disguised portraits of notorious Guatemalan public figures. *The Long Night of White Chickens* summarizes Flor's rags-to-riches-to-death story in its opening two pages, then tells the tale again and again. Each rendition adds new characters and events, increasing the story's complexity. Goldman's long, fluid sentences race through obstacle courses of subordinate clauses as Roger tries to account for all the forces that may have conspired to bring about Flor's murder.

Many of the subplots, while generating vivid scenes, contribute little to clearing up the mystery of Flor's death. But they do help to dramatize the glaring affront to the Guatemalan social order posed by an Indian woman possessing a prestigious U.S. degree. In the end, it seems to be Guatemala itself that kills Flor. But while her death may be subsumed into the novel's symbolic design, Flor in life remains a credible, human character.

The other characters, though evoked with a mass of sharply believable detail, sometimes seem to be kept at a distance by Roger's brilliantly articulate expositions. Goldman's use of Spanish is telling in this regard. Where other bicultural U.S. writers such as Sandra Cisneros and Cristina García leave Spanish dialogue untranslated, forcing the reader to come to grips with the Hispanic cultural presence, Goldman translates every utterance. He sometimes offers two or three English variants in an attempt to convey all the nuances of each expression. In this first novel, Goldman uses fiction to perpetuate his journalist's mission of *interpreting* Central America – in every sense of the word – to a U.S. readership.

While it makes the action more accessible, this approach can hinder the reader's immersion in the book's imaginative universe. The rhythms of Goldman's prose derive from the language of the street – but the streets of New York, not of Guatemala City. Reading *The Long Night of White Chickens* is like being accosted by an edgy, fast-talking New Yorker bent on explaining everything about Central America's most tortured republic. While saying more about Guatemala than has ever before been said in English, the novel ultimately turns its head northwards. Goldman's explanations of Guatemala's history, habits and slang confirm that despite his fondness for hybridization, he has written an American, not a Guatemalan, novel.

If his first book was a United States novel about Guatemala, Goldman's second offering, *The Ordinary Seaman,* is a Central American novel about New York. The time is 1989. Esteban, the seaman of the title, is a nineteen-year-old veteran of two years' combat with an élite unit of the Sandinista army. Lured by the promise of a dizzying wage of more than a dollar an hour, he flies to New York to crew a cargo ship supposedly carrying a load of fertilizer to Costa Rica. The other seamen, also unemployed Nicaraguans and Hondurans, arrive on the same flight. The ship proves to be a wreck. The men work for weeks with minimal supervision and no pay, but the circuit breakers needed to render the vessel seaworthy fail to appear. The captain, an enigmatic Greek-American, becomes an increasingly infrequent visitor. The men's food supply runs low, their clothes rot in the damp, the ship is invaded by rats. A few dull their misery by sniffing paint fumes. The seamen's U.S. visas expire, imprisoning them in the harbour; they cannot enter the city without risking deportation. Their sole group foray into New York leads them into a housing project, where they are mugged by a gang. After this, most of the crew prefer to cower in their isolated corner of Brooklyn Harbour, staring across the water at the Statue of Liberty. Where earlier immigrants sailed past the statue into the U.S.A., Goldman's marooned mariners try, yet fail, to sail home.

The metaphor of the failed return home crystallizes Goldman's concerns. *The Ordinary Seaman* is a snapshot of the peoples of the Americas on the move, carrying their cultures with them even as they grow racially and linguistically more mixed. The only character of undiluted Anglo-Saxon descent, Mark Baker, the captain's hapless sidekick in the swindle whose collapse has stranded the sailors, finds that the streets of New York will not allow him to forget the abandoned Central Americans:

He's sick of being reminded, of feeling angry and guilty everywhere he goes ...

because everywhere he goes he sees them: busboys, McDonald's, even working pizza parlours now instead of Italians and Greeks, lined up outside that taco truck on the corner of 94th and Broadway, in the subways, working in delis ... little brown guys but hardly ever any little brown females, yackety-yacking in Spanish, dark glare of their eyes, squat Napoleon builds and proud, serious Aztec (whatever) faces. By now there's not a Korean deli owner in New York who doesn't know how to say, at least, Qué pasa?

Even Baker succumbs in the end, fleeing one step ahead of the law to the Yucatán and vowing to learn Spanish. As Esteban, the most daring of the sailors, begins venturing into the city alone, the diversity of the Hispanic population startles him. He meets Spanish-speaking blacks from the Dominican Republic and becomes the lover of a brassy young woman from rural Mexico who works as a manicurist in the studio of a macho gay Cuban hairdresser. The harbour authorities are notified of the sailors' plight by an elegant Argentine couple; the official sent to investigate is the fiancé of a young half-French half-Colombian heiress. The Greek-American captain has studied in Mexico, worked in Brazil and Peru, and purchased the doomed ship in Canada. Barely a nation of the Americas escapes Goldman's stew of cultures.

Goldman's language accommodates this free-form merging. *The Ordinary Seaman* is written in long, offhand, present-tense sentences. In contrast to *The Long Night of White Chickens,* Spanish expressions and dialogue stream unitalicized and untranslated through this novel's prose. The book's structure is loose, the forward action checked by flashbacks to half a dozen different countries, but many of these scenes are vivid, even wrenching: the descriptions of Esteban's battle experience in Nicaragua are some of the most powerful prose to have emerged from that conflict. But it is also a prose that mediates between English and Spanish diction, enabling the reader to hear the Spanish rhythms prodding at the English phrasing without ever descending into screen-bandido jargon. This description of the aftermath of a battle in northern Nicaragua is typical:

They were landed near now-empty trenches outside an abandoned hamlet that had been taken over by la contra. There was not that much resistance. And many contra dead, often found in clusters. The dead like the dead always, their deaths so poorly disguised by their grimacing and flinching and astonished and sometimes peaceful expressions, some already bloating, stinking. Vultures everywhere. And dead mules and horses. Milton claimed four hundred contra had died, but that must have been an exaggeration, there weren't that many bodies; but who knew how many dead they had carried back across the border? They recovered at least that many weapons, and radios, all kinds of yanqui equipment left behind when they'd fled. Milton wanted to cross the border and wipe them out, but the Comandancia forbade it. Esteban's entire B LI lost five compas, three to mines, and nine wounded, several by cazabobos, those mines that blow off a foot. But the problem was, supposedly there were a number of dead civilians – women, children – too. Though he, personally, saw only a few, a family sprawled along a riverbank, a mother and three children, two of them chavalitas, their shredded dresses dark brown with blood, their bodies already dissolving into the warm mud.

The horror of the scene is both tempered and accentuated by the troubling sensuality of the bodies dissolving into warm mud. This sort of quasi-magic-realist touch is rare in Goldman's gritty fiction, but it does illustrate the variety of influences acting on his prose. The narrative voice displays Hemingway's stoicism, the method of evocation through deliberate repetition of key words ('dead ... dead ... deaths') is one that Hemingway learned from Tolstoy; there is also the Hemingwayesque stress on the word 'and'. Goldman mingles these stylistic traits with Gabriel García Márquez's epic observation of the sweep of history through anomalous moments of sensuality. In Goldman's overall novelistic designs the reader spots a furious determination to find a linguistic register capable of orchestrating the discordant Mayan, Hispanic and transnational elements present in Central American culture that echoes the ambitions of the Nobel Prize–winning Guatemalan novelist Miguel Angel Asturias (who is alluded to in *The Long Night of White Chickens*). Mixed in with these literary influences are the speech rhythms of the English-speaking Latino, evident in the occasional frankly Hispanic phrasing such as 'those mines that blow off a foot', or in the use of Central American slang such as 'chavalita' – young girl – unitalicized and untranslated.

Goldman is one of the most energetic pioneers in this new American (in the bi-continental sense) literature springing from the encounter of

the English-speaking and Spanish-speaking worlds. Other contemporary U.S. writers who join him in this enterprise include Sandra Cis-
neros (*Woman Hollering Creek*), Cristina García (*Dreaming in Cuban*),
Julia Alvarez (*How the García Girls Lost Their Accents*), Oscar Hijuelos
(*The Mambo Kings Play Songs of Love*), Ernesto Quiñonez (*Bodega
Dreams*) and such Anglo U.S. writers as John Sayles (*Los Gusanos*).
These writers' efforts to weave the heritage of Spanish American lit-
erature into the English-language tradition are crucial to the self-defini-
tion of their U.S. compatriots. But, as Canada's connections with
Europe etiolate and our culture grows more integrated into that of the
Americas, it is important that Canadian writers, also, consider the posi-
tion from which they are writing within the Western Hemisphere.

One of the paradoxes of literary dynamics on this continent is that
while a large number of Canadian writers worship literary U.S. stars,
American writers themselves tend to praise and admire Latin American
writers. Whenever I read one of those end-of-the-year newspaper
surveys where Canadian writers or reviewers are asked to name their
favourite books of the year, I am surprised by the prevalence of chroni-
clers of U.S. imperial high society such as John Updike, or plumbers of
the peculiar, ingrown mythology of the twentieth-century United
States, such as Don DeLillo. These writers, even when critical of U.S.
experience (more the case of DeLillo than of Updike), write from a position of imperial centrality. The Canadian writer can enjoy this work, but
how much can we learn from it?

The malevolent impact of this strain of influence is obvious in that
most supine thread of Canadian writing – eternally present in our
fractured tradition, though never dominant – creeping ignominiously
from Morley Callaghan's *It's Never Over* to Cordelia Strube's *Alex & Zee*,
of books that are set in hazily unnamed, unevoked cities. Products of
the fear that the words 'Toronto' or 'Montreal' might make the U.S.
reader recoil, such books emanate a desperate longing to be American
(in the U.S. sense), a gruesome shame that converts Canadianness into a
family secret too mortifying to mention in the public conversation of
fiction. Just as light-skinned African-Americans used to cut their hair
very short in the hope that they could 'pass' as white, so writers such as
Callaghan or Strube (or a host of others) cut out the description or
naming of shameful Canadian places in the hope that their fiction will

'pass' as American. This kind of neo-colonial self-abasement is embarrassing to behold; but it is also unfulfilled *as fiction.* Strong characters take root in palpable, meticulously evoked settings; the cardboard cutouts of *It's Never Over* or the aimlessly wafting denizens of the faceless city in *Alex & Zee* are weakened by their respective authors' denial of where they come from. Acknowledging the reality of the places one knows, rendering those places with care, is central to investing a writer's fiction with depth and resonance. Writers, like literatures, may have to mature in order to attain this kind of enriching engagement with place and history. Compare the characterization in Mavis Gallant's early novel *Green Water, Green Sky,* where she tries to pass off her Canadians abroad as Americans abroad without possessing a deep enough adult experience of U.S. society to make the characters persuasively American, with the full-blooded richness of *My Heart Is Broken,* Gallant's next published book. *Green Water, Green Sky,* though raptly and even brilliantly written, is hollow at the core; in *My Heart Is Broken,* where Gallant acknowledges the Canadianness of her expatriates in her Parisian stories and plumbs her Quebec youth in 'Its Image on the Mirror', the novella that anchors the collection, all the right details come pouring in to surround, enhance and humanize her creations. Cultural self-respect is an aesthetic, not merely a political, issue.

In 1976 Clark Blaise published in *Fiction International* an essay called 'Writing Canadian Fiction'. This piece, which still stands as one of the most perceptive essays written on the position of the Canadian writer, concludes with the statement that Thomas Pynchon's *Gravity's Rainbow* – the contemporary U.S. novel most widely admired in literary circles at that time – speaks brilliantly for *one* of the American literatures, but, obsessed as it is with superpower paranoia, enjoys limited resonance for readers or writers of the other American literatures: English-Canadian, Québécois, Ibero-American, Caribbean. This observation should have made Canadian writers reconsider their relationship with Latin American fiction nearly a quarter of a century ago. The paradox returns: many Canadian writers admire U.S. writers, but they fail to admire the writers admired by the U.S. writers themselves.

The first reason for Canadian writers to read Latin American fiction is that, as a broad critical consensus affirms, from the early 1950s until at least the mid-1980s, no other world literature produced such a large number of significant novelists or sustained such a consistently high level of innovation in the reworking of literary language or the reshaping of the novel as an art form. After twenty years of reading this literature, I continue to discover new books and writers whose vitality engrosses me. U.S. writers, in general, recognize this achievement. As William H. Gass once said to me across a dinner table: 'They've whupped our asses for the last forty years!' Yet the *popular* reception of Latin American literature in the United States (as opposed to how it has been received by writers) has skewed the Latin Americans' achievement. In the United States – which has been the primary conduit for bringing this literature to the rest of the English-speaking world – Latin American literature became a campus favourite: the Tolkien fad of the 1960s was supplanted in the 1970s and 1980s by the vogue for magic realism. The cocktail of magic realism and violent politics is undeniably a potent one, creating an image of 'a magical continent rising up in revolt', as one disgruntled U.S. critic complained. But the 'magic realism' tag really only applies to García Márquez's *One Hundred Years of Solitude* (not even to his other books) and, arguably, to one or two early works by the Cuban writer Alejo Carpentier. (The novels of Isabel Allende, defined by their self-conscious imitation of the most striking motifs of *One Hundred Years of Solitude* and tending increasingly towards formula fiction as her career progresses, capitalized on magic realism once its commercial appeal had been proved. Allende in turn has bred her own imitators, such as the Mexican best-seller writers Angeles Mastretta and Laura Esquivel, the Colombian Laura Restrepo and the Chilean Marcela Serrano.)

Much Latin American fiction engages in narrative innovation, but only a relatively small, commercially oriented portion enlists the use of magic realism. It is dismaying to see so many vigorous and inventive evocations of marginalized realities dismissed (and praised) as 'magic'. The designation by marketing campaigns, journalists and many book reviewers of the totality of Latin American literature as 'magic realist' is instructive of the prevailing U.S. inability to take other cultures seriously.

Canadian writers can learn to appreciate Latin American literature from writers in the States. But, if we read the books with attention, I suspect we will come to value the Spanish- and Portuguese-speaking literature of the Americas differently than our neighbours. Reading the work of Horacio Quiroga, Clarice Lispector or José Donoso – to choose at random three of the Latin American masters least widely read in English – the Canadian writer cannot help but conceive integration into the Americas in different terms than through the mantra of 'trade harmonization' chanted by our political leaders. In contrast to the welling sameness of proliferating commercial logos and identical shopping malls, one discovers a writing anchored by a multitude of local peculiarities. 'Integration into the Americas', approached through the prism of Latin American literature rather than that of globalized commercial policy, opens the door to the exploration and dramatization of our own differences, turns us back on our own history, as Latin American writers have developed their literature by stretching and twisting the conventions of Iberian prose and the European novel to express the many histories of the Caribbean, Mexico, Central and South America. (It should be said at this point that the Latin American reading experience can be glimpsed in a few Canadian works of fiction. Patrick Roscoe's *Loving Is Starving for Itself* imitates the García Márquez voice almost too perfectly, while disdaining the deeper lessons of the Colombian's fiction; Jack Hodgins's novel *The Return of Joseph Bourne* walks a line between U.S. campus exoticization of Latin American imagery and the adaptation of a mythology of marginalization to a particular peripheral Canadian place, in this case Vancouver Island.)

Prominent among the lessons Canadian writers can learn from Latin American fiction is that if the place you know best is not somewhere famous your writing is most likely to flourish when you immerse yourself in the peculiar details of your own time and space, rather than pretending, like Morley Callaghan, that your characters live in 'the city'. If your reality is marginalized, mythologize your marginalization! Innovation occurs in the moment when you discover that you cannot both remain true to your own experience and write like John Updike (or John Cheever or Saul Bellow or Lorrie Moore or Alice Adams). García Márquez, Carlos Fuentes and Mario Vargas Llosa learned this lesson from William Faulkner, the U.S. writer who made marginality his central preoccupation. All of these writers found they could make the traditions of the European and U.S. novel fit their respective peripheral realities only by wrenching the novel's language and structure into unsuspected configurations – the configurations of Vargas Llosa's *The Green House,* Julio Cortázar's *Hopscotch,* Ernest Sábato's *On Heroes and Tombs,* José Donoso's *The Obscene Bird of Night* – and the novel has been far better for it. Closer to home, the Québécois playwright Michel Tremblay once advised English Canadian writers that the route to universality lay through devotion to local detail. Like most advice coming from Quebec, this wise counsel has been firmly ignored.

The Canadian writer immersed in Latin American literature conceives integration into the Americas not as homogenization, but as communication among a multitude of encampments surrounding a crumbling castle. This is a far more dynamic and creative stance for a writer than docile imitation of the imperial centre. Reading Latin American literature, the Canadian reader (or writer) encounters familiar themes dramatized in provocative, unfamiliar ways: the integration of Native culture into national history in Miguel Angel Asturias's *Men of Maize,* the legacy of eighteenth-century France in the Americas in Alejo Carpentier's *Explosion in a Cathedral,* the impact of B-movies on the individual imagination in Manuel Puig's *The Kiss of the Spider Woman,* the efforts of the city-dweller to assimilate remote backlands into a national outlook in Rómulo Gallegos's *Doña Bárbara,* and many more.

In a similar vein, the bicultural writing of Francisco Goldman, Sandra Cisneros or Ernesto Quiñonez, with its ongoing mediation between English and Spanish, provides a model for Canadian immigrant writers who are stretched between two linguistic traditions. Sandra Cisneros writes:

Urracas, then, big as crows, shiny as ravens, swooping and whooping it up like drunks at Fiesta. *Urracas* giving a sharp cry, a slippery rise up the scales, a quick stroke across a violin string. And then a splintery whistle that they loop and lasso from that box in their throat, and spit and chirrup and chook. *Chook-chook, Chook-chook.*

Cisneros's blending of two languages in this paragraph, from the opening usage of the Spanish word for grackles to the closing onomatopoeic utterance, represents a struggle for a level of expressiveness lying beyond the boundaries of a single language. Even the poor grammar of 'their throat' seems to confirm the author's position in a space where neither of her languages can exert a firm hold on her perceptions.

U.S. Latino prose also opens the door to that never-realized Canadian fantasy of finding a literary language capable of encompassing anglophone and francophone Canadian experience in a single novel.

The subtle interpenetration of our anglophone and francophone literary traditions, too often described as solitary and unrelated, is pervasive. In addition to the obvious cases of bicultural writers such as Mavis Gallant and Gail Scott, little-appreciated bridges exist between the two literary cultures: F.R. Scott's influence on Pierre Trudeau's essays, Nicole Brossard's influence on West Coast feminist poets, Hubert Aquin's influence on Douglas Glover. Margaret Atwood, who at one stage claimed to have been influenced by Marie-Claire Blais, has in turn influenced younger women writers in Quebec. The Franco-Ontarian novelist Daniel Poliquin's novel *The Black Squirrel* contains conspicuous allusions to the novels of Margaret Laurence, Robertson Davies, Matt Cohen and Douglas Glover. The political arch-enemies Mordecai Richler and Yves Beauchemin claimed to admire one another's hefty novels. Even the Québécois nationalist sage Jacques Ferron planted in his novel *The Juneberry Tree* an overt invitation to Northrop Frye to enter into cultural dialogue – an invitation of which Frye, unfortunately, seems to have remained oblivious. Contemporary Canadian intellectuals appear little more disposed than Frye to undertake such a debate. The popularity of postcolonial theory, paradoxically, has directed English-speaking Canadian writers' and thinkers' attention inward, towards the problems of immigrants and Native Canadians within English Canada. The postcolonial paradigm has failed to facilitate an opening to Quebec because even the most progressive English-speaking Canadians resist the notion that Canada colonized Quebec. For this reason, though anglophone and francophone Canada arguably have more in common now than ever before, the increasingly outward-looking fiction of francophone writers such as Daniel Poliquin, Monique Proulx, Louis Hamelin, Sergio Kokis, Ying Chen and others has elicited few echoes in the rest of Canada.

Yet two hundred and fifty years' sharing of ghosts and motifs has bequeathed us the historical and linguistic tools to begin to elaborate a literary language that mediates the experience of the other solitude. (Just as in contemporary Montreal the so-called 'children of Bill 101', many of them from immigrant backgrounds, hop accentlessly from

French to English, often without regarding either language as 'first' or 'second'.) If Latino writers can develop a language that mediates vigorously between English and Spanish, and if some Latin American writers, such as José María Arguedas and Augusto Roa Bastos, have honed prose styles that mediate between Spanish and indigenous American languages, little should prevent Canadian writers from evolving a similar go-between idiom expressing the interpenetration of English and French realities. From our fuller engagement with *all* of the Americas – not just Manhattan or Hollywood – the Great Canadian Novel may yet emerge.

'A Language for the Americas' is adapted from various sources: 'The journey is exotic, but the guide is a little too loud', *Globe and Mail*, 5 September 1992; 'Uniting the Americas', *Times Literary Supplement*, 14 March 1997; and 'Multiple Edges: Latino Fiction, Spanish American Novel, Canadian Writing in the Americas', *The New Quarterly*, vol. xx, no 3, 2001.

Giller's Version

Since its inception in 1994, the $25,000 Giller Prize has become the media darling among Canada's literary prizes. 'English Canada's most glamorous and suspense-filled literary contest', the *Globe and Mail's* Val Ross has rhapsodized. Former *Globe* editor William Thorsell lauded the privately funded Giller as a symbol of 'the power of individuals in the face of systems, governments and organizations'. The Giller Prize banquet has developed into a major media circus.

The Giller's rapid ascent has overshadowed Canada's most comprehensive literary prizes, the Governor General's Awards. Created by the Canadian Authors' Association in 1937, the GGs have been administered by the Canada Council since 1959. Now they are in danger of being nudged out of the limelight by the media's preference for the Giller. Bookstores give pride of place to the Giller's promotional bookmarks and posters, relegating the GGs' materials to the status of second best.

'The Giller,' Thorsell boasted, 'is announced at a lavishly produced dinner in downtown Toronto, attended by an impressive collection of People Who Matter.... Government-linked awards doled out in Ottawa, whether for literature, performing arts or journalism, will never have the same roiled jelly.'

In large part, the Giller owes its rise to the Toronto location of its award ceremony. Major media, which often neglect cultural events in the rest of Canada, have no difficulty covering the Giller.

Until 1997 the Giller had shortlisted only one book published outside Toronto – and that was Steve Weiner's novel *The Museum of Love*, which was published in Woodstock, New York. The only non-large-press book to make the list prior to this year's inclusion of Shani Mootoo's *Cereus Blooms at Night* (Press Gang) and Michael Helms's *The Projectionist* (Douglas & McIntyre) was Leo McKay's *Like This,* published by Anansi, the widely distributed, Toronto-based literary imprint of Stoddart

Publishing. This year's two surprise choices will probably prove to be blips rather than trendsetters. And neither book is the product of a traditional Canadian literary press. Douglas & McIntyre, the largest Canadian publisher west of Toronto, specializes in non-fiction; Press Gang, concentrating on a continental gay market, makes the bulk of its sales in the United States. More importantly, neither Mootoo nor Helms won the Giller. The selection of Mordecai Richler's *Barney's Version* confirms the Giller as the preserve of the 'People Who Matter'. Richler was awarded the prize by a jury that included Mavis Gallant, his friend of more than forty years' standing, just as, in 1996, Margaret Atwood received the Giller from a jury chaired by David Staines, her friend of more than thirty years' standing. Future Giller shortlists, meanwhile, are likely to resemble that of 1996, when two well-heeled Toronto publishers, McClelland & Stewart and Knopf Canada, walked away with all the nominations.

The policy that virtually guarantees big-press, Toronto dominance over the long term is the Giller's *de facto* entry fee. Under the subheading 'Conditions of the Prize', the Giller rules stipulate that: *'Any eligible book which is entered for the Giller Prize shall not qualify for the award unless its publisher agrees: a) for each shortlisted book, to pay $1,250 to The Giller Prize as contributions towards shortlist advertising and promotion; b) to spend an appropriate sum on direct, paid for media advertising for the winning book.'*

'It's a hurdle,' concedes one publisher who expresses frustration at the exclusion of literary press books from past Giller shortlists. Describing his press as being 'at the big end of the small-press spectrum', the publisher suggests that for smaller literary presses the fee 'could be prohibitive'. In an average year, the judges of the Governor General's Award for Fiction consider about 140 books, while the Giller jury looks at only 55 to 60 books. Even this limited sample contains some books whose publishers might not be able to afford the shortlist admission fee and mandatory advertising costs should one of their books be nominated. (Depressingly, Canada's newest fiction prize, the Rogers, awarded by the Writers' Development Trust, has imitated the Giller by also instituting a fee.)

The Giller's monopolization of the spotlight could not have come at a worse time for the Governor General's Awards. Having limped through the 1980s, when the award increased the sales of the fiction prize winner by a measly three hundred copies, the GGs were refurbished by the Canada Council for the 1990s. Thanks to more aggressive publicity, the GGs began turning small-press writers into best-sellers.

The 1990 Governor General's Awards established Ann-Marie MacDonald (who won the drama prize) and Nino Ricci (who won for fiction) as important, rising writers. Poet and travel writer Karen Connelly became a best-seller on the strength of the 1993 non-fiction award; fiction writers Caroline Adderson and Russell Smith first gained wide attention when they were shortlisted respectively for the 1993 and 1994 GGs. The small presses that published these shortlisted books – Coach House, Cormorant, Turnstone and The Porcupine's Quill, respectively – were able to profit from GG publicity because it did not cost them the promise of $1,250 to keep their unknown young writers in contention. The absence of a fee has permitted the GGs to create new stars, while the Giller has merely confirmed the status of writers already possessed of a wealthy publisher. The first two Gillers, reflecting the mid-1990s Toronto obsession with identity politics, were awarded to the Indo-African-Canadian novelist M. G. Vassanji and the Indo-Canadian novelist Rohinton Mistry; the next three Gillers were won by Margaret Atwood, Mordecai Richler and Alice Munro, probably the three most established writers in the country. This is not a prize that is out to shake up our literary preconceptions.

The Giller's exclusive focus on English-language fiction, furthermore, curtails public awareness of other forms of writing. As we hear less about the GGs, we are also less likely to learn who wrote last year's best biography, play or book of poems – or to hear about French-language writing.

Unlike the Giller, the GGs are a national award, with the awards ceremony rotating among major Canadian cities. While William Thorsell was sneering at 'awards doled out in Ottawa', the 1996 GG ceremonies were in fact being held at the National Theatre School in Montreal, a location easily as atmospheric as any Toronto banquet hall. A friend of mine, who ended up at the ceremony by chance, reported finding it 'extremely moving'. But the Toronto-based 'national' media preferred to cover the Giller.

The choice between the Governor General's Awards and the Giller is the choice between a national culture and commercial hype. The Giller has risen on the tide of a big-business dogma that reduces literature to a commodity and drowns a coast-to-coast Canadian culture in the local obsessions of one metropolitan centre. Its crippling shortlist fee, cordoning off the Giller from the wealth of writing being produced across the country, is unlikely to disappear until writers take matters into their own hands. Will one of next year's shortlisted authors turn down his or her Giller nomination to protest the $1,250 fee? I hope so. Any writer who took this stand would gain not only the admiration of literary peers, but a large measure of self-respect: it can't be very satisfying to win the race for the Giller when you know that more than half of the contestants have been locked out at the starting gate.

'Giller's Version' was published in *The Canadian Forum*, December 1997.

* * *

When this piece was published, the editors of *The Canadian Forum* sent out a press release announcing their scoop: the Giller shortlist had a secret entry fee! But the anticipated buzz of controversy failed to sound. No news organization responded to the press release, or even mentioned the entry fee. (Rumour claimed that a commentary on the issue had appeared in an Edmonton newspaper, but my efforts to locate this article were unsuccessful.)

The result of this silence is that the Giller's shortlist fee remains a secret. As the Giller is the consummate cultural expression of the Hollywoodized, neo-conservative, market-driven, user-fee mentality promoted by most of the country's newspapers, it was perhaps unrealistic to expect them to blow the whistle on the caper. In fact, this point had been driven home to me even before the article appeared in *The Canadian Forum*. I originally offered 'Giller's Version' to a newspaper whose books editor had expressed an interest in seeing my work. Shortly after I submitted the article, the paper ran a slaveringly obsequious feature on the 'Glamorous Giller'. I was not very surprised when the editor returned 'Giller's Version' with the comment that it was 'not quite right for our paper'.

As is usually the case in Canada, reaction to the article came in the form of private comments, not public debate. The most persuasive argument I heard against my position was from a writer who had sat on prize juries. I underestimated the strength of jurors' feelings for the books they supported, the writer said. The entry fee was ultimately irrelevant, this writer claimed, because in a pinch the Giller organization would be forced to cover it. A juror whose favourite book was about to be excluded because an indebted literary press could not cough up the shortlist entry fee might threaten to resign from the jury, discrediting the prize. The shortlist fee, the writer argued, was ultimately unenforceable.

If this is true, perhaps next year all publishers should consider withholding their shortlist entry fees.

Another question I faced was: how can you defend the GGs when they have honoured so many awful books? The awarding of the 1997 GG for fiction in English to Jane Urquhart's emotionally vacant, linguistically flat, storyless, characterless novel *The Underpainter* did not make my position any easier. Richler's *Barney's Version* is a structurally clumsy book, awash with sentimentality and an unsavoury nostalgia for the good old days of Anglo suzerainty in Quebec; but it is intelligent, witty and, beneath its cluttered surface, craftily plotted. In 1997 the Giller made a better choice than the GG. Where my argument remains valid, it seems to me, is that between 1990 and 1994, as the subsequent careers of Ann-Marie MacDonald, Nino Ricci, Caroline Adderson, Russell Smith and Karen Connelly attest, the GGs converted small press writers into stars. It is difficult to make similar claims for the Giller, or to foresee this spotlight-obsessed prize playing such a nurturing role in the future. My argument, therefore, is in support of the GGs' superior potential rather than their present form. Arguably the greatest damage done by the Giller has been to reinforce the Hollywoodization of Canadian literary culture, obliging the GGs to redefine themselves as prizes that are also capable of drawing star authors such as Jane Urquhart to their awards ceremonies. Like the CBC straining to compete with commercial television, the post-1994 'competitively oriented' GGs are incapable either of fulfilling their original mandate (choosing the best books, even if the authors are unknown) or of outshining the banquet-hall glare of the Giller. Predictably, the Toronto media have begun to award the GGs a kind of patronizing, second-rate applause now that two Toronto media celebrities, Adrienne Clarkson and John Ralston Saul, have been named Governor General and consort. 'It took the appointment of two celebrated communicators to Rideau Hall for the GGs to get it right,' the eternally zealous Val Ross told her readers in the *Globe and Mail.* She went on to praise the 1999 GG's management of camera angles. One result of this obsession with camera angles was to rule out of order most discussion of the literary merits of the prize-winners. As on any TV show, the host, Clarkson herself, became the story. The GGs have been resurrected in the image of the Giller. In the Clarkson era, the awards ceremony no longer moves around the country to Calgary or Montreal, but has become rooted at Rideau Hall. It is Ottawa versus Toronto.

All of which leads one to ask what the point of literary prizes is in the first place. Between 1860 and 1880 – an astonishingly short period – a handful of the planet's greatest novels were published in Russia. The Russians did have a prominent literary prize at the time, the Pushkin Prize, but who today remembers or cares whether Tolstoy, Dostoyevsky, Turgenev, Goncharov or Saltykov won the award for a particular book? The point is that the novels of these five writers continue to speak to us with a demonic vitality almost unmatched in the history of prose narrative.

In 1941 *The Garden of the Forking Paths,* the first of the two brief collections that Jorge Luis Borges later combined to create *Ficciones,* the book that changed the modern short story, failed to earn a mention in Argentina's National Literature Prizes. Today few people remember the three books that won the awards.

How many people today read *Three Came to Ville Marie* by Alan Sullivan, winner of the 1941 Governor General's Award for Fiction? Far fewer, I would guess, than the number who read Sinclair Ross's *As For Me and My House,* also published in 1941, which received almost no attention at the time and would have disappeared forever but for its rescue by the New Canadian Library sixteen years later.

Our obsession with prizes is one more symptom of our arch-materialist need to reduce each aspect of human existence to a commodity that can be quantified – and priced and sold. But the figure that keeps ringing through my mind is $1.5 million. This, apparently, is the most common estimate of how much money Jack Rabinovitch, the Giller's founder, has spent keeping alive his prize, with its attendant banquets and authors' and judges' flights and hotel bills. If you had $1.5 million to invest in Canadian writing, couldn't you think of a more creative, constructive use for the money than accentuating the commercialization, hype and Toronto-centrism of a literary culture growing ever more estranged from the hard work of forging good prose?

The Canadian Writer
Between Postcolonialism
And Globalization

First video: 1995. I am sitting in a Frenchified café in England. The waiters have stubby dark moustaches and speak in Parisian accents, but the tall, tweedy man sitting opposite me is irredeemably English. Despite the outbreaks of silver at his temples, he has the round, pouting, obedient yet insolent face of a pupil at a boy's boarding school; at seventy-five, he will still have the face of a boarding school pupil. But he is not a schoolboy. He is one of London's most powerful literary agents. Careers take shape at his pleasure. He has read my latest novel and I am awaiting his verdict with writhing impatience.

He says: 'Your novel is beautifully written ...'

I hold my breath.

'... but it's too Canadian. You can't sell a novel set in Canada internationally. The country's image is boring and the fiction plays up to the image. And it's true, you know. I had to go to Toronto once on business. By the time I'd checked into my hotel it was ten o'clock at night and I went outside and there were well-dressed women walking down the street unaccompanied.... Now that's a very safe society! You can't expect exciting fiction from a society like that.'

'Atwood-Davies-Richler-Munro,' I mutter. They sell internationally. What about the recent BBC newscast that opened with a soundtrack of Montreal youths rampaging on referendum night? Is that a boring, safe society?

The agent snorts. Atwood and company established themselves in an era before agents; Montreal doesn't interest him. 'Stephen,' he says, 'you've moved outside Canada. Now it's time to move your fiction outside Canada!'

When I arrived in England in October 1992, an academic who ran a seminar on postcolonial writing invited me to speak to his graduate students. 'We've had Indians, Africans and West Indians,' he said. 'We've had an Australian. But we've never had a Canadian writer talking about the postcolonial writing experience.'

Postcolonial writing, of course, is the trendy, theoretically informed name for the branch of study that used to be called Commonwealth literature. This term was abandoned during the 1980s when some of the writers being studied objected that the word Commonwealth, in addition to being condescending, was an inaccurate description of what seemed to interest students and professors engaged in this field. Salman Rushdie, in an acerbic essay called ' "Commonwealth literature" Does Not Exist', pointed out that while the term 'Commonwealth Literature' insisted that all these different writers had a great deal in common, most essays and lectures produced in the field concentrated on local specificities, examining, for example, the Nigerianness of Chinua Achebe or Wole Soyinka, the Australianness of Patrick White, the Indianness of R.K. Narayan, and so on. The academics, not to be outmanoeuvred, renamed the field postcolonial literature. In response to the writers' assertions that they were all different, the academics had pushed the issue back to a shared historical bedrock. They began to focus on the experience that all of these writers' societies had passed through: the conversion, by one process or another, from rule by the British Empire to independence. This was what made a postcolonial writer.

So was I a postcolonial writer? Until arriving in England, I had never thought of myself in this way. Growing up in stoutly Loyalist rural eastern Ontario, I had certainly been alert to the imperial legacy. In school our morning singing of 'O Canada' alternated with 'God Save the Queen'; a portrait of a youthful Queen Elizabeth II gazed from the walls of my primary school classrooms. We were taught of the Loyalists' heroic rejection of the Revolution in the Thirteen Colonies, taken on school trips to battle sites from the War of 1812, where the Yankee invader had been repelled, and instructed to treat with reverence anyone who signed U.E.L. (United Empire Loyalist) after his name. Loyalty to the enterprise of empire was our history.

Except that it was not my history.

Ottawa Valley culture was mine in that I grew up there, amid its institutions, generosity, inhibitions, prejudices, folklore and linguistic quirks. I learned to pronounce the talismanic Valley phrase 'number nine binder-twine' like a native. But, like other Canadians at that time, and a large number of Canadians today, I was aware that my personal history and the history of my local community did not mesh. I came from somewhere else.

The Mexican novelist Carlos Fuentes has argued that the novel arises from the breakdown of the shared language and assumptions enjoyed by traditional societies. The novel is the comedy or tragedy of our mis-understandings as we interact with others who speak, think and imagine differently from us. As a member of the first immigrant family – or so it seemed – to move into an ingrown Scots-Irish farming district whose earliest settlers had been intermarrying without interruption for six or seven generations, I was acutely aware of the disjuncture between the British English I heard at home and the Ottawa Valley twang ricocheting around me on the long, bumpy ride on the schoolbus every morning. My first serious writing, I can see now, emerged from the clash between these languages: from the ways their disparate intonations and assump-tions jostled against each other on my tongue and in my brain. Yet, at the time, I certainly didn't classify my attempts to reconcile these incongruous world-systems as postcolonial writing. My undergraduate education on the U.S. East Coast accentuated my awareness of the pecu-liarity of the community where I'd grown up. My first novel was, among other things, an attempt to understand Canadian eccentricity in the context of the Western hemisphere. I set off from an assumption that history made Canadian experience different. Until October 1992, when I found myself – somewhat to my surprise – living in England, it didn't occur to me that the history I had trumpeted – the history and institu-tions and even many of the linguistic configurations out of which or against which nearly all Canadian writers wrote – were inevitably, irrefutably, the residue of those deposited on Canadian soil by British imperial rule.

Second video: 1993–1995. Having moved to England to start a graduate degree, I find myself surrounded by budding academics. I used to think of academics as writers in search of a regular income, but my colleagues in England are judicious, solemn, scholarly, analytical. These are people who flourish in archives. I feel starved for a community of writers, for amiably

*obsessed men and women with whom I can discuss the toil of completing
your daily quota, the despair you suffer when a character refuses to live and
breathe, the idiocy of publishers and agents. Then I meet Larry, an American thriller writer living in England. Larry's life resembles what I imagined a writer's life to be like when I was fifteen. The most jaded of New
Yorkers, Larry tells me: 'Whaddya mean ya didn't make any money from
your last book? I started writing when I was thirty-four because I needed
some cash.'*

*This is how Larry's life works: he gets an idea for a novel, writes a
chapter-by-chapter outline and sends it to his agent in New York. Once
the agent has given him her opinion of the outline, he starts writing at a
rate of five pages a day. Within three months he has completed a 400-page
manuscript. Larry sends the manuscript to his agent, she sends it to a
publisher and secures him a $50,000 U.S. advance. Sometimes there is
also a film option. The good thing about film options, Larry tells me, is
that they are time-limited; this means that after a year or two they must
be renewed. Each time a film option is renewed, Larry receives a cheque
for $25,000 U.S.*

*Once Larry has pocketed his advance, he flies to a Swiss ski resort.
Meanwhile his agent sells his novel around the world. His last novel
received sixty-eight reviews in Germany. Every time I run into Larry on
the street, one of his novels is about to appear in translation in the Czech
Republic or Turkey or Japan. Depending on film options and school
semesters, Larry's wife and children may accompany him to Switzerland.
They ski every day until the money runs low, at which point Larry begins
to plot another thriller. Yet he is not particularly famous. When I finally
look for one of Larry's books, it takes me nearly a week to locate a copy. I
read a few pages in a bookstore, but finally decide not to buy Larry's latest
novel because I know I won't finish it: the writing strikes me as embarrass-
ingly clumsy. But his career amazes me. The way Larry talks about the
business of writing is unimaginable even to my more successful Canadian
writing friends – the ones whose books occasionally get published overseas.
One day Larry says: 'Steve! You gotta let me send some of your stuff to my
agent!'*

'Come on, Larry. Your agent isn't going to be interested in my work.'

*'Why not? You've sold a few copies.' I squirm to avoid revealing the
seven book reviews and 450-copy sales figure achieved by my last work of*

fiction. 'I really don't think a New York agent is going to be interested in my work. It's too Canadian.'

'Gimme a break. Steve, how can a book be Canadian?'

I relent. I pass Larry a copy of the manuscript of my most plot-driven work of fiction, a novel set in Montreal on the night of the 1988 Free Trade election. This novel has been turned down by numerous Canadian publishers for being 'too commercial'. One company said it reminded them of the work of John Grisham. This was intended as a criticism, but I suspect that Larry, who is a friend of John Grisham's, will see it as a compliment.

Shortly after I hand him my manuscript, Larry receives a large cheque and disappears from England in search of snow. I leave on a long trip through Eastern Europe. A few weeks after my return I am walking down the street when a patched-up Volkswagen Beetle screeches to a halt beside me. Larry and his wife Gill call out to me. 'Steve! How ya doin'? Hey, I heard from my agent about your book. Great story! Smart writing! Beautifully plotted. But she can't sell it.' He shook his head. 'It's too Canadian!'

In 1984 I returned to Canada from the United States to begin a master's degree in creative writing at Concordia University in Montreal. I drenched myself in Canadian writing, reading dozens of Canadian novelists and short story writers, discovering new writers, bringing myself abreast of who was publishing what, becoming familiar with the different literary journals, magazines and newspaper book review sections. In the United States, I had been a wayward soul plagued by creative ambitions. Returning to Canada gave me a focus; the move restored me to that essential base for the writer of prose narrative – a palpable social reality, with which I had a creatively fraught relationship. Memories of my Ottawa Valley childhood clattered back in a jumble of mismatched accents and phrases; living in Quebec complicated my vision of Canadian history. But, just as important as my creative replenishment was my absorption into a writing community that consolidated my identity and sense of purpose. The institutions of the Canadian writing world – the literary magazines, the small presses, the readings – incorporated me, I felt, into an organic entity. During the mid-1980s, as my first short stories began to appear in journals such as *Descant, The Fiddlehead* and *Canadian Fiction Magazine,* I felt I was contributing to this multiform project. One of this project's most encouraging traits was its openness;

my sense of belonging stemmed from the shared activity of writing rather than from the quest for any particular ideological Jerusalem. The tenor of the collective project did echo the country's preoccupations: during the 1970s the Canadian writing world had become more female; by the late 1980s it was becoming more culturally and racially diverse; and underlying it always was an exploration of our eccentric history, our peculiar social forms, our particular initiation into language. But it was difficult – and creatively fatal – to write with these issues wedged across the gateway of your imagination (though it was perhaps equally fatal to deny that such forces, in a subterranean way, might structure what you wrote). The sense of belonging was crucial because it reminded you, as you sat typing in your dark little room, that somewhere out there in Saskatoon or Moncton or New Westminster sat other figures trying to peg to the page, in their various ways, the scattered realities of life on the northern half of this continent.

Perceiving myself as a member of an emerging generation of Canadian writers heightened my awareness of other young writers whose words and names came pounding over the bush telegraph of magazines and readings; it strengthened my bonds with the other members of my workshops. One evening, at the beginning of a workshop, a few of us were gossiping about journals and readings and grants. Our instructor interrupted us: 'What none of you realize is that the whole Canadian writing world that you take for granted has only come into existence in the last fifteen years.'

We laughed off his comment. We belonged to an impregnable edifice, a chain-mail network. Writing of the emergence from the colonial writing experience, the South African Nobel laureate Nadine Gordimer has evoked 'that other world that was the world': the long, dead time when a country's culture is falsified, estranged, imposed from abroad; the time preceding the elaboration of a language with which to write about life from the perspective of the former colony; the time before autochthonous publishers and magazines and literature. It was Gordimer, in a talk given at Oxford University, who identified Canada's network of literary journals as an achievement envied by other post-colonial nations; as an impressive realization of a particular postcolonial culture. Yet back in the 1980s, I never thought of our cosy, disjointed writing community as a postcolonial formation, an example of what the

British call 'the Empire writes back'. Equally, back in the 1980s, it did not occur to me that the comfortable structures within which I was building my career could ever be threatened with dissolution.

Third video: 1996. For the first time in four years, I return to Canada for the summer. The shock of reimmersion stings me like a bath in iodine. Listening to a customer recounting an anecdote to a storekeeper in the Ottawa Valley, I hear the language grow flesh and fur, alive as a scurrying animal. The Ottawa Valley rhythms and turns of phrase generate a momentum I recognize; I can imagine myself taking up the man's tale, spinning it out over one hundred, two hundred, three hundred pages. This never happens in England, where the intimidating linguistic precision of friends, colleagues and bypassers curtails rather than stokes my fantasies. Silted-up springs of language bubble to the surface of my imagination as I explore the Ottawa Valley. But in more urban, public contexts, language seems to have been stifled. Returning after a long absence, I am startled by changes barely noticed by friends and family members who have lived through their slow accretion. The adjective 'North American', formerly used sparingly by all but continentalists, is on everyone's lips. All debates descend to the bottom line; everyone has become an amateur economist; middle-class conversation swarms with economic buzzwords.

I arrive in Toronto on the day that Coach House Press goes out of business. (Coach House's recent revival could not be foreseen at the time.) More startling than Coach House's death is the reaction to its demise. Where past politicians, even those ill-disposed towards the cultural sector, would have felt it expedient to pay lip-service to Coach House's achievements, Ontario Premier Mike Harris launches into an attack on the press's 'history of total government dependence'. Though Harris's characterization isn't strictly accurate, I am struck by how many of the writers and commentators who respond to Harris argue from the same set of assumptions: they defend Coach House's accounting and marketing strategies, arguing for the press as a viable business rather than an important component of a civilization. Having adopted Harris's vocabulary, the commentators are unable to refute him. Ottawa Valley storytelling may retain its pungency, but Canadian public debate has changed in ways that make it increasingly difficult to justify, or even imagine, the sense of collective endeavour that fuelled the writing community only a few years earlier.

Later in the summer I visit the book-page editor of one of the newspapers I used to write reviews for. When I reach the newspaper's front door, I am confronted by a picket line of locked-out technicians. I negotiate my way past the placards, pick up my pass at the security desk and head for the newsroom. Five years ago this newsroom was a jumbled chaos of voices and machines. Now silence prevails. The open spaces across which journalists and copy editors used to call out to each other have been closed off by cushioned partitions. I look for my editor's desk and can't find it. Then he appears in front of me. 'A lot's changed since the last time you were here,' he says. 'There are more machines and fewer people.'

'Yeah, I saw some of the people out on the sidewalk.'

'Right. We're doing their jobs now. We used to just do our own jobs, but now we do ours and theirs.' His voice drops as he ushers me into the partitioned-off cubbyhole of his office. I notice that he now has two computers instead of the one I remember. 'It makes me sick to see those guys out there. You don't treat people like that.' His voice remaining unnaturally low, he tells me about his efforts to resist wire-service reviews. Reviews of American or British books can be picked up off the wire free of charge, saving the time and money involved in assigning a review copy to a freelance writer. Canadian books are a problem, because U.S. wire services don't review them unless they are published in the States, but even here plans are afoot for prominent Canadian books to receive a single review, which will then be syndicated across the country.

'That means there's only going to be one opinion on each book,' I say. The prospect strikes me as bleak. Without the debate that occurs when reviewers disagree, how can there be a literary culture?

'I made that point,' the editor says. 'But they're not too interested in that. You have to argue it from a readership point of view; that readers in different cities want different angles on a book.'

He mentions a couple of recent books and how they have been received in different Canadian cities. I ask him about the publishing industry. 'The big publishers keep cranking it out,' he says, 'though they don't do much fiction any more; but the medium-sized ones are in trouble. A lot of them are going to go under. And suddenly there are these micro-presses: a couple of people with desktop publishing equipment who do three or four books a year with no real distribution or publicity.'

'Can literature survive through micro-presses?' I ask.

The editor grunts. 'It's going to be a lot more marginalized.'

Perhaps we should have seen this coming.

In a political sense, the collective idea of Canada was demolished on November 21, 1988, when Canadians voted to subordinate our national project to the requirements of continental free trade. Though we were constantly assured that culture was 'off the table', it is obvious that in the absence of some shared national ethos endogenous literature – perhaps all endogenous culture – becomes unsustainable in a medium-sized country speaking two world languages. Richard Gwyn has made the extremely astute observation that while the countries that consolidated their identities in the nineteenth century were 'nation-states', Canada is or was a 'state-nation'. A state-nation erodes in a neo-liberal, free trade environment: dismantle the state and the nation washes away. Deprived of the abstract ideals of a nation, people return to the *Gemeinschaft*: their horizons ever narrower, they vote for the Reform Party or the Bloc Québécois, or define themselves according to ethnicity rather than citizenship. Political support for the national culture evaporates. I hasten to add that this is not merely the howl of a writer bemoaning the disappearance of his Canada Council grant. Let me come clean on this: I received two of these grants at a very early stage of my career, then decided not to apply for any more of them. I'm not convinced that this money helped me get much writing done; at times I felt it had a paralysing effect. In the words of the great Argentine fabulist Julio Cortázar: 'If you want to write, you write.' Cortázar had a full-time job as a translator for most of his adult life, yet he succeeded in creating one of the most impressive bodies of work – particularly in his short fiction – of any writer this century. I don't think that the state is responsible for helping the writer to arrange his or her life. It's your responsibility to get your writing done: if need be, to irritate your boss, your partner, your spouse, your children, with your inflexible writing routine. But the state *is* responsible for maintaining the national publishing industry; for ensuring that there is a cultural debate to which good work may contribute. And here it comes down to a question of will. Portugal, with nine million people and a high level of functional illiteracy, has a viable publishing industry. Denmark, with four and a half million people, has a strong publishing industry. Greece, with barely one-third Canada's population and a much lower standard of living, has, I have been told, 17,000 published poets. All of these nations also enjoy an advantage Canada lacks: they are protected by a language barrier. Protected from what? From globalization, postcolonialism's bleakly homogenizing successor.

U.S. Trade Representative Mickey Kantor has identified 'so-called Canadian culture' as a significant irritant to the smooth functioning of global markets. This is where the question of national will becomes important. If we wish to continue to express the eccentricities of our experience, of our own idiosyncratic historical development, through our writing, if we wish to read and understand each other from the Atlantic to the Pacific to the Arctic Oceans, if we wish to project a vision unmistakably ours out into the stratosphere over the World Wide Web and the satellite link, then we need the base of a functioning cultural infrastructure. Living next door to the world's dominant cultural and economic power, with whom most of us share a language, we cannot achieve this by tossing culture to the wolves of the marketplace. The cuts to individual arts grants are trivial. What matters is the demolition of our infrastructure: without the literary presses, the CBC, policies to facilitate the national distribution and marketing of Canadian books and magazines, we will, literally, cease to exist as creative producers. If we cannot garner public support for these policies, we will vanish. In time, even the widget-makers will regret this, because in the twenty-first century it will be the smack of a distinctive cultural identity that allows a country to flog its services over the Web. We as writers need a cultural infrastructure in order to keep working; but many of those who denigrate our demands have greater need of us than they suspect.

Globalization and fragmentation are the twin faces of a single dynamic. As I said a few minutes ago, perhaps we should have seen this coming. Evidence of our inexorable transferral from a postcolonial realm to a globalized sphere has been building for years. Until 1977, the Canadian rights to a book published internationally were assigned automatically to the book's British publisher. In the years since then, Canadian bookstores have become crossroads where U.S., U.K. and local editions rub spines. This is a stimulating situation, though it is perhaps less stimulating that as time passes, the U.S. editions predominate. The other movement of the early 1980s, which no one seems to have noticed at the time, was the retreat of literary publishing to the regions. In a dress rehearsal for today's political Canada, where each slice of the country votes for a different party, cultural Canada split up into a chain of linked local markets. Local heroines and heroes emerged, published and praised in their own backyards and little read beyond. As in politics ten years later, southern Ontario's claim to inclusive Canadianness masked a regionalism as obdurate as any other, with all but a few of the fiction writers promoted by the so-called 'national' presses in Toronto residing in or close to the city where they were published.

If postcolonialism united us in our differences, globalization divides us in sameness. The thumping of the bush telegraph has grown faint before the jabber of CNN. I have difficulty feeling my old sense of participation in a nation-wide generation of writers. I think this has less to do with my absences than with the breakdown of the national cultural infrastructure. It is difficult to sustain a broad consciousness in a country splintering into shards, each one becoming embedded at a different angle in the impervious hide of the elephant to our south.

The ways in which we are being 'globalized' or 'Americanized' – the two terms grow daily more indistinguishable – are peculiarly ours, due to our proximity to the U.S., but they also connect us to dilemmas shared by other cultures. The enfeeblement of the bush telegraph stems not only from the erosion of our cultural infrastructure, but also from the recasting of arts coverage in private media along neo-conservative lines. This, too, was presaged during the 1980s. The right-wing Toronto magazine *The Idler* generated a model replicated today by editors throttling cultural debate in a number of publications, most notably *Books in Canada* and the 'Weekly' section of the Ottawa *Citizen,* where *Idler* apostles have been put in charge. Both of these publications have abandoned their former comprehensive coverage of Canadian writing, preferring to squander thousands of words on reviews of academic books about Aristotle or Thucydides. Only a perverse sprinkling of Canadian books is deemed worth a mention.

The *Idler*ites applaud the annihilation of our infrastructure, claiming that the literary presses published a lot of second-rate books. Their rationale is that fewer publishing opportunities will mean that, due to 'competition', the books which are published will be of a higher literary quality. This simplistic application of market economics to cultural analysis overlooks the enormous subjective element involved in assessing contemporary writing. History is littered with writers now regarded as classics who were ignored in their own lifetimes; and, in even greater numbers, with writers worshipped in their lifetimes who disappeared into irrelevance after their deaths. Anyone who has spent time in publishing circles knows that, once professional competence has been established, which books get published is determined by a host of factors only tangentially related to any notion so abstract as 'quality'. The perceived marketability of a work's theme, the current trendiness of the author's cultural identity, an attractive publicity photograph, the author's association with powerful cultural or media figures; these – at least for larger publishers – are the criteria on which publishing decisions are based. We can have a good idea about which were the 'quality' books of 1530, 1630 or 1930, but in most cases we will never know which books from our own lifetime turn out to be enduringly readable. Last year I heard a reader ask the English novelist David Lodge which late-twentieth-century British writers would be read in a hundred years' time. 'The only thing we can be sure of,' Lodge said, 'is that if we came back in a hundred years, we would be very surprised.'

But I think the *Idler*ites know this. Their stance is disingenuous. Their true concern is not promoting literary 'quality', but contributing to the suffocation of the Canadian national project, which they see as inimical to their particular dogma. Anyone possessing the most fleeting acquaintance with literary history understands that fewer books almost always means worse books. Think of the eighteenth century in Spain. Think of Canada in the 1940s. Then think of the titanic gush of writing that flooded out of Victorian England. Most of this writing was appalling schlock, but the same publishing industry that thrived on this tripe also permitted the publication of the novels of George Eliot, Dickens, Thackeray, Trollope, Gaskell. The outpouring of books created a culture in which literature was discussed, literature was an event. The aftershocks of such debate form a large part of the reason why, more than a hundred years later, we still turn to Victorian writing to find 'quality'. Then as now, many of the best writers were not huge bestsellers; even Dickens sold only moderately well by comparison with the megasellers of his day.

It is at this point, I think, that globalization leads us back to postcolonialism. The cultural globalizer – the *Idler*-trained editor – urges us to read less Atwood and more Aristotle. This is presented as a concern for 'quality', but in fact it is a colonial attitude; it assumes that writing originating in centres of political power will by definition be of a higher 'quality' – that word again – than writing from a peripheral, postcolonial northern land. The assertion also sets up a false dichotomy. As writers writing in a Western European language we must read Aristotle, or at least be familiar with the cultural tradition Aristotle represents (even if only to argue against it). But as Canadian writers we cannot opt out of the cultural debates of our present, though we must bear in mind that the writers we regard as important today may not turn out to be the most crucial figures in the long run. The problem, for the globalizer, is that cultural debates have a way of connecting to political debates. When Mickey Kantor says that Canadian culture is an impediment to the smooth functioning of global markets, he is not speaking merely of tariff barriers; he also means that readers and citizens who are conscious of their history are less likely to become compliant consumers of a homogenized planet. In the words of the Chilean novelist Antonio Skármeta: 'A book read by the people whom it describes is a community act. Through a book one can imagine better and understand not only the difficult reality of a fabled world but also the difficult reality in which the book is read.'

The political agenda encouraging the cultural right's enthusiasm for ancient Greece became transparent recently at Carleton University in Ottawa. A report recommended closing the departments of Classics and Religious Studies while at the same time money was being lavished on the creation of a new liberal arts college within the university. The first draft of the proposal for this liberal arts college announced that it hoped to concentrate on students educated at private high schools and that its curriculum would consist of the great books of the Western tradition – the books that used to be taught in Classics and Religious Studies – interspersed with contemporary neo-conservative tracts such as Francis Fukuyama's *The End of History*. Western cultural history, made inaccessible to the average student through the closing of the pertinent departments, would now be taught only to an economic élite, Plato's *Republic* perverted into the budding manager's guide to keeping the techno-serfs in their places. The founders of the liberal arts college, like the editors trained at *The Idler,* are – to adapt a phrase from V.I. Lenin – the 'useful idiots of globalization': intellectuals furthering their careers through the craven propagation of a destructive ideology.

This facet of globalization is helpfully illuminated by an acquaintance with postcolonialism. An awareness of postcolonialism alerts us that we are heading back into what Gordimer calls 'that world that was the world': a time when our voices are displaced by those of alienated élites, a time when most people are blocked from the resources to learn their own national cultures and histories. A time when literature, by definition, becomes something stodgy and worthy and ancient and foreign, used to bolster the ruling class's sense of superiority; a time when debate withers. Rather than experiencing these suppressions in a colonial environment prior to the articulation of the nation, though, we will now experience them in the globalized sphere that seems to be the successor to the nation. Yet the nation, for all its warts, is a forum that allows the development of civil society, a democratic culture, a fertile engagement with history and language. The nation offers broader vistas than the phoney universality of globalization. The fading of the bush telegraph that allowed Canadian writers to keep up on each other's work is inseparable from our national vivisection.

I draw this image of vivisection from the Mozambican novelist Mia Couto. In his novel *Terra Sonâmbula (Sleepwalking Land),* Couto charts the nation's dissolution into diaphanous instability; in one scene he likens the nation to a beached whale being sliced up with knives. But why should we care about this? Aren't writers independent spirits, free souls, wandering troubadours? Isn't our work most likely to become wooden and predictable when we yoke ourselves to the ox-cart of the nation? And yet how else can we bathe ourselves in history, the fluid in which the spores of language are dissolved? In a recent issue of *Index on Censorship,* Salman Rushdie wrote: 'Kadaré's Albania, Ivo Andrić's Bosnia, Achebe's Nigeria, García Márquez's Colombia, Jorge Amado's Brazil.

'Writers are unable to deny the lure of the nation, its tides in our blood. Writing as mapping: the cartography of the imagination [...] In the best writing, however, a map of the nation will also turn out to be a map of the world.'

This map of the nation may be our best defence against the

impoverishment of our imagination represented by the dissemination of an ever-shrinking variety of words, habits, soft drinks, sitcoms and life-possibilities across the surface of our planet. In its absence, we may all be condemned to view each other through the same limited stock of stereotypes: the stereotypes of mass culture propelled around the globe by the U.S. entertainment industry. Think of that literary agent who told me that Canada was boring. The most interesting fact about his statement is that he was not expressing a traditional British stereotype about Canada, a stereotype growing out of Britain's history as a colonial power in this country. The equation of Canadianness with tedium is in fact a U.S. stereotype, one which the U.S. media – particularly *The New Republic* – glories in repeating. But as U.S. mass culture spreads, so do its assumptions. A British literary agent and a New York literary agent will view Canadianness with the same disdain because, increasingly, they share the same words and imagery. More and more, we all view each other through U.S. cultural categories. More and more, we share a single imaginative repertoire. Perhaps this is why, five years later, my visit to that postcolonial professor's graduate students still hasn't materialized. Each time we talk, the professor mentions a date a few months hence, saying: '*Then* you must come and tell my graduate students about Canadian writers and postcolonialism.' But *then* never comes. I am beginning to suspect it never will. We have moved on from the postcolonial world, and now we are afloat in the ether of globalization. We are who the teleculture says we are. I am no longer a writer bearing the residue of a particular history, but merely a resident of America's boring appendage.

Let me give an example of this change: In the early 1980s a Canadian writer, who later became a friend of mine, began writing g book reviews for a very snooty English magazine. He wanted to review novels but was told that, as a Canadian, he was qualified only to review non-fiction books on the Arctic and on Native Canadians. Fifteen years later he is still reviewing those kinds of books for that magazine. By 1994, when I began writing for the same publication, preconceptions about Canada had changed. A Canadian had become simply a duller sort of American. I was allowed to review novels, but, initially, only those written by writers from the United States. My interest in the literatures of other Commonwealth countries was dismissed. How could I know anything about that?

This ahistorical view of life is precisely what the novel resists. I am not among those who believe that the new communications technologies will, on their own, kill the novel. I harbour a perverse belief that there will always be readers for compelling prose narrative. But, returning to Fuentes's definition of the novel as the comedy or tragedy of our differences, we do seem to be condemned to having fewer and fewer differences to write about. The greatest peril to literature lurks in our all becoming alike – though perhaps I am overlooking homogenization's grim associate, fragmentation. We may all work and eat and dress and categorize in the same ways, but as long as, sequestered in our respective Quebecs and British Columbias – our Serbias, Bosnias, Croatias – we *believe* ourselves to be irreconcilably different, we may preserve enough imaginative territory to keep misunderstanding each other in creative ways. To sustain such creative misunderstandings must be the ambition of all writers everywhere – and perhaps especially of Canadian writers, perched on the front lines of globalization.

Yet it seems undeniable that our imaginative powers are being sapped by the assimilation of the world's small and medium-sized cultures into one big one. A few years ago, in a frontier town in Eastern Europe, a woman told me about the day famished refugees from the neighbouring country had come pouring across the border. Wanting to hear more details, I asked: 'What did it look like?'

She thought for a long time. At last she said: 'It looked like something on television.'

Fourth video: 1997. I am staring at a screen which distracts me from my purpose. My office computer, in the East London college where I work, freezes the cursor in my word-processing program each time I receive an e-mail message. One afternoon I sit for hours ploughing through administrative work on the screen, interrupted by messages that come pinging in from friends in Montreal, Toronto, Rome, Dublin, Prague. All of these messages are written in the same offhand English; none is as satisfying as receiving a letter or phone call from these same people. I feel wired to the whole world, yet intimately in touch with no one. At the end of the day, my eyes glazed from the screen, I stumble out of the office and trail through Muslim East London, where little girls, veiled to the cheekbones, flaunt denim jackets over their robes and tiny boys come capering around the corner wearing circular flat-topped white caps, shiny imitation-leather copies of the Koran clutched in their hands as they rush into the Ambala Sweet Shop. Around me leather-jacketed teenagers converse with mullah-like elders grumbling over moustacheless beards in a language I don't understand. It strikes me that I have experienced the perfect high-tech, multicultural day. This is a foretaste of the twenty-first century: communication via global technology and communion within the ethnic group, but no public sphere, no generalized sense of belonging, no shared words, identifications or assumptions. I realize that all of us who wish to keep reading and writing fiction must find a language to make the screen and the street connect.

A brief excerpt from 'The Canadian Writer Between Post-Colonialism and Globalization', entitled 'The Unmarketable Obscurity of Being Canadian', was published in *Matrix*, no. 49, Spring 1997 and reprinted in the *Ottawa Citizen*, 27 July 1997. The article in its entirety was first delivered as a lecture to the Maritime Writers' Workshop at the University of New Brunswick in Fredericton, July 1997, then published in *The New Quarterly*, vol. XVIII, no. 2, Summer 1998.

Linking Short Stories
In an Age of Fragmentation

Writers and professors treat each other with suspicion. Writers view academics the way small-town insurance salesmen look upon government bureaucrats: as intrusive, lazy, overpaid, encrusted in jargon, and out of touch with the trade of daily life, with the dip and soar of literary language. Academics, for their part, wish that writers would quietly die. Then they could be examined in peace, shorn of their awkward contradictions and temperamental outbursts, and laid in the neatly carpentered coffin of a well-made theory. As someone whose makeup contains elements of both these fratricidal ethnicities, I find myself spotting chinks in the armour of each. In the long run, I am on the side of the writers. I was a writer for many years before I succumbed to the siren call of a professor's salary and, unless I am hit by the proverbial bus, I expect to continue being a writer long after I have ceased to be a professor. For this reason, I would like to focus on a chink in the armour of professordom: on one of the facets of literary art to which academics pay insufficient attention.

In studying the short story, academics, depending on their critical predilections, look at theme, character, the structures of individual stories, point of view, voice, language, cultural assumptions, implicit or explicit ideology. In my experience they rarely look at how the collection is structured. For the writer, on the other hand, the question of why one story comes first and another second and another in the middle and another next-to-last and which one to end with is unavoidable. In the absence of a cogent response to these problems, there is no book.

By 1990, for example, I had published more than half a dozen stories in literary magazines. I had written dozens of other unpublished stories, among them seven or eight that I considered respectable. Having published a novel, it seemed to me that the next step in my literary career should be to bring out a collection of stories. I pulled together manuscripts of my best stories: stories about the Ottawa Valley, stories about Montreal, stories about backpackers in Latin America, even fantasy stories. The manuscripts went out in the mail and, a few weeks or months later, came bouncing back. 'I liked the Ottawa Valley ones, but not the others,' one editor said. Other editors liked the Latin American stories or the Montreal stories. All seemed to feel that while I had written a number of publishable short stories, I had not written a collection. It took a few months for this message to sink in. One day, sitting at home, I decided to put my Latin American stories together in a pile. Realizing that I had nearly enough of these for a short collection, I wrote two more. I bundled the stories into the mail and, within a few weeks, found a publisher.

But this was not the end of the lesson. I had grasped that the imperative of thematic unity within a short story prevailed also at the level of the collection of stories. This was true both for valid artistic reasons and invidious marketing motives: not only did thematic unity make for a more satisfying reading experience, it was also easier for a sales rep to persuade a bookstore to stock a book when she could say, 'This is a collection of stories about travellers in Latin America,' than when he had to mumble embarrassed platitudes about the fine sensibility of a new small-press author.

Having resolved to put together my Latin American stories, I had to decide *how* to put them together. Initially, the collection contained ten stories, three set among politically committed foreigners in Nicaragua at the time of the Sandinista government in the 1980s, and seven set among travellers in the Andean countries. My editor, Seán Virgo, encouraged me to write some new Latin American stories, one of which eventually made its way into the finished book, which was called *Nights in the Yungas*. The central problem I faced in structuring the collection was how to hone a harmonious development in spite of the disjuncture that left me with three stories whose setting in a time and place of revolutionary political urgency invested them with a tone – at once more earnestly idealistic and more destructively ironic – that differed, to my ear, from the rather distanced lyricism I had practised in the Andean stories. I decided to arrange the stories in two cycles, the Nicaraguan stories first and the Andean stories second, each cycle opening with a story describing a journey to Latin America and each concluding with a story dealing with the difficulty of finding a morally respectable way to come home. A brief closing parable, the only piece in the collection employing a Latin American narrator, summed up the theme of outsiders' illusions about the worlds they think they discover when travelling. I describe this process in detail to point out that organizing a collection of stories involves as many difficult artistic choices as structuring the order of the scenes in a long, layered short story of the sort written by Mavis Gallant or Alice Munro. I wrote the stories in *Nights in the Yungas* haphazardly over a period of eleven years – the first when I was twenty-one, the last when I was thirty-one – never suspecting that they would be called upon to harmonize their voices within the chorus of a single book. During those eleven years I experimented with a variety of registers, structures, and voices, with documentary realism and magic realism, with pared-down diction and lyrical evocation, rooting out in my own way the possibilities of the short story form, as young writers do. The presentation of *Nights in the Yungas* as a unified collection is an illusion, as all art is an illusion. But I recognized that the illusion of my book had to be more persuasive than the illusions of my characters, many of whom I had pummelled with the realization that they were not changing their essential beings by travelling to faraway countries.

A book, once it is finished, is the book that it is: there can be no looking back. The artist must always drive forward towards the next new work, the next illusion, which, inevitably, seems destined to be more glorious than the last creation, now revealed in the hard light of paper, ink and glue as not quite the wonder it promised to be when it was still glowing inside the author's head. 'Try again, fail better,' as Samuel Beckett advises. Yet on occasions such as this one, I allow myself a brief backward glance to wonder how different an aesthetic profile *Nights in the Yungas* might have cut had I mixed the stories, allowing the political urgency of the Nicaraguan stories and the limpid, somewhat enervated distancing of the Andean stories to mingle and curdle. Would the Nicaraguan stories have heightened the muted tones of the Andean pieces, and would these have tempered the rough edges of the Nicaraguan stories' politicization? Or would the abrupt hopping from one locale to the other simply have irritated readers? I cannot say, I have no regrets and by this time in any event I would have consigned the book, whatever its organization, to honourable Beckettian failure; but I do want to point out that this decision would have made *Nights in the Yungas* a completely different book. Had I not placed the parable-like story at the end, but buried it in the middle, it is unlikely that reviewers would have read it, approvingly or critically, as the key to the collection. If I had dispersed through the book the three stories set in Sandinista Nicaragua, rather than setting them squarely at the collection's front gate, I doubt that I would be perceived, even today, as such a relentlessly political writer. Nearly any reorganization would have produced a different literary work. Different passages would have been highlighted, reviewers would have identified different themes as important and reached different conclusions about what I was up to.

When we put stories together with other stories, we change them. Just as personal identity is often forged against the identity of another – parent, partner, sibling – so stories assume different shapes in the company of other stories.

I had learned something of this by the time, seven years later, that I began to assemble my second story collection, *North of Tourism*. Here, where the stories defied unity of setting, character or historical period, I had to depend on the common theme of cultural displacement to provide cohesion. I worried, though, that shared themes alone might not supply sufficient glue to hold together a collection in which the stories' settings ranged from Azerbaijan to the Ottawa Valley, from Brazil to Yugoslavia. I recalled having read a dyspeptic review of another writer's short story collection, in which the reviewer complained about being wrenched from continent to continent as one story succeeded another. I decided that it would be in my interest to smooth the reader's passage from each setting to the next. After examining the eight stories I planned to include in *North of Tourism*, I realized that some of the stories contained facets of setting or theme that echoed those in other stories. I decided to start with stories set in Latin America, since that seemed to be what readers expected of me, then ease into other parts of the world. I led from a story about an elderly Frenchwoman travelling in Brazil to a story about a young Frenchwoman, who had studied in Spain, working in Guatemala. From here it was an easy leap across the Atlantic to a story set in Spain, in which one of the minor characters was Guatemalan and another was an American expatriate. Having introduced the European expatriate theme, I was able to pair the Spanish story with a story about Canadian expatriates in England. This story in turn contained enough Canadian material that I could, without jarring the reader, set my Ottawa Valley story alongside it. The next story was about a young woman in Toronto dreaming of entering an Orthodox monastery in post-Soviet Moldova. This story introduced the Eastern European setting and the theme of post-Soviet disintegration, allowing me to pair it with the story about post-Soviet Azerbaijan. The treatment of the collapse of empires in eastern Europe prepared the ground for the long closing story, set in Yugoslavia during the last days of the Ottoman and Austro-Hungarian empires at the outbreak of the First World War. By the time I had finished arranging this collection I felt that it was so tightly meshed *as a collection* that I could not move a single story without causing the whole book to crumble. Like the stories in *Nights in the Yungas,* those in *North of Tourism* were written on a series of whims, in a variety of literary moods and styles, over a period of roughly a decade. They were written in innocence of any notion that they would ever have to coexist in a book. This time, though, in assembling the stories into a collection, I had developed less obtrusive and arguably more effective organizing principles than I had in *Nights in the Yungas.* I am convinced that one of the reasons *North of Tourism* has received better reviews than my three previous books is because it fits together better. As individual stories, the stories may be more mature than those in *Nights in the Yungas,* but at least as important is the fact that my conception of structuring a book of stories had also matured. I had learned more not only about the art of the short story, but also about the art of the short story *collection.*

It is with this insight in mind that I approach the work of other Canadian short story writers of my generation. Most of the writers I will be discussing were born within five years, one way or the other, of 1960. I plan to tilt the scales by focusing primarily on books which adopt the format of the story cycle, or collection of linked short stories, where the imperative to maintain structural unity becomes more pressing than in an ordinary short story collection. The book of linked short stories is often claimed as the quintessential Canadian literary form. Some critics have traced a rising Canadian tradition originating in nineteenth-century pioneer sketches and evolving, through the sketch-like stories of

Duncan Campbell Scott at the end of the century and the satirical anec-
dote-like tales of Stephen Leacock early in the twentieth century,
towards the linked-story collections of Margaret Laurence and Alice
Munro. In a book called *What Is a Canadian Literature?*, John Metcalf
has argued that this interpretation of literary history is nonsense.
Metcalf accuses these critics of fabricating a national literary tradition
where no real literary heritage, in the sense of writers reading other
writers and being inspired by their use of language and form, truly
exists. Metcalf's assessment of the lasting resonance of Scott's *The Village of Viger* is irrefutable. In the dying weeks of our millennium, the
critic who sets out to find a thirtysomething Canadian writer of short
fiction proud to uphold the literary legacy of Duncan Campbell Scott
will be severely disappointed. From the perspective of the turn of the
millennium, the nationalist critics of the 1970s whom Metcalf attacks –
the Margaret Atwood of *Survival*, literary journalists such as Wayne
Grady, academics such as Sam Solecki and lunatics such as Robin Math-
ews – appear trapped in a contradictory enterprise. They emphasize
Canada's cultural marginality, then go on to try to forge for Canada a literary tradition as chronologically coherent as those of Great Britain and
the United States. The contemporary cultural theorist would poke a
hole in this charade in an instant, arguing that the literary cultures of
marginal countries are bound to be marked by ruptures, inconsistencies
and long silences; this is the cost of being more a receiver than a
producer of the stock of global mythologies. Only empires enjoy the
privilege of consistent historical narratives. We should not expect a
chronologically coherent Canadian tradition to map out our literary
history in epic fashion. John Metcalf, little though he suspects it, is in
perfect accord with some of today's most jargon-drenched academics.
Both insist on the hit-and-miss unevenness of Canadian writing over
the decades. Both, I think, would agree that foreign models have often
been more important to Canadian writers than domestic examples; neither would be surprised to hear that I cannot remember having met a
Canadian writer who draws sustenance from the work of Duncan
Campbell Scott. Stephen Leacock does remain a shadowy presence, even
though most of us read him under duress in the classroom. But
Leacock's Mariposa represents a quaintly archaic take on a disappearing
Canada; his British-tinged irony makes his sensibility increasingly

foreign to a society that is fast descending into earnest literal-mind-edness.

The 1970s, though, mark a change. From this point on, partly because of the activities of nationalist critics, I think we can assume that we are dealing with a literary tradition in the proper sense of new gener-ations of writers creating their work out of an awareness of what has gone before. For the purposes of my discussion of the contemporary linked-story collection, I assume that Linda Svendsen, Michael Winter, Connie Barnes Rose, Debbie Howlett, Russell Smith, Patrick Roscoe, Steven Heighton and Elyse Gasco are aware of books such as Alice Munro's *Lives of Girls and Women* and Margaret Laurence's *A Bird in the House*, and in most cases will have read them. This is not to say that linked-story collections from other traditions – Ivan Turgenev's *A Hunter's Sketches*, William Faulkner's *Go Down, Moses*, V.S. Naipaul's *Miguel Street* – have not also helped to shape their literary conscious-nesses. But where foreign examples may elicit admiration and imitation, the achievements of other Canadian writers demand a response. All writing is to some extent a sharp retort to previous writing. We feel most compelled to produce a riposte to the writing that is praised around us. From the 1970s onward, Canadian writers have become more aware of other Canadian writers and more likely, it seems to me, to write in response to their compatriots' creative visions.

What is the model which younger Canadian writers of linked-stories collections begin to write *against*? *Lives of Girls and Women* and *A Bird in the House* transport Leacock's Mariposa into the modern era by shift-ing the focus of the linked-stories collection from the life of the collec-tivity to that of the individual's elaboration of her personality and identity. The small town, still reassuringly eccentric, becomes a place that must be outgrown if the individual – particularly the female indi-vidual – is to fulfil her potential. Munro's socially small-minded Jubilee cannot contain Del Jordan's questing intelligence; Laurence's Man-awaka, a place of harsher moral judgements and outbreaks of violence and racial prejudice, will prove fatal to Vanessa MacLeod's literary ambitions. Both of these collections place the artist at the centre, redrawing society's contours from the artist's standpoint. Each book opens as its female protagonist approaches puberty. The two books close with Del and Vanessa in their late teens, having experienced their first romantic relationships, preparing to leave town. Del Jordan's intellectual and sexual maturity grow in tandem, though this linkage is less explicit in the case of Laurence's Vanessa MacLeod. Rather than the complex temporal shifts characterizing Munro's later short fiction, it is the straightfoward chronological approach of *Lives of Girls and Women* that has become a literary model. (Both books are presented as the recollections of adult women who have become writers; to the extent that we hear the voice of the older woman regarding her younger self, the narration can be said to be include elements from different timeframes. But the action, none the less, traces a linear trajectory from girl to woman.) Women writers of succeeding generations, such as Isabel Huggan in *The Elizabeth Stories* and, more recently, Frances Itani in *Leaning, Leaning over Water,* have taken up this model without altering it substantially; Itani even signposts the linear progression of her collection by placing a date at the top of each story. I would like to argue, though, that younger writers have found the Munrovian pattern of following the protagonist through a small-town upbringing from near-infancy to intercourse impossible to sustain. They have had to structure their collections differently.

One of the unspoken conditions of the *Bildungsroman* – and the Munrovian story cycle is nothing if not a *Bildungsroman* in instalments – is that it takes place against the backdrop of a relatively stable society. Choosing the protagonist's education as a theme implies the existence of a fixed set of moral references for the young hero or heroine to be educated into. This sort of stability has been scarce for writers of my generation. Many of us grew up as the children of the first big wave of middle-class divorces to hit Canadian society around 1970 – the same divorces that liberated women writers such as Alice Munro, Margaret Laurence, Marian Engel and Elisabeth Harvor from traditional female roles, and were instrumental in enabling them to gain access to a broader range of dramatic possibilities for their female protagonists. But for the children of those divorces the upheaval was more disorienting than liberating – one has only to read Patrick Roscoe's *Birthmarks,* its quest for understanding floundering in a blur of prostitution, drugs, family disintegration and compulsive travelling, to see the extremes which such alienation can reach. It is no coincidence that where *Lives of Girls and Women* unfurls in an easy linear flow, *Birthmarks* is a fractured, fragmented, self-consciously mutilated collection. Similarly, women writers have been compelled by changing sexual mores to abandon the Munro-Laurence formula of signalling the female protagonist's maturity and readiness to move on to adult life in the city by providing her with her first boyfriend at the age of eighteen. The female protagonists of both Debbie Howlett's *We Could Stay Here All Night* and Connie Barnes Rose's *Getting Out of Town,* casually sexually active by early adolescence, oblige their authors to find other ways to dramatize the culmination of their protagonists' educations. The *Lives of Girls and Women* formula has been dented also by the experience of rapid movement around the globe. In a generation for which teaching English as a Second Language in a distant country has been almost a rite of passage, crucial stages of the young protagonist's education are as likely to take place in Jakarta or Osaka as in Jubilee or Manawaka. This is one of the themes of Steven Heighton's collection, *Flight Paths of the Emperor.* Similarly, unlike the writers of the Munro-Laurence generation, many of us were born outside the country – the case of Roscoe, Michael Winter and Russell Smith; some of us, perceiving ourselves as immigrants, retain links to foreign cultures and literary traditions. Finally, one needs to bear in mind that just as Munro and Laurence, consciously or unconsciously, took over and feminized Stephen Leacock's Mariposa model, so Munro's model has been adopted not only by younger women writers such as Connie Barnes Rose, but also by younger men such as Michael Winter, who have reshaped the linked-stories collection to reflect male coming-of-age experiences.

It is in Atlantic Canada that the model seems to have changed least. Connie Barnes Rose's *Getting Out of Town,* ironically, is about not leaving town; about what happens to young women who fail where Del Jordan and Vanessa MacLeod succeed. In spite of the gaunt, Raymond Carver-like minimalism of its style, this is a sprightly, surprisingly affecting collection. It begins where *A Bird in the House* ends. Eighteen-year-old Nancy MacKinnon, the daughter of the town police chief, is visiting her criminal boyfriend in the local jail. Condemned to an almost eternal adolescence – a common feature of nearly all these books – Nancy drifts through mediocre jobs, bouts of late-night drinking, one intense female friendship and sexual encounters with various hard-drinking local men. The most ungainly aspect of the book's structure is also the most revealing. When, in her late twenties, Nancy finally does leave town, the tough, unreflective voice Barnes Rose has created for her protagonist seems unable to dramatize how she arrives at this decision. The penultimate story, interrupting the book's neat linear row of first-person narratives, describes in the third person a conversation between Nancy's ex-boyfriend and his new lover, during which we learn that Nancy has moved to Vancouver. In the final story Nancy, now married with a family, returns in the first person as, visiting Nova Scotia, she participates in a town tragedy that underlines the self-destructiveness of the life she has put behind her. The glitch that requires Barnes Rose to intervene in the third person in order to set up the conclusion illustrates the imperative, for the writer of a book of linked stories, of finding a voice that not only works at the level of the individual story, but also serves to unify the collection. It is Barnes Rose's minimalism that makes the leap into the third person feel jarring. Minimalism is the ideal stylistic choice for describing bleak, circumscribed lives; but once the characters' experience broadens, the author's stylistic repertoire must grow also.

Michael Winter's collection *One Last Good Look,* employing a lusher, more supple language than that of Barnes Rose, successfully negotiates the transition from first person to third. In both voices, the point of view remains locked on the protagonist, Gabriel English. For Gabe English, as for most of the central characters of writers of this generation, growing up is a process that begins in his late teens and culminates around the age of thirty, with marriage and commitment. Gabe himself is painfully conscious of the fact: 'I realized that, at twenty-nine, I was still unmarried, had never lived with anyone (except roommates, for financial reasons). I didn't own a house, was still ignoring a hefty student loan, had no real job, or prospects, was not accumulating R R S P s.... I was living the same way I had in university and I understood this was due to my lack of commitment to the world.'

The narrative of *One Last Good Look,* reflecting Gabe's experience, advances by fits and starts. In the opening story Gabe is working at a summer job while waiting to leave his native Corner Brook to attend university in St. John's; in the final story he is married. Yet the book's linear trajectory is constantly diverted by flashbacks to adolescence or backward steps to events or characters referred to two or three stories earlier. Winter has created a structure mimetic of the kind of growing up experienced by wayward adults in their twenties, when conspicuous rites of passage are in the past and the growth of a personality becomes increasingly difficult to calibrate. The entire collection works like a long, multi-layered short story; even the three or four stories that stand up less well as individual stories are essential to Winter's portrait of Gabe's fitful journey towards adulthood. The ambiguousness of this journey contributes to the expanded-short-story feel of the book: *One Last Good Look* lacks the narrative decisiveness to masquerade, in the favourite phrase of publishers trying to market linked-stories collections, as 'a novel in stories'.

In the Munro-Laurence tradition, Gabe English is a writer. Unlike Del Jordan or Vanessa MacLeod – perhaps because he is a man of the 1990s rather than a young woman of the late 1940s, or perhaps because he is from Newfoundland – Gabe does not feel that he must move to Toronto to succeed as an artist. (Though it is probably worth noting that his creator has made this move.) Gabe does not even remain fixed in St. John's. After meeting the woman who will become his wife, he moves back to the countryside. Gabe's awareness of 'how small life is under Newfoundland's big ear' coexists with an appreciation of the Rock's vitality. Nor is the vigour Winter depicts purely that of the great outdoors. The reader eavesdrops on conversations where Gabe and other St. John's intellectuals discuss writers from all over the world.

This is a very different portrait of home than that drawn by Russell Smith, another young writer who has moved from Atlantic Canada to Toronto. The structure of Smith's collection *Young Men* represents a radical and revealing shake-up of the linked-stories formula. Smith's protagonists, like those of other writers of his generation, become aware of the grim necessity of growing up only in their late twenties. By this time they are all living in Toronto, though many of them have come from other places. Rather than following the maturation of one young man through ten or eleven stories, Smith slices his book into four sections. Each of the first two sections contains three stories about a different young man working on the fringes of the Toronto arts scene; the third section consists of two stories about a character named James, who has appeared in Smith's novel, *Noise;* the fourth section contains three stories about young women occupying the same Toronto arts milieu as the men. Some of the characters allude sneeringly to those in other sections, contributing to the illusion of an almost Leacock-like collectivity: the Annex as a mediaphile's Mariposa. Smith's inability to follow a single character through a succession of rites of passage speaks more eloquently of the transience of contemporary urban life than all of the book's manic satire of its protagonists' pretensions. Trapped in a value-free eternal present from which nearly all cultural or historical references have been stripped away, Smith's characters do not have the option of growing up. After following them through two or three stories, the author must abandon them, and move on to other members of the same tribe. Nothing irrevocable ever happens in Smith's fictional world: lovers exchange partners, restaurants change their decor, film companies rewrite scripts; but no one ever dies or is born or has to wrestle with a serious moral dilemma. Smith's painfully self-conscious characters, themselves aware of these limitations, can find no way out of the glittering morass of their lives. Toronto is phoney, the collection argues, but the rest of the country is both boring and boorish. 'The Stockholm Syndrome,' the longest story, describes a Toronto writer's hellish reading tour of rural Nova Scotia. Unlike Michael Winter, Smith can imagine the hinterland only as the butt of jokes; the locals' provincialism is played strictly for laughs. The story's closing lurch towards affirmation misfires. When Lionel, the protagonist, meets a dignified old woman who has led a dramatic life on two continents his attitude resembles that of a nineteenth-century British explorer encountering a noble savage among unwashed heathens. The story patronizes the old woman while purporting to praise her. (The story's title suggests that Lionel's respect for this Maritimer is a symptom of isolation-induced madness.) The scene is typical of the tension opposing Smith's conservative, disciplined prose style to the fragmentation of his structures. This tension, bolstered by Smith's faultless ear for dialogue, makes his work very readable, but it also suggests that in a media-driven urban world severed from history and tradition, the future of the linked-stories collection is to disintegrate into ever-briefer cameo shots of individuals unable to evolve.

Women writers have responded differently to the urban milieu. In fact, in *We Could Stay Here All Night* the reader is struck by how little Debbie Howlett has modified the Munro-Laurence structures. The narrative trajectory of Howlett's collection, following her protagonist Diane Wilkinson from a childhood swimming outing near her suburban Montreal home to her move away to Vancouver in her late teens, matches the Munro-Laurence pattern. Howlett's language has an unmanicured, spoken quality, spare yet less stylized than Barnes Rose's deliberate minimalism. Her material rehearses the main sources of social fragmentation experienced by her generation: Diane's parents fight, separate, reunite, then separate again; her father disappears to British Columbia, her mother has a succession of dubious lovers, while in the background Quebec's language tensions spark and flicker. Howlett's characters, working-class anglophone Montreal Catholics, respond to these upheavals with a kind of straightforward pragmatism that almost refuses to acknowledge their abandonment of conventional values. The traditionalism of the characters' responses to the collapse of traditional lifestyles affords Howlett the possibility of sustaining what remains, with small interruptions, a linear narrative. This book comes closer than any of the others discussed here to being 'a novel in stories', with the result that some of the stories, though crucial to the ongoing development of the narrative, do not stand up particularly well as stories. At the level of the story, Howlett's endings are often abrupt and forced; at the level of the collection, the conclusion, where Diane returns to Montreal from Vancouver for her father's funeral and has casual sex in the airport with a fatherly man she has met on the plane, achieves greater resonance than my improbable summary of it might lead a reader to expect.

In ending the book with a story linking death to sex with incestuous overtones, Howlett echoes the concluding story of *Marine Life* by Linda Svendsen, Howlett's mentor at the University of British Columbia. Svendsen's 'White Shoulders', with its depiction of an apparently decent man who drives his daughter to her death by molesting her while his wife is undergoing treatment for cancer, is a subtler story than any of Howlett's work, yet the overall impact of *Marine Life* adds up to less than the fine artistry of its various parts. Svendsen, the oldest of the writers I am discussing here, arguably writes the best-crafted stories. Her treatment of time is so sophisticated that summarizing the span of her protagonist Adele Nordstrom's life covered by *Marine Life* becomes almost futile. Most of the stories are told by a woman in her thirties, based in New York, who is looking back on her Vancouver childhood as the youngest daughter in a family complicated by multiple marriages, divorces and disappearances. Women readers, I am told, often find Svendsen's work emotionally cold by comparison with the fiction of other Canadian women writers. To me the book seems prematurely dated, too much a product of the self-obsessed Columbia University creative writing workshops of the 1980s, where students such as Svendsen were taught to bare their psychological scars to their peers before putting pen to paper. The writing of the eight slender stories in *Marine Life* was supported by two years at Columbia, followed by residencies at the pleasure of eight major U.S. and Canadian arts foundations; when so much care is lavished on so little material, preciousness is bound to creep in. One example must stand for many: in another motif echoed by Debbie Howlett, Adele Nordstrom at one point has casual sex with a man she meets on a hovercraft. As in Howlett's collection, this scene takes on incestuous overtones when Adele confesses the encounter to her much older half-brother Ray and he responds by telling her how he had sex with a twelve-year-old girl at a time when Adele, too, was twelve years old. Svendsen writes: 'Ray and I were thirty-five and twenty-one, old and comfortable enough to talk openly. I'd just admitted that the true story wasn't revealed in the photographs, and told him about making love with a stranger on the Hovercraft between England and France.' The phrase 'making love' jars in its genteel inappropriateness to the kind of sexual encounters Ray and Adele are discussing. (Howlett, narrating the analogous moment in her collection, opts for 'we did it'.) And, sure enough, if one looks back at the version of this story that was originally published, then reprinted in various anthologies, Svendsen's first formulation was 'and told him about fucking a stranger on the hover craft between England and France.' This language matches the experience far better than the final version. It is all too possible for writers to revise too much: to sink too deeply into their own psyches, to refine their prose to the point where they suck the life out of their creations. If Smith's *Young Men* alerts the reader to the danger that the linked-stories collection may fracture for lack of measurable emotional development on the part of its protagonists, Svendsen's *Marine Life* raises the possibility of an implosion into a narrative self unable to imagine or evoke the world beyond purely personal, private myths. This, it seems to me, is what is on the verge of occurring in Elyse Gasco's collection *Can You Wave Bye Bye, Baby?*

Gasco is the youngest of these writers. Some would argue that she is also the most talented. *Can You Wave Bye Bye, Baby?* is a book of stories, though not of linked stories. Yet Gasco's stories are so deeply imbued with common motifs, obsessions and images, and so haughtily disdainful of evoking the world outside the author's mind – only in the final story do characters with names appear – that one can be forgiven for reading this collection under the impression that it is a book of linked stories. For me the most startling moment in this book which has been praised for its emotional shock value was when I finished the last story and flipped back to read the blurb inside the front cover. There I found a series of plot summaries that seemed to have nothing to do with the book I had just read. After thinking long and hard, I was, with effort, able to match the blurb's summaries with the stories, rather in the way that one might match police descriptions of criminals with masked shadows glimpsed through the fog. Gasco's writing represents the logical extension of Svendsen's aesthetic: Gasco also completed her creative writing degree in New York, though more recently than Svendsen and at New York University rather than Columbia. No reader could deny Gasco's high intelligence, but her work ultimately recalls Paul Valéry's complaint that the mind is a force without an object. The repeated images of mothers who cease to love their babies, mothers who abandon their babies, even the descriptions of the young couples having the babies, insist on their story-by-story resemblance; the book that accumulates is an unacknowledged linked-stories collection, tied together by its refusal to evoke the differences of character and place that exist outside the mind. One of the book's rare attempts at creating a scene occurs on the first page, where Gasco describes the institution where an unwed mother is having her baby: 'a convent-type thing where it is hoped that all the hushed holiness will keep the girls from heaving and grunting too loudly. One of those places. You know. You've seen the same movies I have.' The presumption of shared images derived from popular culture underscores Gasco's assumption that narrative has been hijacked by film, leaving the human psyche as the sole territory worth exploring through prose. Near the bottom of the first page the reader learns that the convent is in Quebec. In the rest of the book, names of provinces, cities or streets more or less vanish; descriptions of external features of reality, such as houses, rooms, furniture, trees or human beings, are sparse to nonexistent. This effacement of where the stories are taking place – presumably Montreal, where Gasco has lived for most of her life – becomes highly detrimental, since it shears away the context of the deviously inventive punning that is one of the most striking features of Gasco's style. Punning, as a linguistic phenomenon, tends to arise when people view their own language through the prism of other languages, which is why, as a literary phenomenon, punning is the domain of exiled or expatriate writers such as Joyce or Nabokov or Cabrera Infante or Anthony Burgess, or of writers belonging to linguistic minorities – such as Elyse Gasco. Being a Quebec anglophone may not be central to Gasco's literary preoccupations, but when her book makes unavailable to the reader a fact so crucial to her use of language, something important is missing. *Can You Wave Bye Bye, Baby?* represents the almost total dissolution of Leacock's Mariposa into the individual psyche. It carries the process initiated by Munro and Laurence's delineation of personal, rather than collective, concerns to an extreme that threatens not to involve the reader, but to close her out.

Can Mariposa be recovered? The answer appears to be yes, but with a caveat that the Canadian writer now finds his small towns overseas. Like Gasco's book, Steven Heighton's *Flight Paths of the Emperor* is not really a collection of linked stories. An intriguing feature of this book of stories is that it presents itself as being more linked than it is. Many of the stories are about foreigners teaching English in Japan during the 1980s, though some admit glances backward to Canada, or spill over into China. The experience of young Canadians confronting questions of identity through their encounters with the intricacies of Japanese culture or the weight of Asian history are common to nearly all the stories. A few characters recur, including a young English teacher named Steven and a married couple named Nick and Sandra. The book opens with a two-page city map. Above the map is written: 'In the Sumiyoshi ward in Osaka, Japan, the area near Nagai Park and around the Nagai train and subway stops is a place of cheap accommodation where a good number of foreigners live – though often without ever meeting. Most of them teach English to Japanese students in the burgeoning schools of downtown Osaka.' Unlike Russell Smith's characters, who snipe at each other from different corners of his collection, Heighton's English teachers are unaware of one another's existences. The map, which indicates where in the Sumiyoshi ward the different characters are living, represents a narrative intervention that imposes cohesion on the characters' dispersal, salvaging a vestigial small-town Canada from the globalized fragmentation of which the migration of so many young Canadians to Asia is a prime symptom. Heighton unifies his collection by binding together his recognition of the collapse of traditional structures – the book is full of wrecked marriages – with his insistence on the endurance of a certain notion of common experience. The book's balancing of such contrary impulses invests Heighton's work with a resonance that is sometimes lacking from the overseas Mariposas of the final writer I would like to discuss, Patrick Roscoe.

Roscoe, as noted earlier, is the author of *Birthmarks*, the most relentless Canadian fictional exploration of the legacy of alienation that 1960s hippie parenting bequeathed to its children. The material is insistently autobiographical, playing repeatedly on the motifs of a childhood divided between Africa and British Columbia, siblings who run away from home and never return, male prostitution in California, the evolution of a literary vocation and eventual impoverished expatriation in Spain. The progress of *Birthmarks*'s autobiographical narrative, which ends not with an arrival at maturity but with a dive back into childhood to plumb the origins of the central character's restlessness, is interrupted, diffused, enlarged upon by the inclusion of similar stories about unrelated characters. The book's structure, complicated by an artificial division into four sections, each preceded by one or two pages of mostly gratuitous citations from newspaper clippings or rock songs, underscores a self-indulgence that is the most offputting feature of a book which contains many moments of lyrical insight. This trait is reinforced by a story where the author's fingerprints are splashed on the middle of the page and by the book's design, which imprints a negative of the author's face, in blazing red and black, in the centre of the front cover. If Gasco's collection threatens to submerse the book of linked stories in the depths of the individual psyche, *Birthmarks,* while in some respects inventively adapting the genre to a drastically altered world, often seems to be on the verge of diminishing this sort of writing from *Bildungsroman* to garish advertisement for the author's public image.

But *Birthmarks* represents only one side of Roscoe's work. His two other linked-story collections describe life in an isolated village on the west coast of Mexico; a third volume about this village is promised. The first of these collections, *Beneath the Western Slopes,* published when Roscoe was twenty-five, is imaginatively thin; but the second, *Love Is Starving for Itself,* is Roscoe's most integrated book. The epic distance of the narrative voice comes as a shock after the gruesome confessions of *Birthmarks.* The opening paragraph begins:

The world seemed very far away, and separated from the town. Though everyone knew that only thirty miles across the hills waited a city with bright lights and with wide paved roads leading to all points upon the globe, it might have been a million miles away, for only a narrow twisting track of dirt connected the capital city to the town, and this was unbearably dusty during the dry season, washed away during the rainy season, and always rough and potted with holes.

One might almost be reading the opening of Leacock's *Sunshine Sketches of a Little Town:* 'I don't know whether you know Mariposa.... There it lies in the sunlight, sloping up from the little lake that spreads out at the foot of the hillside on which the town is built.' Roscoe seems to be seeking an idyllic rural world as a refuge from the kinds of experiences described in *Birthmarks.* Yet it is important for critics attentive to the discontinuities interrupting the quest for a Canadian tradition to note that Roscoe's model is not Leacock: it is Gabriel García Márquez. The echoes of the early chapters of *One Hundred Years of Solitude* are unmistakable: the epic voice, the long narrative paragraphs and sparse dialogue, the appearance of magical phenomena (in Roscoe's case a small white horse) later banished by the advance of technology, the dominance of a matriarchal figure who outlives her descendants – Roscoe's Señora Lopez corresponding to García Márquez's Ursula Buendía. The book's most perplexing feature is the depth of Roscoe's mimicry of the García Márquez voice. *Love Is Starving for Itself* reads like an imitation of a translation. At the level of language, as well as at the level of material, the rift with *Birthmarks* is dramatic: it feels like the work of a different writer. Roscoe writes like someone afflicted by what German linguists refer to as *doppel Halbsprachigkeit* – the condition of having two second languages but no first language. His eccentric deployment of prepositions feels non-native; when he writes that two people have known each other 'since forever', the reader can hear the Spanish *desde siempre* obtruding through the awkward English diction. Yet Roscoe omits accents from Spanish surnames, or puts them in the wrong places, and the book's Spanish-language dedication does not mean what I think Roscoe intends it to mean. His cultivated estrangement – linguistic, stylistic, thematic – from Canadian experience does not engage significantly with Spanish American reality. When, halfway through the book, a man is described as carrying a machete as he walks to work in the fields, the detail pulls the reader to attention, permitting a discordant glimpse of grinding Mexican reality to penetrate the shimmering lyricism of Roscoe's lofty narrative voice. Roscoe has imitated García Márquez's narrative voice, but dispensed with the historical engagement that furnishes García Márquez's prose with its myth-making power. The result is that not much happens in the stilted eloquence of Roscoe's long paragraphs. Even more than in Leacock's world, the narration focuses on events as they affect the collectivity. The expression 'the townspeople' recurs as the subject of narrative sentences. Nearly the only defined characters in the book are Señora Lopez and her three daughters, who grow up, fall in love and, like the children in *Birthmarks,* disappear one by one. Unlike the runaway tales in the earlier book, which end in needle-strewn alleys at night, the disappearances in *Love Is Starving for Itself* are ethereal and ecstatic: more metaphors for how we efface our personalities when we fall in love than experiences reflecting the pain of family breakup.

If a common motif emerges from the diversity of approaches taken by the linked-story writers I have discussed it is that of the flight from history. Russell Smith's characters flee from history into the eternal present of fashion and trend; Elyse Gasco's characters elide history through their ingrown obsession with personal demons; Patrick Roscoe's characters escape from history first into drugs, sex and travel, then into a utopian rural past. The pattern alerts the reader to a paradox: that Jubilee and Manawaka, though representing social stability, participate in history through their memories of the pioneer past and their disruption by the Second World War. 'Writing's going to change a lot after the war,' Vanessa MacLeod's boyfriend Michael tells her at the end of *A*

Bird in the House. 'It did after the First War and it will even more after this one.' How right he was! But, seen from the perspective of the Munro-Laurence linked-stories collection, the paradox of contemporary linked-stories fiction must be that, though buffeted by social instability, it seems powerless to take the pulse of history.

At this point, I probably need to question my own neat linear narrative, which has led this essay from stability and tradition to postmodernity and dispersion. Just as each generation believes that it is the first to discover sex, so each is convinced that no previous generation experienced cultural fragmentation. Even *Sunshine Sketches of a Little Town* concludes with an urbanized character, alienated from his small-town childhood, returning to a Mariposa that is no longer his. My portrait of the development of the Canadian linked-stories collection would have been complicated had I chosen as a model for the present generation not Alice Munro or Margaret Laurence, but Mavis Gallant. In common with many younger writers, Gallant comes from an immigrant background, experienced family disintegration, various types of instability, compulsive travelling and long-term expatriation. The six first-person stories about Linnet Muir that close Gallant's collection *Home Truths,* like many of the collections by younger writers that I have discussed, open with the protagonist at eighteen, trying to clear up the confusions of her identity. They shuttle back and forth between past and present in defiance of linear chronology. At the same time, though, like Munro and Laurence and unlike most of the current generation, Gallant remains acutely aware of history. I had good reasons for not choosing Gallant as an ancestor, namely that *Home Truths* was published only in 1981, and that the coolness verging on hostility with which Gallant was treated by nationalist critics means that she was accepted into the canon much later. Today's writers, in most cases, will have been exposed to Margaret Laurence and Alice Munro earlier than they were to Gallant's fiction. These traditionalist ancestors were more available to my generation during our formative reading years than was the precursor who might have offered us a model of how to find historical engagement within social fragmentation. In the slow accretion of a tradition that occurs as writers read the work of other writers, that kind of discontinuity matters.

A segment of the above essay, then entitled 'What Comes Last? Linking Short Stories in an Age of Fragmentation', was delivered as a lecture at the conference, 'A Visionary Tradition: Canadian Literature and Culture at the Turn of the Millennium', held at the University of Guelph in November 1999.

Part Two
When Words Deny the World

The kernel of 'When Words Deny the World' appeared in 'Beyond Postcolonialism: The News from Canada', a lecture delivered at the Open University, Milton Keynes, England, in October 1997, while the first sketch of this piece was published as 'A Novel for the 90s', *Montreal Gazette*, 27 February 1999. A condensed version of 'Vulgarity on Bloor' appeared in *Quill and Quire*, March 2002, as 'From CanLit to TorLit: There's a problem at the centre of the universe'.

1
Free Trade Fiction, or the Victory of Metaphor over History

It probably makes sense that times dominated by the spirit of the marketplace see as their true counterpart those poets who have nothing at all to do with their time, who do not besmirch themselves with the topical concerns of the day but supply only pure poetry, as it were, addressing their faithful in obsolete idioms on great subjects, as though they were just passing through on earth, coming from eternity, where they live, like the man who went to America three years ago and is already speaking broken German on his first visit home.

– Robert Musil, *The Man Without Qualities*

In June 1997 U.S. novelist John Irving, who lives for part of the year in Toronto, published an article in the *Globe and Mail* under the headline 'If Craig Nova were Canadian ... he'd be Timothy Findley.' Bemoaning the neglect suffered by literary authors in the United States, Irving urged Canadians to recognize the exceptional quantities of media attention, prizes and sales available to writers of literary fiction in Canada. Irving compared December 1996 best-seller lists from the *New York Times* and the *Globe and Mail*, noting that the former was dominated by the formula fiction of writers such as Tom Clancy, Danielle Steel and Sue Grafton, while the latter featured 'literary authors' such as Margaret Atwood, Guy Vanderhaeghe, Mavis Gallant, Timothy Findley, Ann-Marie MacDonald and Anne Michaels. 'I wonder if Canadians appreciate how literary the book business in Canada is,' Irving wrote.

Irving's insights proved influential in Toronto journalism circles. The dictum that 'in Canada the literary writers are the best-sellers' has been popping up ever since on the lips of literary chat-show guests and in the lines of articles and reviews. Irving had put his finger on an intriguing phenomenon: the growing glamorization and commercialization of literary fiction in Canada.

But if literary novels are the country's bestsellers, it becomes true, also, that a novel, in order to sell well, must appear literary: ideally, it should advertise its literariness through 'beautiful' imagery, exotic settings, exquisite production and other features calculated to flatter its purchaser with evidence of his own aesthetic refinement. The 'literary bestseller' became the dominant Canadian literary form of the 1990s. Led by such self-consciously artistic artifacts as Michael Ondaatje's *The English Patient* and Anne Michaels's *Fugitive Pieces*, the Canadian novel of the 1990s evolved from an artistic work engaged with language and history into an *objet d'art*.

It is worth examining in detail how this occurred.

The British historian Eric Hobsbawm has argued that the 'long nineteenth century' began in 1789 with the French Revolution and ended only in 1914 with the outbreak of the First World War. The 'short twentieth century', by contrast, ended in 1991, with the collapse of the Soviet Union. The subsequent division of the globe into trading blocks and the digitalization of commerce, propelled us into a new century a decade before we reached the new millennium.

But if you live in Canada, globalization means Americanization. The North American Free Trade Agreement is not the European Union, where give and take among a multiplicity of members provides smaller countries and minority cultures with the latitude to sustain their vitality. 'Harmonization' meant not only the crippling of familiar local or national businesses, or educational, medical or cultural institutions, but, more profoundly, an assault on the stuffy, provincial, overweeningly decent, obstinately regional, conservative yet residually communitarian Canadian ethos. Society's dominant institutions turned against the population, ridiculing its culture. Canadianness itself came to be perceived as an impediment: as embarrassing baggage to be jettisoned in the quest for global competitiveness.

The jolts of the 1990s accentuated invidious tendencies already ingrained in Canadian culture: a propensity for self-abasement, an insufficiently creative and critical approach to foreign models, a craving for the approval of powerful friends, a latent desire to dispense with the awkwardness of being Canadian and meld into some larger, simpler entity.

The English-language literary tradition has been at odds from the start with Canadian experience. The anti-theoretical bias inherited from the two empires – nineteenth-century Great Britain and the twentieth-century United States – that forged the modern English-language literary tradition puts blinkers on the Canadian writer striving to take the measure of her marginalized northern society. Unlike the Mexican, the Pole, the Angolan, the Japanese, we have experienced difficulty in focusing in our art on our historical position: first as a British colony and a country oriented towards Great Britain, then, after 1945, as a neighbour of the most powerful nation on earth. It is not that these themes have never been touched upon; it is that they have been dealt with in simple-minded, tract-like ways (as, for example, in the illiterate nationalist thrillers of Richard Rohmer), rather than becoming springboards for artistic innovation, as has occurred in other countries on the world's cultural margins.

The absence of artistic engagement with our historical position need not be a serious drawback for the poet or short story writer, whose art can flourish at a hermetic remove from history. This probably explains why short story writers and, to a lesser extent, poets have produced the best English-language writing in Canada. The novel, famously described by Stendhal as a mirror dawdling along a road, expresses, implicitly or explicitly, a statement about society. To narrate the life of a protagonist during a significant period of personal development is to render a judgement, however oblique, ironic or contradictory, on the context within which that development occurs. Not even the most effete art novel can elude this vocation. The great nineteenth-century European novels were eminently engaged with national history, but so were the three great novelistic masterpieces of European modernism: Marcel Proust's *In Search of Lost Time,* James Joyce's *Ulysses* and Robert Musil's *The Man Without Qualities.* The form of Proust's mythologization of language and memory is unimaginable outside the boundaries of the France of *la belle époque;* Joyce's linguistic shenanigans dramatize a colonized country's fractious relationship to European history and the English language; and in Musil the crumbling of the certainties of 19th-century rationalism and the disintegration of the Austro-Hungarian empire become elaborate metaphors for one another. In more recent, neo-modernist or post-modernist times, it has been impossible to imagine the fiction of Günter Grass or Christa Wolf without the partition of Germany, of Salman Rushdie without the multiple partitions of the Indian subcontinent and the Indian diaspora, the fiction of Gabriel García Márquez without Colombia's civil wars, the fiction of Nadine Gordimer without South African apartheid and its aftermath, the fiction of Thomas Pynchon without U.S. intervention in the Vietnam War, the fiction of Milan Kundera without the Soviet invasion of Czechoslovakia, the fiction of Pauline Melville without the destruction of Native American communities in Guyana, the fiction of Cristina Peri Rossi without the crisis of gender definition provoked by the eruption of a macho military dictatorship in the peaceful backwater of Uruguay, the fiction of Haruki Murakami without the legacy of Japanese militarism lurking beneath the placid surface of modern Japan. In all of these writers, the making of the individual, the historical trajectory of society and the dynamics of the novel as an artistic form intertwine. Artistic innovation, particularly in the novel, feeds on communal crisis. 'The great novelist is a kind of vulture,' Mario Vargas Llosa has written. 'The putrid flesh of history is his favourite nourishment and has served to inspire him to his most audacious undertakings. And those societies in crisis are precisely ... the ones that have inspired the most daring and total novels ever conceived.'

In Canada, though, the vultures are confined to Bay Street and the oil patch. In the arts, and particularly in literature, crisis has bred conformity, suffusing our novels with a desire to transcend history into a commercially congenial strand of non-engaged high art: to ascend to the best-seller list while retaining the 'literary fiction' label. Crisis, in short, has enhanced complacency.

One possible rejoinder to this is that, for all the job losses, constitutional tempests and evaporation of familiar cultural touchstones, the crisis of the 1990s was not that severe. This is Canada, after all. Thousands of people were not killed. The gap between rich and poor grew wider, most people were living with less cultural and financial security than in the past, but, being Canadian, many developed a masochistic sense of duty about living with insecurity. They were persuaded that it was good for them: that the threat of losing their jobs made them 'competitive', that the disintegration of their culture made them 'post-modern'. Perhaps the upheaval was not all that serious.

Yet I think this interpretation is wrong. I feel it to be intuitively wrong at a personal level, having returned to live in Canada in the late 1990s to discover that many of the common assumptions and ways of doing things that I had grown up with had vanished. The texture of life, life's capacity to permeate experience with significance, had thinned. Life felt like television – American television. (Richard Gwyn, who returned to the country in the early 1990s, also after a long absence, reported in his book *Nationalism Without Walls* that he came back to find that Canada 'had evaporated'.) In retrospect, history seems likely to view the early 1990s as a time of wrenching cultural change, even of collective trauma.

How have our novelists responded to the annihilation of our intimate selves?

Primarily with averted eyes. Rather than feasting, vulture-like, on the putrid flesh – and how putrid it is! – of the history of the last decade, many of our most prominent novelists have collaborated in rewriting history as a stately foreign pageant, fleeing the gnarled corruption of our slow subsiding into the hide of the elephant to our south for a realm of noble metaphors. It may be objected that, though literature is commonly conceived to be 'news which stays news', one should not expect the novel to report on the present. Yet there is no gainsaying the importance of history to fiction. Even so resolute an art novelist as Henry James declared that it took a great deal of history to make a little literature. History, of course, often requires the clarifying binoculars of time in order to concentrate itself as literature. Only fifty years after Napoleon's failed invasion of Russia did Tolstoy write *War and Peace*. But it is also true that the novel, as Georg Lukács argued, is the bourgeois epic, and an integral part of the novelist's task is to keep his eye on the follies of the bourgeoisie. It is difficult to think of recent Canadian novels that do this in a compelling, innovative way. The Canadian bourgeoisie, it is true, has been an embarrassing spectacle over the last ten years, rarely missing an opportunity to conform to its own beaver-like self-image by biting off its testicles and offering them up to its pursuers. Yet the novelist must do what she can with the materials at hand. Simply because a writer comes from a country whose bourgeoisie lacks a backbone does not absolve him from engaging with the dilemmas of spinelessness. (James Joyce's short story 'Ivy Day in the Committee Room' offers one example of how to do this.)

The great nineteenth-century Portuguese novelist Eça de Queirós was fond of decrying his position as 'the Balzac of the insipid'. We cannot gauge whether, given the material that Balzac found before him, Queirós would have evolved into a greater writer than his French counterpart. What is indisputable is that had he not persisted in dramatizing the 'insipid' Portuguese bourgeoisie, Queirós would not have left a legacy of dauntingly accomplished novels such as *Cousin Basilio* and *The Maias*. Coming from a peripheral nation such as Portugal, Queirós will never be read as widely as Balzac. But he is better known as a superb chronicler of Portuguese folly than he would have been had he renounced his surroundings and tried to write about miserly old men in the French provinces.

· · ·

The two novels which set the tone for the 1990s in Canada were *The English Patient* by Michael Ondaatje and *Fugitive Pieces* by Anne Michaels. I do not mean by this that all Canadian novels of the 'Free Trade Fiction' era adopted the same metaphor-saturated aesthetic as these two, merely that *The English Patient* and *Fugitive Pieces,* by virtue of their conspicuous commercial and critical success, channelled much literary debate. In their striving for high art, their settings remote in time and place from the Canadian present, they came to be seen as salient indicators of where the Canadian novel was going. When you talked to writers and literary people, these were the books they were discussing. They were also the Canadian novels most likely to have been read – or at least attempted – by people outside the literary world.

It is easy to make fun of *The English Patient*. A standing joke dictates that most people who start reading the book do not finish it. The British thriller writer Frederick Forsyth has enumerated the improbabilities of the novel's plot. Philip Marchand has poked holes in the pompous self-regard of the narrative voice. Terence Byrnes's '10 Sentences of Poetic

Prose from Michael Ondaatje's *The English Patient*, published in *Matrix* magazine, demolishes the book with a few choice quotes. The novel's defenders respond to these attacks by arguing that Ondaatje is a serious artist who is taking risks with language in order to elaborate a profound vision of life. If his prose lacks the clarity of that of, say, Russell Smith (Marchand's example), it is because Ondaatje sees beyond the screen of contemporary fashion to profound, lasting verities.

This quest for 'lasting verities', for a 'profound vision of life', is integral to the novel's flight from history. *The English Patient* transforms the Second World War from history into metaphor. Events with human consequences dissolve into predigested images: an Italian villa, the desert, a burned man, a valiant nurse. The novel's tactics are identical to those of television commercials and rock videos, which destroy the past by recycling familiar tunes or images severed from the historical context that lent them meaning. Anthems of 1960s revolt recycled as soap jingles, Che Guevara no longer an outraged Argentine doctor marching through the mountains with a gun in his hands but a red-ringed icon of post-modern chic, and the Hungarian Nazi Almásy stripped of his fascist allegiances to become the centrepiece of a literary *objet d'art*, his 'penis sleeping like a seahorse' – all belong in the same category. Middle-class readers have acclaimed *The English Patient* as art because it employs an art they recognize: the neutering of the past into harmless, ecstatic visions. The contemporary assumption, in Canada at least, that the adjective 'beautiful' is the highest praise that can be accorded a work of literature betrays the corrupt guilty conscience of a class that has collaborated in the destruction of its values and culture in exchange for a tax cut and the promise of easy profits from global markets. Would 'beautiful' be the first word that came to mind to describe *The Iliad*? Was Milton seeking to generate mere beauty through the austere Latinate verses of *Paradise Lost*? Is 'beauty' a significant consideration in our appreciation of *Middlemarch* or *Bleak House*? Would anyone attach so anodyne an adjective as 'beautiful' to Joyce's achievement in *Ulysses* or Thomas Pynchon's achievement in *Gravity's Rainbow*? These works shake or move us because they are *resonant:* they connect language with human history, and in so doing absorb us as readers into a breadth of experience that surpasses the customary limits of individual understanding.

The English Patient does the opposite: it closes off meaningful comprehension of the past, substituting an understanding that is either purely mechanical, as in the detailed descriptions of the bombs Kip defuses, or vulgarly romanticized, as in the novel's histories of interwar desert exploration. The past evaporates into an eternal present captured in visions of sand dunes and a burned man lying in a picturesque villa.

The English Patient distances us from the experiences it purports to describe.

The maddening part of this is that, line by line, Ondaatje can be one of the best writers around. He has little grasp of the novel as a literary form – of the novel's possibilities, pacing and conventions, of how its architecture can be massaged into revealing new shapes – but, at its best, his prose is unbeatable. The opening four paragraphs of *The English Patient*, describing Hana walking into the villa as she feels the rain coming on, display a pitch-perfect ear for prose rhythms. Only that garish, attention-grabbing image of the 'penis sleeping like a seahorse' mars the tone. Ondaatje has enjoyed his greatest success in the tossed-salad forms of *Coming Through Slaughter* and *Running in the Family*, where fractured structures enabled him to duck out of scenes before they dragged on into pomposity and barnacled metaphors. When he can animate his poet's gift for image with a quick sluice of narrative he is at his most effective. What Ondaatje cannot write is interaction between people. The weakest scenes of *The English Patient* – and, alas, among the most numerous – are those where Hana, Kip and the improbable David Caravaggio waft around the villa pontificating about their lives. The diaphanousness of the characters – who, like everything else in the book, are first and foremost images – means that the narrator seems to be unsure what they want in a particular scene. The ancient Greeks argued that character was fate: that kind of motivation is sorely lacking in *The English Patient*. The characters are there to glow and be admired for their immanence. When they interact emotionally the results are stilted; their physical horseplay in the villa's darkened rooms is both ungainly and unfathomable. For example:

Then everything in the room seemed to be in movement but Caravaggio. He could hear it all around him, surprised he wasn't touched. The boy was in the room. Caravaggio walked over to the sofa and placed his hand down towards

Hana. She was not there. As he straightened up, an arm went around his neck and pulled him down backwards in a grip. A light glared harshly into his face, and there was a gasp from them both as they fell towards the floor. The arm with the light still holding him at the neck. Then a naked foot emerged into the light, moved past Caravaggio's face and stepped onto the boy's neck beside him. Another light went on.

In scenes like this one Ondaatje the poet conceives human interaction almost solely in terms of image. The scene to which this description belongs reflects no emotional event, only an attempt to rig up a certain vision of human bodies and lights arrayed in a particular configuration. The strain on Ondaatje's prose rhythms is palpable. The *non-sequitur*-like rifts between the sentences, the awkward syntax of 'placed his hand down towards', the weak verbs ('went', 'there was', 'went on') betray the exertions of a writer who thinks visually rather than viscerally or psychologically. Yet when Ondaatje's characters sit and talk, the consequences are even grimmer. Caravaggio may be the worst offender (unless one counts the entire sections narrated in the voice of the scorched yet encyclopedic patient), but none of the characters is exempt from dialogue of a narcissistic self-regard. Here is Hana talking to Kip. It is worth noting that her expression while she utters these words is reported to be 'quizzical':

I thought I was going to die. I wanted to die. And I thought if I was going to die I would die with you. Someone like you, young as I am, I saw so many dying near me in the last year. I didn't feel scared. I certainly wasn't brave just now. I thought to myself, We have this villa, this grass, we should have lain down together, you in my arms, before we died. I wanted to touch that bone at your neck, collarbone, it's like a small hard wing under your skin. I wanted to place my fingers against it. I've always liked flesh the colour of rivers and rocks or like the brown eye of a Susan, do you know what that flower is? –

On and on Hana's monologue flows, along the brown river and over the brown rocks and into the brown-eyed Susans. Hana, who is twenty years old and has been a war nurse since the age of seventeen, uses words like 'trenchant'. Though she reads a lot, her preciousness stretches credulity. One of the books she is reading, *The Charterhouse of Parma*, is used to reinforce the novel's romanticization of Italy as a landscape fit for swashbucklers. (Ondaatje's one-dimensional interpretation of the novel conveniently overlooks Stendhal's mordant ironies, such as Fabrizio's non-witnessing of the battle of Waterloo.) Had Hana been reading a different Stendhal novel – his mature work *Lucien Leuwen,* for example, with its organic integration of individual and societal destinies – the reader might have been obliged to pause and reflect upon Ondaatje's dissolution of history into metaphor.

The novel's central metaphor is the burned patient. The sections of the book narrated in his voice read like the long, stodgy, erudite monologues in the later novels of Robertson Davies. Educated at a British school, able to pass for an Englishman though irredeemably foreign, Almásy resembles one of Davies's Oxford-educated colonials. Where Davies values the Comic Spirit in such characters, Ondaatje values Passion. Almásy is Passionate. And, oh yes, he is a Nazi. But this does not worry the other characters. As Hana says, 'It doesn't matter who he is. The war is over.'

This is almost certainly the novel's greatest implausibility. In early 1945 three battered veterans of the Allied campaigns in Italy and North Africa, after years of fighting fascism, being mutilated by fascists (Caravaggio), losing both a father and the father of a would-be first child to fascism (Hana), having a surrogate father killed by a fascist bomb (Kip), find themselves in a villa with a man whom they suspect of being a fascist spy. And they do nothing? They don't even discuss whether they should turn this man over to the Allied authorities? The lapse illustrates more strikingly than any other feature of the novel Ondaatje's flight from history into metaphor. Almásy's historical identity (and Almásy is an actual historical figure) as a 1930s desert explorer who worked for the Germans during the Second World War melts before his immanence as an image.

As the English patient, Almásy is a symbol, and what he symbolizes is the death of the British Empire, to which the Second World War dealt a mortal blow. Hana, Kip and Caravaggio are all orphans of that empire, about to be cut loose into a post-colonial world. It is appropriate that the English patient should not be English, as most of the subjects of the British Empire were not English, though, like Ondaatje himself – a graduate of Dulwich Academy – Almásy has a posh English education.

This is why the love affair that dominates the film version is of secondary importance to the novel. In the novel, Almásy's primary role is to embody the kind of Africa-obsessed Boy Scout ethos that ensured that the sun never set on the Union Jack. John Buchan and Rider Haggard are not that far away, the line separating the Cave of Swimmers from King Solomon's Mines being a relatively fine one.

Almásy matters most as a monitor of the death of the common world – or Commonwealth – to which Hana, Kip and Caravaggio have been brought up. The best material in the book, and the only scenes which are authentically moving, describe Kip's relationship with his aristocratic English mentor, Lord Suffolk. If the English patient is the book's symbolic centre, Kip is its emotional core. His proud yet troubled absorption of the upper-class English ethos propounded by Suffolk may well echo Ondaatje's own experiences as a South Asian studying at Dulwich. In light of these contradictory preoccupations, the novel's structural asymmetry – dominated by the image of the English patient, its conclusion is dictated by Kip's flight from the villa – is not surprising.

Ondaatje's abandonment of history for metaphor cripples his ability to develop his post-colonial themes. The novel approaches 1945 Italy through the lens of early 1990s Toronto. Hana, for example, is characterized through the Free Trade maxim of North Americanism. When Kip tells her about his upbringing in the Punjab, she replies, 'I'm from Upper America,' casting her own colonial relationship outside the bounds of the British Empire, whose history they share. This jab of early 1990s Toronto ideology imposes on Hana a consciousness of a merging with the U.S.A. that does not belong to her generation of Canadians. The anachronism is compounded when Almásy criticizes the way she reads aloud from Rudyard Kipling's *Kim* by telling her, 'Your eye is too quick and North American.' Again, Toronto of the 1990s is projected onto the Toronto of the 1940s: a sedate, colonial, intensely Anglophile city where public buildings flew the Union Jack and people talked about 'motoring' in their cars rather than driving them. The rhythms of Kipling's language, though alien to a young Toronto woman today, would have been familiar to a woman of Hana's generation. The language of Rudyard Kipling, in fact, would have formed a crucial part of the Imperial cultural baggage shared by a woman like Hana and a man like Almásy. In a similar, post–Gulf War vein, Ondaatje speaks of 'North

American troops' in a war that Canada entered two years before the United States and under very different conditions.

The novel's eradication of the particularities of Canadian history in favour of a continentalist vision that had little currency during the period when the story takes place stymies Ondaatje's attempts to describe the post-colonial experience. In spite of his own apparent intentions, Ondaatje allows Kip his post-colonial perceptions, but denies Hana and Caravaggio theirs.

When Kip renounces European culture after the American nuclear bombing of Hiroshima, Ondaatje frames his renunciation in terms of the ahistorical identity politics of early 1990s Toronto. This brandishing of pigmentation as a banner of identity, in isolation from the cross-currents of history, was one of the most salient traits of the trauma that gripped Canadian cultural circles in the aftermath of the passage of the Free Trade Agreement. As the ship of Canadian identity sank, ethnic belonging bobbed to the surface for many as the most convenient spar to cling to. In 1995, in an essay called 'Borrowed Blackness', André Alexis, one of the most perceptive critics of this largely Torontonian phenomenon, wrote: 'I miss hearing black Canadians speak *from* Canada.' Alexis was dealing specifically with the overwhelming presence of black American culture for Canadians of African ancestry. But his observation of the ways in which identity had become separated from history, particularly within the Toronto media cockpit (Alexis wrote as a bemused outsider who had moved to Toronto from Ottawa), holds true across a range of identities.

In portraying Kip's reaction to the bombing of Hiroshima, Ondaatje struggles to equate the Americans with the British and the Japanese with the Indians. 'You had King Leopold of Belgium and now you have fucking Harry Truman of the U.S.A. You all learned it from the British,' Kip says as he prepares to abandon the villa. The correlation comes across as strained because Ondaatje's ahistorical approach has not prepared us for it. (Compare, by contrast, the elegant inevitability with which the Second World War transfer of imperial dominance from the U.K. to the U.S.A. occurs in the closing pages of Graham Swift's *Waterland,* a novel which animates and engages with history.) In the end, Ondaatje has nothing to fall back on but, to adopt André Alexis's phrase, 'borrowed blackness'. Racial essentialism cloaks the novel's final scene in the assumptions of Toronto identity politics. The description of Kip – now restored to his original name of Kirpal – having dinner with his family some time after Indian independence in 1947 reports that: 'At this table all of their hands are brown. They move with ease in their customs and their habits.' The order which is restored at the novel's close is one in which history has evaporated, yet the races live separately, each prolonging its own customs – a Utopia whose internal contradictions could be viewed as harmonious only in post-Free Trade, ahistorical, identity-obsessed early 1990s Toronto.

The English Patient's influence and popularity make it worth discussing in detail. Though a cumbersome novel whose gutting of history is troubling, it contains passages of excellent writing (in addition to pages of awful writing). And it has provoked a response. Jack Hodgins's novel *Broken Ground,* published six years later in 1998, often reads like a deliberate inversion of *The English Patient.* Hodgins reaches back to the First World War, the war that for many defined Canadian nationhood. He focuses on a small British Columbia town in 1922 where most of the men are veterans. Portuguese Creek is as earthy as Ondaatje's villa is ethereal. Hodgins's descriptions of his protagonists' experiences in the trenches and during the forest fire they fight upon their return to Canada are cast in prose of graphic specificity, with scarcely a metaphor to be found. A scene narrating the execution of a teenage boy accused of having deserted his post on the front lines is gruesomely memorable. Where Ondaatje's Kip is an expert in defusing bombs, two of Hodgins's central characters specialize in blowing things up. This detail, combined with subplots about how history written by Americans and movie directors has erased Canada's contribution to the First World War, suggests that, among its other concerns, *Broken Ground* is a retort to Ondaatje. Hodgins does his characters greater justice than does Ondaatje, tracing in detail their long, painful recoveries from their wartime ordeals. In the end, the novel goes on too long. Hodgins's folksy tone is not well suited to delineating psychological trauma. His orchestration of Faulkneresque monologues and shifting narrative viewpoints, though impressive, lacks the emotional intensity to invest such techniques with real power. Yet *Broken Ground,* the strongest book in Hodgins's prolific career, seems to gain part of its energy from a deliberate sparring with *The English Patient.*

The true companion piece to *The English Patient*, in a variety of important ways, is Anne Michaels's novel, *Fugitive Pieces*. This novel's action originates in the central fact of Second World War history omitted by Ondaatje: the mass murder of European Jews by the Nazis. Broaching the issue of the Holocaust in *The English Patient* would have risked converting Almásy from metaphor to historical figure, causing the novel's disengaged symbolic edifice to crumble. *Fugitive Pieces*, like *Broken Ground*, can be read as a retort to *The English Patient*'s historical omissions; but it also represents a shameless imitation of Ondaatje's metaphor-laden aesthetic and a consolidation of his suppression of Canadian history. Published in 1996, Michaels's novel epitomizes the second half of the 1990s as Ondaatje's book does the first half of the decade. A less complex work, it can claim a nearly equal significance in the reshaping of the Canadian English-language novel.

Douglas Glover once argued that Marian Engel's novel *Bear* was intended as a parody of Margaret Atwood's *Surfacing*. In the same vein, *Fugitive Pieces* pays *The English Patient* the sincerest form of flattery, surrounding with metaphors the crucial fact of Second World War history suppressed by Ondaatje's novel. Michaels's novel can be read as a parody of *The English Patient*, though it may not have been intended that way. (The digression on Antarctic exploration that concludes with the Canadian explorer punching out his British colleague for calling him 'the American', reads like a deliberate lampooning of Ondaatje's sanguine sketch of multinational harmony among 1930s desert explorers.) But the parallel with Engel's relationship to Atwood breaks down. In terms of its literary aesthetic and its public impact, it is *Surfacing*, not *Bear*, which *Fugitive Pieces* resembles.

Fugitive Pieces is to the mid-1990s what *Surfacing* was to the early 1970s. The similarities are irresistible: the poet-turned-novelist etching the values of a generation in metaphor, the geological imagery compensating for hazy characterization and negligible plotting, the remote public persona of an author whose head is armoured with curls, the worshipful admiration of the Toronto media acting as a launching-pad into markets farther afield. *Surfacing* became a banner for the nationalism of the young, liberal Canadian bourgeoisie of the 1970s; the popularity of *Fugitive Pieces*, which one journalist estimated was present in households in the Annex to the tune of one-and-a-half copies per home, coincides with and confirms the same generation's middle-aged slide away from nationalism into a yearning for cosmopolitanism, its renunciation of Canadian historical particularity while still paying lip-service to Canadianism – or Torontonianism, at least – as a basic value. *Fugitive Pieces* is *Surfacing* for former nationalists growing rich on NAFTA. It is Canadian, part of it is set in Toronto, yet, at a time when Toronto's streets are filling up with homeless people, it depicts the city in terms of its *geology:* 'a city built in the bowl of a prehistoric lake'.

Athos, the Greek protector of the young Jewish-Polish protagonist, Jakob, is invited to Canada to help found the geography department at the University of Toronto. Not only does the novel divert the reader's attention from Toronto *society,* it makes her feel good about herself for thinking in this way. At the same time that the reader is overlooking local historical or social references by admiring Michaels's metaphors, he is thinking about the Holocaust, undeniably an important subject. In Robert Musil's words, Michaels is 'addressing (her) faithful in obsolete idioms on great subjects'. Yet the presence of *the* great subject evoked by Michaels's novel, the genocide of European Jews, is often as ethereal as Ondaatje's Italian villa. In a novel about memory and the legacy of mass murder, the evocations of the Holocaust grow disquietingly lush. Surveying the battered landscape of post–Second World War Greece, the young Jakob thinks:

The landscape of the Peloponnesus had been injured and healed so many times, sorrow darkened the sunlit ground. All sorrow feels ancient. Wars, occupations, earthquakes; fire and drought. I stood in the valleys and imagined the grief of the hills. I felt my own grief expressed there. It would be almost fifty years and in another country before I would again experience this intense empathy with a landscape.

Would an adolescent boy mourning the death of his parents and his sister conceive his pain, even in retrospect, through the expression of such a complacent credo as, 'All sorrow feels ancient'? Most sorrow does not feel ancient. It feels immediate and agonizing, and grates on the bone with the unfairness that calamity has sought out *me*. 'I stood in the valleys and imagined the grief of the hills,' is as close as Michaels comes at this point to rendering Jakob's existence as an individual Holocaust survivor.

Michaels's recourse to metaphor is inseparable from her failure to imagine the particularities of Jakob's humanity. Like his mirror-opposite, the Nazi Almásy, Jakob remains an ethereal cliché: the heroically erudite Holocaust survivor. His thinness as a character finally forces Michaels, in the novel's most ungainly lurch, to wrench the narrative point-of-view away from him. When he takes over the narration, two-thirds of the way through the novel, the young academic Ben refers to Jakob as 'embalmed', a description that rings sadly true. Jakob the paragon is too static to develop. His woodenness is evident even in the early scenes set in Greece. Michaels's cursory catalogue of epic dislocations ('Wars, occupations, earthquakes') feels almost off-hand, reducing Jakob, like other victims and survivors over the centuries, to a speck in a vast panorama – 'A single death is a tragedy; a million deaths is a statistic.' If Josef Stalin's brutal maxim were rewritten by Anne Michaels, it might read: 'A single death is a tragedy; six million deaths is a metaphor.'

This is the most perturbing aspect of *Fugitive Pieces*. A number of thoughtful readers – particularly Jewish readers – have suggested that the book is immoral because it 'aestheticizes the Holocaust'. Lines such as Jakob's description of the moment when he realizes his sister has been murdered ('Bella becomes flooded ground. A body of water pulling under the moon') drape mass murder in elegant metaphors. It is worth observing that the most successful Holocaust writing of recent decades, that of Primo Levi, relies on a scientific precision and an objectivity resistant to flights into poetic generalization. The Nazis' fondness for grandiloquent speechifying made many of their victims suspicious of poetry. A number of Canadian journalists have gushed that *Fugitive Pieces* 'shows that it is possible to write poetry after Auschwitz', but it is clear from their utterances that they do not understand the context in which this doubt arises, or how high the stakes are. Even more appalling is the literary ignorance betrayed by this remark. The question of writing poetry after Auschwitz, posed by Theodor Adorno, dominated the work of the Jewish-German-Romanian poet Paul Celan, one of the major figures of twentieth-century European literature (and, indeed, of many of the other members of Gruppe 47, the loose gathering of talents to which Celan belonged, such as Hans Magnus Enzensburger, Günter Grass and Heinrich Böll). Since Celan wrote that, 'Es sind / noch Lieder zu singen jenseits / der Menschen' ('There are still songs to sing beyond mankind'), it has not been possible to pretend that this material is uncharted territory. The critic who perceives *Fugitive Pieces* as courageous because it raises the question of writing poetry after Auschwitz has not read Paul Celan. The stark lines of Celan's collection *Fadensonnen* (roughly translatable as *Threadsuns*) are barbed by a wordplay that is not at all playful: a rough tugging that hauls concealed meanings out of common expressions, exposing the hidden cargoes sheathed by metaphorical language. Revolted by the Nazis' gusty reappropriation of the lofty verbiage of German Romanticism, how would Holocaust survivors such as Celan and Levi have reacted to *Fugitive Pieces?* There is a good chance that they would have seen the book as collaborating with the kind of linguistic corruption they loathed. Yet the vital issue is not the book's specious 'originality', but *how* Michaels writes 'poetry' (or poetic prose) after Auschwitz. What history do her metaphors make available? What do they obscure?

In the novel Michaels defends the use of metaphor, arguing that the Holocaust occurred because 'the German language annihilated metaphor, turning humans into objects.' This process is equated, predictably, with the development of the atom bomb. In following Ondaatje's lead on metaphors in general, and nuclear weapons in particular, Michaels misconstrues what the Nazis did to language. In fact, she contradicts herself only a few pages later when she points out how euphemisms and metaphorical depictions of Jews as animals facilitated the atrocities committed during the Hitler years: 'Non-Aryans were never to be referred to as human, but as 'figuren', 'stücke' – 'dolls', 'wood', 'merchandise', 'rags'. Humans were not being gassed, only 'figuren', so ethics weren't being violated. No one could be faulted for burning debris, for burning rags and clutter in the dirty basement of society.'

This is the strongest case against the language of *Fugitive Pieces.* By dismembering the world into images, the novel blocks the reader's ability to imagine the movements of history, including both the ghastly crimes of the Nazis and the comparatively extremely mild yet nonetheless worrying disruptions within contemporary Canadian society. The most striking feature of Michaels's metaphors is their free-standing, aphoristic nature. They are not *earned* metaphors: they do not blossom from a mass of richly evoked experience, as, for example, the metaphors of Malcolm Lowry do in *Under the Volcano.* Rather, they stand at the heads of paragraphs or chapters, superficially profound pearls of wisdom such as: 'Time is a blind guide', or 'Irony is scissors, a divining rod always pointing in two directions', or 'Complicity is not sudden, though it occurs in an instant', or 'Privacy is the true profundity of a marriage'. There is a fortune-cookie quality to these utterances – not all of them graced by full metaphors – that holds them apart from the development of character or scene. The metaphors, for the most part, are not coordinated to create a unified artistic effect. A typical scene begins with an aphorism, often containing a metaphor, slips into recollection, then, as the scene's momentum wanes, coughs up a fresh aphorism and starts over again. With a few exceptions, the metaphors remain discrete and arbitrary. At the beginning of one short paragraph the narrator reports that 'History is the poisoned well, seeping into the groundwater'; two lines later we are told that, 'Every recorded event is a brick of potential'; three lines after this the paragraph ends with the sentence fragment: 'Out of fertile ground, the compost of history'.

Poisoned wells, bricks, compost – while all these images are vaguely rustic, their deployment in the paragraph is random. One could shuffle the images, or move them to a different section of the book, and the novel would remain unchanged. One of Michaels's European translators told me that at first *Fugitive Pieces* seemed exceptionally difficult to translate. The translator was trying to recreate in the translation a metaphorical coherence that was presumed to exist in the original. Once the translator realized that most of the book had no meaning, that the metaphors were there to shine rather than to build towards artistic resonance, the task became easier. 'I just guessed,' the translator said. Most of *Fugitive Pieces* is shapeless showing-off: poetic wanking in stagy, forced diction. The imagery's few consistent motifs, therefore, become doubly revealing.

Where Ondaatje's imagery draws on the four elements – earth, air, fire, water – Michaels develops a scheme where images of weight are counterpointed against those of weightlessness. The juxtaposition, as simple as it is tendentious, chimes perfectly with the ideology of the age, serving to explain the widespread breathless acclaim of the novel's 'profundity'. Works hailed as profound by large numbers of people at the time of their publication nearly always promote, overtly or covertly, the dominant trends of the day. *Fugitive Pieces* assures a Canadian bourgeoisie in the midst of relinquishing its national culture of that culture's triviality, promising that cultural weight resides elsewhere. The first inkling of this arises with that foolish Canadian Antarctic explorer walloping his British counterpart for calling him an American. But the contrast between the 'lightness' of the characters possessing a culture identified by the narrator as Canadian and the 'heaviness' of the characters possessing a culture identified as European makes explicit the triviality of Canadian identity. (With the exception of a fleetingly mentioned 'Chinese girl', Michaels's Toronto, though a city of immigrants, does not include immigrants from continents other than Europe.)

The second sentence of Jakob's narration establishes his identity as the 'bog-boy'. Jakob, Athos and Bella ('A body of water pulling under the moon') are associated with images of weight. The Canadian characters are linked to images of weightlessness. This is most evident in the portrait of Jakob's first wife, Alexandra Maclean. Where Jakob comes from 'the drowned city' of Biskupin in Poland, Alex's father devoted his energies during the Second World War to creating a papier-mâché model of Alexandria, Egypt, that distracted German bombers from the real place. The contrast between Jakob's origins in the cultural heaviness of a drowned city and the Canadian's fashioning of an illusory city 'that vanished at dawn', set up the contrast that causes Jakob, the first time he meets Alex – who is named after her father's counterfeit city – to describe making her acquaintance as being like 'the gift of a beautiful bird'. The bird image returns in the scene where their marriage is breaking up: 'She is thin and light, the bones of a bird.' A third bird reference links Alex's avian lightness to the triviality of Canadian culture:

I begin to feel that Alex is brainwashing me. Her Gerrard Street scene, her jazz at the Tick Tock, her coffeehouse politics at the River Nihilism, owned by an origami artist who folds birds out of dollar bills. Her Trudeaumania and her cornet mania. Her portrait painted by the artist who wears half a moustache, the length of her, the edgy sexuality of which she's now fully in control – all of it is making me forget. Athos replaced parts of me slowly, as if he were preserving wood. But Alex – Alex wants to explode me, set fire to everything. She wants me to begin again.

John Ralston Saul has argued that one of the dominant falsehoods of the neo-conservative campaign to eradicate Canadian cultural history lies in the constant repetition of the dictum that Canada is a 'new country'. As Saul points out in *Reflections of a Siamese Twin*, Canada is in fact one of the world's oldest functioning states, its geographical boundaries and basic institutions having been moulded more than two hundred years ago; significant aspects of our present arrangements reach back almost four hundred years. Few other countries can match this record of geographical and institutional continuity. One reason that Canadian neo-conservatives experience orgasm while reading *Fugitive Pieces* is that the novel's denial and denigration of Canadian history coincide flawlessly with the neo-con project of recasting Canada as a 'new land' where everything can be torn down and 'begun again'. This fad for 'newness' represents an annexing of Canada to the United States ideal of the eternal new dawn, the erasure of the Canadian past and Canadian traditions that may not mesh well with the corporate motto of 'harmonization', and the consequent belief that one must 'begin again', this time according to the American Way, because no culture of substance exists here in the first place. It is the attitude that European colonizers once carried around the world with them to justify the suppression of other cultures. By reducing Canadian history to a cartoon version of the flakier side of 1960s Toronto student life, Michaels loads the dice against Canadian particularity. Being Canadian is bird-like: it is for the birds.

The most consistent motif perceptible in the imagery of this otherwise imagistically scattered novel goes a long way to explaining its success. The novel's appeal to neo-conservatives is obvious – the never-explained decision that led the neo-conservative editors of *Books in Canada* to award *Fugitive Pieces* the magazine's First Novel Prize after the judges had split three ways is a good example of the special pleading undertaken on this book's behalf by the right-wing media.

But many Canadian readers who are not neo-conservatives have also lauded *Fugitive Pieces*'s 'profundity'. The combination of 'beautiful' imagery and the Holocaust subject matter no doubt explains part of this reaction, but the subconscious impact on an upper-middle-class readership adapting to a globalized corporate order of Michaels's image-wrapped conversion of the dissolution of Canadian history into something 'beautiful' and 'cultured' can also claim responsibility for the praise's breathless quality.

(This is emphatically not the reason for *Fugitive Pieces*'s European success. The resurgence of neo-fascist politics in 1990s Europe meant that books about the Holocaust were championed by the left, but regarded with suspicion by the right. In Britain, for example, it was conservative publications, such as the *Daily Telegraph*, that expressed scepticism about *Fugitive Pieces*, questioning what a writer born in Canada in the 1950s could know about the Holocaust. By contrast, Orange Prize jury president Lisa Jardine, herself the daughter of a famous Holocaust survivor, greeted Michaels's novel as a godsend to her campaign to berate British women writers for their lack of political engagement. One of Jardine's graduate students was instrumental to the novel's publication in one major European market. Help came also from the British writer John Berger, who diminished himself as an intellectual by penning a long, effusive review – reprinted in various European newspapers – pronouncing *Fugitive Pieces* the most important novel of the last forty years. In this context it is intriguing to observe that Berger's work is mentioned in the text of the novel, that Berger is accorded further praise in Michaels's acknowledgements, that Berger's name and that of the novel's protagonist Jakob Beer resemble each other, and that, tantalizingly, the book's dedication reads 'for J'. No wonder he thought the book was important!)

Finally, there is the love affair, during the 1980s and 1990s, of the now aging Jakob Beer and 'his ardent and glorious Michaela' (to quote the cover copy), whom some critics have seen as a stand-in for the author. If Nabokov's *Lolita* was about young America debauching old Europe, this section of *Fugitive Pieces* depicts neo-conservative 'new beginning' Canada being rewarded for cultural compliance by the adoration of 'heavy' Jakob, the bearer of authentic history and culture. At this point in the novel, Jakob has been spending half the year in Europe for the last eighteen years, so he is even more the voice of European culture than he was during his Toronto adolescence. This is what he thinks when he meets Michaela, who is twenty-five years younger than he:

Her mind is a palace. She moves through history with the fluency of a spirit, mourns the burning of the library at Alexandria as if it happened yesterday. She discusses the influence of trade routes on European architecture, while still noticing the pattern of light across a table ...

There's no one left in the kitchen. All around us are glasses and small towers of dirty dishes. The noise of the party in the other room. Michaela's hips lean against the kitchen counter. Voluptuous scholar.

To anyone who has spent time in European intellectual circles, this passage is beyond inanity. Persuading continental European intellectuals to take seriously the thoughts on Western culture of a Canadian – even a recognized authority of the weight of, say, the literary critic Northrop Frye or the philosopher Charles Taylor – is excruciatingly difficult. The likelihood of a man of Jakob's generation and background admiring Michaela's *intellect,* let alone perceiving it as a 'palace', is precisely zero. (Her 'voluptuousness', of course, is a different matter.) For the culturally anxious Canadian reader, Michaela represents the novel's moment of triumph: the discovery of a Canadian mode of being that foreign arbiters of high culture will not deride as bird-boned or bird-brained. Since we do not have palaces in Canada, Jakob's use of this image to define Michaela's mind pays her the high compliment (within the novel's colonized symbolic framework) of de-Canadianizing her, translating her back into the implicit cultural superiority of Europe. The city of Alexandria returns to confirm Michaela's triumph. In contrast to the papier-mâché model of modern Alexandria constructed by Alex's father, Michaela is associated with ancient Alexandria, which she inhabits as though it formed part of the present. Alexandria, of course, is just down the Nile from Cairo, an important locale in *The English Patient.* Almásy and Alex's father turn out to have been in the same place during the same historical period. B.W. Powe once suggested that 'the hidden ground' of Canadian literature was the university campus; in the 1990s, one could argue, the Canadian novel's 'hidden ground' lay somewhere along the lower reaches of the Nile River.

The definition of culture in *Fugitive Pieces* as something ancient, foreign and lifeless coincides with the neo-conservative promotion of a particularly stultifying vision of the 'Great Books' of Western civilization. Most of these books are truly great, and must be read. But a creative and open-minded reading of ancient Greek literature, medieval or renaissance literature, or any of the other classics, will lead to an appreciation of the culture, literary and otherwise, of one's own time, not to the denigration and annihilation of the history of one's own

FREE TRADE FICTION

country. The neo-conservative reading which Michaels embellishes with pretty images is inextricably linked to an upper-class, *socially exclusive* conception of scholarship, to increasing social stratification, to an alienated comprador élite drawing its culture from other times and places as a bulwark against the claims of the history of its own place, which this same class has denied, suppressed, disdained, betrayed and now wishes to pretend does not exist. Hence the focus on Toronto primarily in terms of its geology. Michaela subscribes to the magazines *Nature, Archeology* and *The Conservator,* but does not appear to read a daily newspaper. Readers occupying privileged social positions (or yearning to share some of the assumptions of such a position) will discover in *Fugitive Pieces* a soothing balm and the confirmation of their prejudices.

Most of the world's literatures preserve a pocket for the 'poet's novel,' a book governed by metaphor rather than the vital interlinking of character and story. Such works generally attract a few appreciative readers who then pay more attention to the poet's next book of poems. A literature dominated by 'poet's novels' is an anomaly. A culture whose reading public requires this sort of fiction – self-consciously 'artistic' without posing the challenges of authentic art – is ill. It is not unexpected that such art should prevail in a country where a belief in a kind of democratic egalitarianism is shredding before an ever-greater gap between rich and poor. In such an environment the bourgeoisie's applause for the 'artistry' of books such as *The English Patient* and *Fugitive Pieces* forms an indispensable part of its self-redefinition as a class of inherently superior people whose allegiances are to similar, even wealthier people in richer, more powerful countries rather than to the nation where they live, to their own history, institutions or art, or to the neighbours who used to be their near-equals. Reading such novels becomes a means of asserting one's social distinction. As Arthur Koestler once observed about reading Kierkegaard, *The English Patient* and *Fugitive Pieces* make you impressed with yourself for having read them. These novels also provide an interpretative scheme for ignoring the unravelling of surrounding reality. Like wealthy early nineteenth-century Parisians admiring their own faces in the suffocated portraiture of Jean Auguste Dominique Ingres while the echoes of the Jacobin tumbrels ring out over the cobblestones, upper-middle-class Toronto

155

readers enthuse over metaphorical depictions of Toronto's geology to sustain their denial of the people sleeping in cardboard boxes at downtown bus stops; they gasp in delight at a Danforth burglar philosophizing in an Italian villa in order to ignore the new security systems they are installing in their homes. To return to Robert Musil, *The English Patient* and *Fugitive Pieces* are the work of writers who are speaking 'broken German' – or, more accurately, 'broken Canadian' – after only three years in America (translatable in the context of 1996 as three years into NAFTA). But such a self-negating literature does not take root in a void. Its creation depends on the formation of literary institutions designed to direct attention away from the reality in which most readers live.

2

Vulgarity on Bloor
Literary Institutions From
CanLit to TorLit

Literatures, like trees and plants, are born of a land and in it flourish
and die. – Octavio Paz, *Sor Juana, or The Traps of Faith*

It seemed that there was but one virtue in the world, commercial
enterprise. – Anthony Trollope, *The Way We Live Now*

In the aftermath of a round of cuts to the budget of the Canadian
Broadcasting Corporation that was destined to curtail regional
programming, the journalist Robert Mason Lee commented that if the
CBC were reduced to telling the rest of the country 'how powerful and
important everyone in Ottawa is' and 'how clever and talented everyone
in Toronto is' it would become a divisive, rather than an integrating,
force in Canadian life. The bottom-line policies responsible for the
erosion of the CBC have also contorted the publishing world. Ever more
concentrated in one city yet drenched in an ambience of cautious
careerism that throttles the kind of ferment sometimes generated by
lively urban literary cultures, the Canadian writing world has been ossi-
fied by the promise of wealth. The less the state intervenes, the more
activity devolves upon Toronto, and the more profoundly literary culture is shaped by the market and its attendant values drawn from
advertising and television. In the last ten years we have seen a painfully
sincere, myopically provincial literary scene strung out across the country in a government-supported bracelet of literary journals and small
publishing houses superseded by a slick, image-obsessed, Toronto-

centric commercial publishing industry serving as a supply depot for the global book market. This culture is substantially more parochial than the one it dislodged.

In the CanLit scene, as it existed from the mid-1960s until the early 1990s, only Margaret Atwood, Robertson Davies, Mordecai Richler, Margaret Laurence, Mavis Gallant, Alice Munro and possibly two or three other writers scraped a living from writing fiction. Canada Council grants were the currency of literary respectability. Small-press books were distributed throughout the country as well as any other books were, which was not always very well. There was an equality of torpor, a comfortable collegiality where everyone knew everyone else through their work, even though they might not have met. It was not a particularly challenging milieu, although for a few years during the late 1960s and early 1970s the task of national self-definition lent some of the writing a certain urgency. By contrast to today's literary world, the culture was welcoming to new writers regardless of their geographical location within the country. (Immigrants, particularly those from continents other than Europe, may have felt less welcome. Those who could, such as Michael Ondaatje, Canadianized themselves; those who could not, such as Austin Clarke, were neglected.)

In this world, if you sent out enough manuscripts to enough slush piles, they would eventually be read and, if they showed promise, the new writer could begin to build a career. By reading the literary journals you could keep up with other writers whose careers were also evolving. In spite of this laudable accessibility (or perhaps because of it), CanLit culture often had a provincializing effect on those who participated in it. (George Woodcock, having built a respected career in London writing biographies of complex figures such as Peter Kropotkin, lapsed, after his return to Canada, into comparing Margaret Laurence to Tolstoy.) Short fiction was strong in the CanLit world, poetry was both strong and extremely weak, the novel was uneven but popular and most literary criticism was limp and servile. The most impressive feature of CanLit, perceived from the tawdry vantage point of the neon-soaked shopping mall that has been built on its premises, was its commitment to *literature*. As I recall the boosterism inflating the literary culture of the 1970s, I am surprised to find myself writing these words. But the naïve nationalism of the past, it is becoming clear, sucked up less aesthetic air than the vapid commercialism of the present. Discussion of writing as writing remained possible.

TorLit, the successor to CanLit, is about money. During the 1980s, most Canadian literary publishing developed a strong regional emphasis. With the advent of the globalized 1990s, the regional publishing industry of southern Ontario was plugged into the global marketplace, and most other publishing scenes became corralled within their own regions. Dwindling government support and hard-ball tactics on the part of the new chain bookstores demanding large discounts from small publishers whose slender output gave them little leverage to negotiate, shaved profit margins to the bone. Publishers located in New Brunswick, Manitoba, Saskatchewan or Newfoundland, where overheads are low, have been able to scrape by within their regional markets. But one can no longer take for granted – as might have been the case even in the early 1990s – that a collection of short stories published by Goose Lane, Turnstone, Thistledown or Breakwater will receive consistent national distribution. (British Columbia ranks as a special case, sharing aspects of both the regional presses and the Toronto ones. The B.C. publishing industry has grown in recent years, through a combination of the growth in population and prosperity of its own region and the connections Raincoast, which has emerged as the region's largest publishing conglomerate, has established with U.S. West Coast markets.) In Ontario, middle-ranking literary publishers – the 'large small presses' that sustained the country's writing during the 1970s and 1980s – have undergone the fate of medium-sized businesses in any market-driven system. They have been bought up by larger companies (Anansi, Cormorant), gone out of business (Coach House), or shrivelled into triviality (Quarry, Oberon). A rift has opened between the upper and lower tiers of our literary culture, with Toronto-based commercial publishers now enjoying a clout, in terms of distribution, publicity budget, media attention and, consequently, sales, many times that of their small-press rivals. The advantage of being published by, say, McClelland and Stewart rather than Talon Books, has become many times greater than it was in the 1980s. This is especially true in the realm of access to the media, where promotion has become gruellingly difficult for smaller publishers. In 1990, as an unknown author promoting a first novel published by a minor press, I embarked on an extensive promotional tour including nearly a dozen radio and print interviews; by 1999, when, as a moderately well-known literary author promoting a well-reviewed fourth book published by a small press whose publicity was centralized in its large-press parent company, my tour was much shorter: several of the radio stations where I had been interviewed in 1990 were no longer accessible to me, having become the exclusive province of 'name-brand' authors. Here, as in other domains of our society, a certain rough equality has vanished. Writers published by the 'national' publishers – most of which are not national at all, but are U.S. branch plants (whose ultimate ownership may be in Germany, England or elsewhere) such as HarperCollins, Knopf, Random House and Doubleday – occupy a different universe, financially as well as socially, from other writers. A national sense of literary community, with its accompanying possibility of creative exchange, has been split by a literary class division. In cultural terms, the relationship between Toronto and the rest of the country has come to resemble the relationship between Americans and Canadians: they know nothing about our country, but we are obliged to know everything about theirs.

All Canadian publishing is primarily regional. The southern Ontario commercial presses are no exception to this. Like other Canadian presses, they publish local writers; the Toronto media, like other media, report on local stories. The hollowing-out of the media in the rest of the country means that, rather than telling Canada about itself, more and more Canadian newspapers and television stations tell the country about Toronto. This is a decisive factor in determining writers' career trajectories. The two best-known Canadian writers from Atlantic Canada, Wayne Johnston and David Adams Richards, live in Toronto; to some extent, and without denying the talent of either of these writers, they are well-known *because* they live in Toronto. Johnston, one of the most striking successes of recent years, began his career by winning the *Books in Canada* First Novel Award for *The Story of Bobby O'Malley*, a novel that was published as long ago as 1985. At the time, Johnston was living in Fredericton, New Brunswick, so the award meant little in terms of financial reward or more ample publishing opportunities: Johnston's second novel, like his first, was published by Oberon Press. Johnston's achievements commanded more attention once he moved to Toronto. Today the media portray Johnston as a recent literary discovery. He is not. He has been a solid performer for a decade and a half. What is relatively recent – and what counts for the media – is Johnston's move to Toronto. Neil Bissoondath, by contrast, was showered with attention for his gloweringly overwritten though energetic early books; his later, more accomplished, work has been little hyped, in spite of his Governor General's Award nomination for *The Worlds Within Her*. Bissoondath's media profile has faded as his writing has improved, mirroring his moves from downtown Toronto to English Montreal to suburban Quebec City rather than the development of his prose.

The transitory nature of an increasingly media- and marketing-driven culture means that absence from the southern Ontario scene quickly translates into oblivion. The work of Norman Levine and Seán Virgo, two substantial short story writers who departed for self-imposed exiles (in England and rural southwestern Saskatchewan respectively), has disappeared from bookstore shelves and no longer seems to be mentioned even by other writers. Among the non-southern Ontario writers currently published by the Toronto presses, many – Audrey Thomas, Rudy Wiebe, Guy Vanderhaeghe, Jack Hodgins – came in on the CanLit wave of the 1970s and early 1980s, when the country could still lay claim to a national literature. While some new writers from other provinces have broken through in recent years – Gail Anderson-Dargatz, Sharon Butala, Greg Hollingshead – the direction of the trend is clear. One has only to pick up an issue of *Quill and Quire* to verify that a disproportionate number of the new writers being signed up by the Toronto presses live in or around Toronto. Toronto residence alone often magically confers large-press status on writers who have not previously published fiction – and the absence of a Toronto residence or references can, just as unremittingly, deny publication or media attention. Gerald Lynch's novel *Troutstream*, for example, which is drenched in eastern Ontario language and allusions, was rejected by the southern Ontario presses. Only after Fourth Estate in London accepted *Troutstream* did Toronto publication become possible. A contract with an English publisher overcame the liability of the Ottawa-area setting – though *Troutstream* still received less attention in Canada than in Britain. Even a foreign literary prize does not always compensate for the deficiency (in Toronto media eyes) of residence outside Toronto. Jeffrey Moore's novel, *Prisoner in a Red-Rose Chain*, a humorous, highly readable, hyper-literary romp through Montreal's Plateau Mont-Royal district, which won the 1999 Commonwealth Prize for Best First Book, passed virtually unnoticed by Toronto reviewers or feature-writers – almost undoubtedly because the author was from Montreal and the publisher was in Saskatoon. (When a Toronto writer wins the Commonwealth Prize we hear about it – oh yes, we hear about it.) The fact that the protagonist of *Prisoner in a Red-Rose Chain*, like its author, was a bilingual anglophone living and working unselfconsciously in a predominantly francophone milieu, confounding the Toronto media's 'racist francophones / oppressed anglophones' formula for covering Quebec, deepened Moore's plight. It is important to bear these cases in mind when considering the status enjoyed by writers resident in Toronto. Writers as varied as Cordelia Strube and Russell Smith ('Nationally famous in Toronto', in the words of one literary agent), if they lived elsewhere in Canada, would be classified as regional writers. Their focus on the mores of their own city would mire them in obscurity if that city were Winnipeg. Feeling little obligation to look beyond its own front yard, the Toronto arts media are significantly more parochial than those in the rest of the country.

The writer who enters the Toronto literary world finds himself hemmed in by prickly insularity. I cannot pretend detachment in this matter. When I travel to New Brunswick or Saskatchewan, the other writers I meet are aware of my existence as a writer. They may not have read anything more than a book review or a short story in an anthology, but, since geographical isolation requires them to discover other Canadian writers by *reading*, they will usually know other writers' names. In Toronto all this is different. A blank stare, an offended expression, as though I have made an impertinent suggestion, greet my side-of-the-mouth allowance that, well, actually, I've published a few pieces myself. 'I guess you must be a poet', is one of the more common responses to this remark. 'That's why I've never heard of you.'

Toronto writers, unlike those in the rest of the country, define 'national' literature in terms of who they know rather than who they read: in terms of the faces at the most recent party or banquet, or perhaps on the television screen, rather than the words on the page. Appearance, not prose style, becomes the currency of a writer's identity. 'Robertson Davies?' a successful young Toronto writer might ask. 'Is he the guy with the white beard?' I have changed the famous name and prominent trait, but I did hear an analogous remark made by a very successful young Toronto writer about a central figure of Canadian literary life over the last three decades. My point is that Toronto's media-channelled obsession with image *obliterates the transmission of a literary heritage.* The relationship between one generation of writers and its successors is no longer cemented by the act of reading and responding creatively to literature. Relationships are defined within an eternal present. The figure who toiled for thirty years to modernize Canadian prose or poetry or criticism is distinguished by his fashion accessories rather than his use of the semi-colon. As a result, the new generation writes with a faulty knowledge of what has come before, what has been tried and what has not been tried, what has succeeded and what has failed. Literature is either a dialogue with earlier literature, or it is detritus. Do not expect to see much lasting work emerging from the vacant core of TorLit TV-Land.

As glossy with eternal newness as the world bounded by TV shows such as *Hot Type* and *Imprint,* and the ever-more Oscar-like Giller Prize dinner may be, it reposes on the phlegmatic foundations of Toronto's past. The domain of literary celebrity is the Family Compact wired. Rooted in a consensus culture that has been deeply uncomfortable with debate since long before Northrop Frye dubbed southern Ontario 'the most brutally uncommunicative culture in the Western world', the élite literary milieu flits unthinkingly from trend to trend without ever questioning why one trend has been discarded and a fresh one adopted. The trends involved rarely deal with words on the page, but more often with superficial approaches to political issues, or with the writer's wardrobe or haircut. Here, too, history plays a roll: port cities such as Vancouver and Montreal have long experience of feisty interaction with the outside world; mid-continental Toronto, far from the sea, has always responded to inbound influences with a blend of passivity and insularity. Trends rule without taking root, then, in a moment, they vanish. This sort of built-in obsolescence is typical of much modern life, but it is also peculiar to Toronto, based as it is on the suffocation of dissent and the assumption that no one who matters could live elsewhere in the country. 'Most writers live in Toronto', an otherwise admirably open-minded Toronto writer informed me. This statement is inaccurate. But in an incongruous way it is also true. A writer is someone who is recognized by others as a writer. The old CanLit method of garnering recognition – sending out manuscripts, collecting rejection slips, rewriting until the rejections turn into acceptances, arduously accumulating a list of published stories or poems, then published books – no longer counts for much. Indeed, it is a liability. By publishing extensively you may become pigeonholed as a 'small press writer', hence eliminating yourself from the running to become this year's 'undiscovered' first novelist.

Under the aegis of TorLit, one becomes a writer by being seen at certain parties, mentioned in tabloid gossip columns, establishing a distinctively glamorous personal identity in tune with this month's social and political fashions, appearing on television *as a writer*. Publication is less important, literary accomplishment barely relevant. If you have not been published, then once you appear on television identified as a writer, a literary agent will ensure that your fledgling work is bound in hard covers and honoured with a healthy advance and a few foreign rights sales. Your prose may be wobbly by comparison with that of the losers out there in Moncton and Moose Jaw who go on toiling at their art in snowbound obscurity, but as long as your publicity machine is sufficiently well-oiled most reviewers will be browbeaten into tight-lipped Torontonian politeness. Criticism, after all, has become simply one wing of the publicity machine. Corporate pressure on book review editors to allot excessive numbers of column inches to highly promoted books by name-brand authors has mounted in recent years, squeezing out the column inches available to authors lacking big publicity machines and resulting in a spate of stories, particularly at certain newspapers, of reviews suppressed by editors because the reviewer had reached a judgement other than one of unalloyed praise. In this environment, the writer who wishes to continue reviewing learns to measure the work under review according to its author's clout within the book business. This guts book reviewing of its legitimacy. The growing concentration of the book business in Toronto, increasing the chances that the reviewer will know the writer socially, contributes to this culture of pulled punches and book-report reviewing prose. Writers who blurb each other's books, writers who award one another soft, friendly reviews, have undermined confidence in the autonomy of reviewing. This is one of the reasons for the increasing influence and glamorization of Canadian literary prizes. A writer living outside Toronto who aspires to a large-press contract can collect an almost infinite number of favourable reviews for her small-press novel or story collection without anyone in the southern Ontario commercial presses deigning to notice, since the assumption from within Toronto is that all praise is corrupt. Only if this writer is short-listed for the Giller, the Trillium or the Governor General's Award can her status suddenly change.

What has permitted this vulgarity to hijack our literary culture? In part it is the willingness of authors themselves to be seduced by Mammon. The tone of our writing may have become more superficial and commercial in recent years, but more Canadian writers are living from their work than at any time in the past. To claim that this signals an advance for *literature* (as Toronto-based commentators are fond of doing) is to confuse art with commerce. It is like arguing that Ontario has never been better off than under Mike Harris: it ignores disparities in wealth, overlooks the increasing marginalization of authors whose work is not highly commercial and represses knowledge of the long-term artistic cost of retooling the publishing industry to serve the global market. To extend the analogy with Ontario politics, the literary 'poor' who end up 'homeless' (i.e., without decent publicity and distribution) may be precisely those people indispensable to literary society, since innovation usually originates in marginalized precincts of the artistic world. A literature that fails to make a place for the 'less fortunate', even more profoundly than a society that fails in this way, will stagnate. It is difficult to see how this pattern can be broken as long as Toronto remains our literary conduit to the rest of the world. If only the comparative advantage principle of globalized commerce had allocated our English-language publishing industry to a less staid city! Fractious, gloriously eccentric Montreal, or energetic, tough-talking Calgary, or poised, bicultural Ottawa – any of them, writ large, would have projected a more alluring Canadianism out into the world than constipated Toronto. Any of them would have responded with more spirit and less quiescent conformity to the task of generating a literary culture capable of stimulating *literature* – for when the camera is switched off and the World Wide Web connection is mouse-clicked into silence, we are back to those same twenty-six letters slumping across the page, so they had better be saying something stimulating. To achieve literary novelty the words must engage with writing: with past writing, with a culture of writing rather than a culture of image where the individual's work is supplanted by her hairstyle or his beard.

TorLit would not have been possible without the crumbling of the institutions of CanLit. In some cases, such as the competition between the Giller Prize and the Governor General's Awards, the two cultures continue to run parallel. The reaction against an increasingly Toronto-centric national literary culture during the 1980s in the literary scenes in places such as English-speaking Montreal, Vancouver and Edmonton began the process of uncoupling the links in the chain. Writers emerged who belonged to those places only, setting the stage for the full-bore release of market forces in the early 1990s that carried Toronto away into a globalized sphere remote from the rest of the country.

Specific institutions were also weakened. The Canada Council's reading and travel budgets, which helped to make writers in different parts of the country more aware of each other, stagnated while the number of writers increased. The Toronto-centrism of purportedly national journals such as *Quill and Quire*, accentuated the problem. Commercial pressures also changed the country's literary journals, the traditional proving-ground for new talent. Forced to increase subscriptions to offset rising costs and compensate for shrivelled government largesse, all but a few of these magazines have embarked on a perpetual round of contests for short stories, long stories, postcard stories or creative non-fiction, with each entrant being obliged to purchase a subscription. Special issues showcase the winning stories, while other special issues are devoted to particular themes, the issue's costs sometimes being underwritten by interested parties. All this is TorLit writ small. The infiltration of the prizes-and-showbiz mentality into the literary journals has debilitated these publications' capacity to cultivate new talent through the quiet, issue-by-issue refinement of a focus and an aesthetic. The steady sifting of submissions is unsustainable in an environment where a publication is incessantly lunging headlong towards the next prize announcement. The imperative to find 'a winner' also tends to favour certain types of flashy stories over their more solid but less grabby counterparts.

Perhaps the saddest casualty of an era of crumbling institutions was *Books in Canada*. During the 1980s and early 1990s this was the country's most comprehensive book review magazine, the one publication nearly all writers read to keep up with the Canadian literary world. In spite of lapses into facile trendiness, *Books in Canada* succeeded in producing a wide-angle picture of literary activity in Canada. Its approach to issues sometimes betrayed its Toronto base, but its varied national pool of freelancers ensured that opinions from Vancouver, Montreal and Edmonton, and even Victoria, Frederiction and St. John's, continued to be heard. Amazingly, *Books in Canada* managed to review nearly every work of fiction or poetry published in the country, in addition to a sprinkling of non-fiction books. In the mid-1990s, *Books in Canada* was bought up and turned over to a pretentious, comically provincial coterie of self-infatuated Toronto right-wingers. The magazine's glossy, readable format bloated to a *New York Review of Books* portentousness – devoid, needless to say, of the *NYRB*'s first-rate intellects. The result was long, dim pages of weary prose. Books of fiction or poetry, unless written by neighbours of the editors, passed largely unreviewed. Academic books about ancient political theory, U.S. neo-conservative tracts, loopy opinion columns praising fascist dictators and the longest book review in Canadian magazine history (an epic boot-licking of Conrad Black's memoirs) earned pride of place in the new format of a journal whose name began to seem increasingly irrelevant to its contents. When the new editors did turn their attention to Canadian fiction, neither they nor the few freelancers enjoying their ideological trust were competent in the field. The old *Books in Canada* was light and journalistic, but a pleasure to read; the only source of amusement offered by the new *BiC* came from spotting the remarkably numerous factual errors strewn through the reviews on Canadian subjects. Some of the highlights included misspelling Mordecai Richler's name on the magazine's cover and printing a review analysing Matt Cohen's *Elizabeth and After* – Cohen's thirteenth novel – as 'Matt Cohen's third novel'. (How would this new young writer develop?) Not surprisingly, *BiC*'s circulation dropped by two-thirds. In October 1997, in a gesture that was all too telling of all that was wrong with Canada's literary institutions, *BiC* published its own obituary. A discreet note tucked inside the back cover announced: 'As of Oct. 1, 1997 *Books in Canada* will have a new home in the downtown Toronto Yorkville district. We hope this central location will prove more accessible and convenient for our contributors....'

The message was clear: any writer residing more than a dozen blocks from the corner of Yonge and Bloor need not apply. The days when writers in Halifax or Regina could contribute to magazines in Toronto were passing. CanLit had yielded to TorLit, ToryLit, Toy-Lit.

It took three more years for *Books in Canada* to run itself out of business. An attempted relaunch in 2001 was marred by controversy surrounding the new editor's scheme to finance the journal by selling old *BiC* reviews – whose electronic rights he did not own – to Amazon.com. Deprived of its national reach, *Books in Canada* oscillated between purely local, Torontonian support and that of the global market, without finding a secure niche in either.

. . .

Strongly market-driven systems concentrate wealth geographically just as they concentrate wealth socially. But in the era of globalized communication, the old bohemian myth of the city as a site of artistic ferment – Paris in the 1920s, New York in the 1940s and 1950s, Barcelona in the late 1960s – can no longer be taken for granted. (Prague, the city which came closest to playing this role in the 1990s, produced a commercialized international youth culture but little art.) Nourished by news from the Web and books ordered from on-line marketing services, good writers are far more able to sustain themselves in remote outposts than was the case in the past. A writer living in Fort Simpson might be lonelier than a writer living at the corner of Yonge and Bloor, but there is no reason for her not to be just as literarily up to date as the inhabitant of a metropolis. It is Toronto's drab fate to have acquired the media and public-relations trappings of a metropolis at a point in history when metropolitan status alone no longer assures the challenging, innovative culture of debate traditionally associated with large, polycultural cities.

As the Canadian media become more centralized in Toronto and publishers grow more reliant on literary agents and less disposed to hire teams of unemployed English literature graduates to read mountains of unsolicited manuscripts, the regionalism of southern Ontario publishing grows more pronounced. (To the point of distorting not only present achievements, but also our vision of our literary past: Katherine Ashenburg has suggested that the relative obscurity of Ethel Wilson outside her native British Columbia is a product of the Ontario base of most of the people who define Canada's literary history; looking to the other coast, the same could be said of Ernest Buckler's reputation.) Today, the disadvantage faced by the writer in Fort Simpson is not artistic but commercial. No impediment exists that will prevent her from writing a novel as good or better than that written by the Yonge-and-Bloor writer. But, whereas in the old days of CanLit she could have mailed her manuscript to half a dozen major publishers confident that most of them would eventually read it, TorLit requires her to attract the attention of an agent. To do this she must become recognized as a writer within the agent's sphere of operation – downtown Toronto. If her job, finances, personal preferences or private life make it difficult for her to leave Fort Simpson, becoming known in Toronto may prove to be an even more daunting task than writing a good novel.

One would think that writers, with their famous anti-authoritarian temperaments, would revolt against this system. A few years ago, when publishing in the United States was rendered one notch more commercialized by the decision of a number of large U.S. publishers to shift marketing personnel to the editorial offices, U.S. writers howled in protest. Toronto's enduring obedience-to-authority culture ('authority' here taking the form of fashion and trend) has ensured that the increasing dominance of agents and commercial fiction has elicited no similar utterances from Toronto writers. Our would-be Young Turks regard the commercializers with chummy complacency. Andrew Pyper, a young writer who published a promising first collection of short stories before going commercial and producing a thriller notorious for the mammoth advances secured by his agent, offers this bracing critique of the role of the agent in the publishing process:

So we've got a good product, international interest, and domestic publishers willing to shell out the dough in order to reap greater rewards in the long-term future. But there are still far more manuscripts out there than are worthy of publication, and you still have to select those that are most promising and sell them. This is where Anne [McDermid] comes in. She makes editors see that the manuscript they have before them isn't just another big new thing, but The Real Thing.

Pyper's vocabulary in this passage ('good product, international interest', 'big new thing') is that of a freshly minted M.B.A. The tone of invincible equanimity and Panglossian we-live-in-the-best-of-all-possible-worlds complacency showcases some of the more off-putting traits of the TorLit outlook. These are people who are writers in the way that other yuppies are software developers or management consultants; all questing, all uncompromising ferocity of inquiry into life and human experience, has been tamed. The acceptance of commercial criteria as the arbiter of a book's worth, and of the agent rather than the editor as literary gatekeeper, is total. Pyper even claims that the globalization of the publishing industry has given Canadian writers a 'new freedom ... to set their work in Canada', when to most observers, the changes he extols have had the opposite effect. Where, I wonder, does Pyper imagine that *The Mountain and the Valley, Swamp Angel, The Apprenticeship of Duddy Kravitz, Fifth Business, Lives of Girls and Women* and *The Diviners* are set? Far closer to home, by most estimates, than *The English Patient, A Fine Balance* or *The White Bone*. (Though it must be allowed that in the case of genre fiction, such as Trevor Ferguson/John Farrow's *City of Ice* or Pyper's own *Lost Girls*, the proven international saleability of the mystery or thriller formula grants a larger margin of freedom to adopt Canadian settings.)

I am not arguing that it is evil, or a betrayal of one's heritage, to set one's fiction outside Canada. I would be in a poor position to make this argument, having set much of my own fiction in other countries. As an immigrant, I am aware that many writers from immigrant backgrounds retain significant baggage from ancestral cultures. The tensions between the old culture and the new, the almost inevitable feeling of no longer belonging to the culture of origin while remaining imperfectly integrated into the Canadian world, can make for fine fiction. Writers who came here later in life are even more likely to write about another country. It is natural for Rohinton Mistry to write about India, where he lived until the age of twenty-two. (It is depressing, though, that some of his foreign publishers have tried to conceal his residence in suburban Toronto out of a fear that his work would lose its Oriental allure if readers realized he was a Canadian. This enabled Germaine Greer to cause a minor sensation on British television by 'outing' Mistry: 'It's a *Canadian* book – a *Canadian* book about India – what could be more boring!')

My concern with the gimmick of setting fiction 'anywhere but here' centres on the self-effacing, colonized way in which Canadian writers alight upon foreign settings. The literature of the United States contains novels such as *The Ambassadors, The Sun Also Rises* and *Tender Is the Night.* All are set in Europe; all are intensely American novels. Similarly, what could be more British than *Goodbye to Berlin, Women in Love, The Heart of the Matter* or *A Passage to India?* Substantial parts of all these novels are set in Europe, India or Africa, but no one doubts their resonance as emanations of a peculiarly British cultural outlook. During the 1970s Canadian writers, too, discovered the self-confidence to use overseas settings to play out our national preoccupations. Large portions of Richler's *St. Urbain's Horseman,* Laurence's *The Diviners* and Davies's Deptford Trilogy take place in Europe. Yet the characters do not pretend to be Europeans; they sally forth eager to test their Canadian culture (which, obviously, is not exactly the same for Richler as it is for Davies) against the contours of other cultures. This self-assurance began to wane in the 1980s, as fiction became less ambitious and more commercial. With the advent of the Free Trade Fiction of the 1990s, our recolonization was complete.

The colonized literature of the 1990s, like the nationalist literature of the 1970s, attracts its grovelling academic apologists. Much poisoned ink has been spilled denouncing the 'brainwashed CanLit academics' of the 1970s who told us that reading Frederick Philip Grove was good for us. A new generation of Canadian academics abases itself by praising commercial fiction calculated to hook foreign rights sales as the pinnacle of artistic 'sophistication'. In an ardently boot-licking article in the April 2000 issue of *Quill and Quire,* for example, an academic named Allan Hepburn commends M.G. Vassanji's novel *Amriika* for avoiding Canada: 'I assumed the protagonist would eventually move to Toronto. It never happened.' Hepburn portrays this avoidance of a Canadian setting as evidence of the growing 'sophistication' of Canadian writing – a pathetically provincial attitude. Can anyone imagine John Updike being cheered as 'sophisticated' for writing a novel set outside the U.S.A.? Hepburn's praise of Vassanji's decision to set his novel in the U.S. overlooks the obvious commercial motives for adopting this setting – a craven attempt to make it in the lucrative U.S. market – and ignores the fact that *Amriika* received the worst reviews of any of Vassanji's novels, in large part because many critics felt that Vassanji was writing about a society he did not know or understand. The parochial self-hatred saturating Hepburn's article, which opportunistically goes on to praise all rising TorLit stars regardless of whether or not they fit into his argument, suggests that the more things change in CanLitCrit, the more they stay the same. Unflinching support for the trends of the day, even at the price of intellectual incoherence, remains axiomatic.

Our inability to imagine ourselves against the backdrop of foreign settings, the increasing use of those settings, as in *The English Patient* and *Fugitive Pieces,* as vehicles for steamrolling Canadian history, betray both large-scale psychological trauma and the derisive message our publishing industry is sending to our authors. Comments such as those of Germaine Greer (supported by flocks of foreign literary agents) illustrate why Canadian writers pretend to be someone else. Globalization has made Canadianness – deep, historically rooted Canadianness such as that of Richler, Davies or Laurence – a commercial liability. Canadian books do well overseas, but new writers must not cross the line that causes foreign agents or publishers to press the button that says, 'too Canadian'. The artistic problem, of course, is that it is often only by engaging with the dilemmas that lie on the far side of this line that the author creates groundbreaking work. What is 'commercially correct', in other words, is often at odds with what is artistically desirable. This is arguably *the* key impediment to the growth of a significant novelistic tradition in Canada today. Having been told by literary agents in both New York and London that my fiction was 'too Canadian' for publication in their respective countries, I do not underestimate this problem. But to a large extent, the problem begins at home, in the growing gap between Toronto and the rest of the country that prompts many of our own metropolitan writers and commentators to disparage anywhere 'north of the 401' as, to borrow Dionne Brand's words, 'Reform country'. This kind of national self-execration – or metropolitan execration of the rest of the nation, and hence of national history – feeds foreigners' prejudices about books concentrating on distinctively Canadian events or social tensions being 'boring'. If contemporary Canadian writers were less hasty to capitulate to what the international market appears to want, they might eventually create novels sufficiently committed to local detail to achieve universal resonance.

The problem boils down to our failure to find either a creative or a critical vocabulary to dramatize our relationship to the society around us in the way that some of the Australians and Anglo-Indians and many of the Latin Americans have done. Free Trade and globalization have made this task more difficult. The consequent slide towards greater commercialism squelches the contradictions and complexities on which good fiction thrives. 'I would have preferred a much simpler story', one of Toronto's top editors wrote recently to an author whose manuscript contained a mild use of flashbacks. Within the TorLit garrison, narratives which depart from linear simplicity are increasingly regarded with extreme suspicion. Yet Canadian material and narrative innovation are inseparable: each makes the other necessary; and both have the potential to fascinate the world. If the gnarled histories of small towns in Colombia can pique the curiosity of a planetary readership, why not the history of a town in rural Canada?

The main obstacle to luring others into the labyrinths of our history is our own lack of daring – our inability to conceive our history in a creative, mythologizing way. Here we return to the problem of vocabulary. The Anglo-American tradition, with its unbridgeable chasm between bad political or sociological fiction and ostensibly detached high art, inappropriate to Canada's off-centre, 'fifth business' position in the world, paralyses us. I was reminded of this arid division while listening to a 1999 broadcast of the C B C radio program *Talking Books*. The show's guests were discussing two first novels by young Canadian writers. Both novels were set in other countries. The discussion degenerated into a squabble about whether these writers, whose novels contained little recognizably Canadian material, could be called Canadian. Kenneth J. Harvey, the Newfoundland novelist and short story writer, maintained that the writers were not Canadian, while Bert Archer, a Yonge-and-Bloor book reviewer, said that they were Canadian. (The third panel member, Montreal short story writer Denise Roig, wisely confessed to being an American and withdrew from this unsavoury conversation.) When challenged to explain why these writers were not Canadian, Harvey said: 'They're not speaking with the national voice.'

'There is no national voice,' Archer answered. 'There are only individual voices.'

These two clichés exemplify the sterility of contemporary Canadian literary debate. In the gap between the sentimental-nostalgic approach of Harvey ('The nation! The land! The voice of the people!') and the TV-lobotomized, all-American simple-mindedness of Archer ('Gee whiz ... Duh, like we're all individuals and we've all got our own opinions') lies most of what is crucial to a literature. Harvey's dogmatic insistence that the two young writers are 'not Canadian' obscures an important dilemma: that many writers who are Canadian currently find themselves incapable of writing fiction set in Canada. Archer's neo-conservative slogan-speak suppresses the same dilemma by propagating the lie that a literature is simply a cacophony of random individual utterances rather than the consequence of a group of people who share some of the same places, sense of language and history responding, year by year and generation by generation, to the best of one another's work. A more nuanced position between these two ideological stereotypes represents not simply a balanced middle ground, but a position alien to the imperial Anglo-American tradition: a location where history need not be either romanticized or repressed, where historical engagement can create myths and stimulate literary innovation. This is a location familiar to many writers from other peripheral nations. Writers from Canada, the only industrialized North Atlantic nation where – as in the Third World, but in opposition to the rest of the supposed First World – nationalists occupy the left and anti-nationalists the right of the political spectrum, should feel intimately at home with such a stance.

But the growth of TorLit culture, in tandem with larger trends in our society, will make it difficult for writers to reach or sustain this fertile position. The national literature embodied in CanLit days by the more or less coast-to-coast distribution of small press books has disintegrated. Returning to live in Canada in the late 1990s, I was startled by the condescension, even disdain, with which I heard Toronto literary people dismiss the country's smaller publishers and their authors. An American showbiz value system, according to which anyone not earning 'big bucks' was a 'loser', now governed discussion. The only literary movement displaying any vitality was the school known as Careerism. The *Globe and Mail,* increasingly 'Toronto's national newspaper', looking no further than Yonge and Bloor, or perhaps College Street, for its feature articles on literary life, trumpeted Torontonian artistic supremacy over the rest of the country. One of the most notorious *Globe* features rounded up four young, male, white, media-friendly Toronto writers and labelled them the 'Book Boys'. The most striking characteristic of this article was that this group was not linked by aesthetic concerns. (The article made a feeble attempt to classify the four writers as 'urban', at a time when three of them had recently published books set in the Ontario hinterland.) Montreal in the 1940s had First Statement, in the 1960s Vancouver had the Tish movement and Toronto had Coach House and the Four Horsemen – and Toronto in the 1990s had the Book Boys, a group united not by an artistic quest, but by a shared concern with looking good in front of a camera. Nothing illustrates the dissolution of art by image more convincingly than the replacement of groups brought together by the way their words hit the page by a group whose unity stems from a similarity of facial features and career goals.

In the spirit of every other facile trend to ripple through Toronto over the last hundred and fifty years, authors defined by their images more than their art have been hailed (by the Toronto media) as evidence that Canada (for which, read Toronto) is really, truly, finally up to date and just as civilized as the rest of the Western world. Like the incessant anxious assertions of Toronto newspapers that Toronto is a 'world-class city', authors whose reputations are built on the foundations of public relations prowess rather than rapt prose can look foolish in the international arena. Being a Toronto media hero or heroine is simply another form of Canadian localism. Revolutions in marketing know-how have little to do with literary accomplishment. As a teenager, I happened to be in England for three weeks at the time when *The Lark in the Clear Air* by Dennis T. Patrick Sears, one of the best-selling Canadian novels of the 1970s, was published in Britain. (*The Lark in the Clear Air,* which in its day rivalled *The Diviners* for acclaim, is about as widely read today as the work of Jane Urquhart, Timothy Findley or most of the Book Boys will be in thirty years' time.) The first British review of Sears's novel that I came across began: 'In Canada, where one moose is presumably much like another moose, this novel has been extravagantly praised and its author compared to Faulkner.' It was one of those moments when you tell British acquaintances who mistake you for an American that yes, in fact, you are from Texas. Recently, reading a British review of *The Lion in the Room Next Door* by Merilyn Simonds, whose photogenic qualities and media skills may have landed her in the unfortunate position of publishing a book which another writer would have been obliged to leave in the drawer, I experienced a fresh rush of allegiance to Houston and the Alamo. A few short excerpts will underline the perils of elevating writers on the basis of public image: '... the solipsistic narrator herself is the main event.... This book's fundamental problem lies in an inability to distinguish between the raw material for stories and stories themselves.... Her writing dumps untreated material on to the reader and unconvincingly passes off disjointed scraps as reflections of the fragmentation of postmodern living.... The only irony at work here is of the dramatic type, in which the writer is blind to the ludicrousness of the figure she cuts.'

Thirty years ago our authors were being ridiculed as semi-literate backwoodsmen. Today they are being disparaged for confusing their own media images with artistic invention. This is not evidence of increased sophistication: it is a change in the form of our provincialism. By fulfilling George Grant's glum prediction in *Lament for a Nation* that southern Ontario would wish 'to be integrated into the [U.S.] Great Lakes region', Toronto relinquished its own position as a potential hub of pan-Canadian English-language cultural activity. No longer the place where a Canadian way of creating literature could be imagined, the city has declined into a cultural assembly plant supplying a global market with literary widgets of predetermined sizes, shapes and colours. By embracing globalization, Toronto has made itself irrelevant as a site of cultural innovation. Hence the paradox of Toronto in the 1990s: a booming publishing centre devoid of literary energy or artistic innovation, a place that dominates the country not by virtue of its dynamism but because of its passive insertion into a transnational assembly line.

On its own, the sniping of foreign book reviewers should not concern us; every national literature contains books that are central to local readers, but which do not travel. The filter of foreign publication, particularly in translation, distorts writing in ways that make it difficult to discern what is being picked up by the foreign readership. The French thought that the U.S. gangster novelist James Hadley Chase was greater than Dostoevsky, the Russians love the lumbering Theodore Dreiser, informed German readers fly into a rage when they see which modern German writers are available in English ('Do you only translate books about the Nazis?'). The incongruity of the Canadian conundrum stems from Toronto's supine obedience to the commercial dictates of the global publishing industry. As foreign rights sales surpass local popularity as the barometer of a book's worth, Canadian fiction is increasingly assessed *by Canadian agents and editors* – though not by Canadian readers – according to its anticipated foreign reception. (One author of my acquaintance was told by a *Canadian* literary agent that her novel was 'too Canadian'.)

This is a situation without parallel in the world. Benedict Anderson, the respected theorist of nationalism, portrays the novel as the essential glue of the nation. Nations, he contends, are created by middle classes that imagine themselves as having something in common. These 'imagined communities' are expressed through writing, since middle classes are by definition both literate and too numerous and far-flung for everyone to be acquainted with everyone else. Novels such as Laurence's *The Diviners* or Richler's *Solomon Gursky Was Here,* their plots roving over broad swaths of Canadian real estate, create this sort of presumed unity of shared experience. Since the economics of film-making has determined that driving to a cinema and watching a movie dramatizing Canadian life is an experience most Canadians will never have, the novel, almost anachronistically, has retained in this country a pivotal importance in sustaining our 'imagined community' more reminiscent of the role played by novels in Argentina, Peru, India, South Africa, Australia or the Czech Republic than of the way novels are received and read in the United States, Great Britain or France. This confers a tremendous responsibility and a commensurate opportunity upon the novelist – a responsibility which is currently not being met, an opportunity which is being squandered.

In this context, John Irving's observation about the difference between New York and Toronto best-seller lists becomes easier to understand. Much of the influence of the United States flows from its ability to flood the planet with junk culture for the masses. In such an environment, the best U.S. writers are bound to get buried beneath the schlock. In many countries, this aggressively marketed U.S. schlock drives out local schlock, leaving national writers to the task of sustaining the country's 'imagined community' by producing the books bought by the local middle class to confirm its cultural superiority and sense of identity. Popular culture is imported, high culture is local. This is true in

Canada, but, in a reversal of traditional tendencies, it is also becoming true in many other countries. The difference characterizing the Canadian experience lies in the traumatic demolition of our national sense of being by Free Trade- and NAFTA-based 'harmonization', to the point where our particular individual experiences of society have become intangible and inexpressible. One can understand the rash of Canadian novels with non-Canadian settings as a reflection of our middle class's feelings of emptiness, or (as in the case of *The English Patient* or *Fugitive Pieces*) as evidence of the middle class's need to transform itself in order to 'belong' to the evanescent globalized world while still clinging to a certain residual imagined community within which reading a novel about a faraway place *written by a Canadian* represents a last tenuous homage to a disappearing self. It is possible that as 'harmonization' proceeds, the quotient of Canadian fiction on the best-seller lists will diminish. Three Canadian novels among the top ten fiction best-sellers during the busy fall season is more the norm than the eight out of ten spotted by Irving during one remarkable week in 1996. But what will these books be like? The novel always arises in a national context. No literature in history has sustained itself on works set elsewhere, in which national concerns are absent – less for simple reasons of reader identification than because the catalyst for most artistic innovation within the novel form has been an engagement, whether in an affirming or a debunking mode, with national history: with the shared myths of an 'imagined community'. As the linked Hollywoodization of our literary scene and artistic focus on faraway times and places makes obvious, the 1990s were a transitional decade. But, in literary terms, a transition towards *what?*

To gather a few clues, one must examine the novels.

3
'They Can't Be About Things Here'
The Reshaping of the Canadian Novel

Sempre onde chego é um lugar. Mas abrigo maior não encontrei senão nas paragens da memória. (Where I arrive is always a place. But no greater shelter have I found than in the stations of my memory.) – Mia Couto, *Contos do Nascer da Terra*

Originality is the return to origins. – Antonio Gaudí

No one will know how we lived.

A mature literature is a varied literature. It has its fantasists, its realists, its lunatics, its kitchen-sink, its crusaders, its nostalgia-mongers, its epic storytellers, its bohemians and its company men and women. It exhibits a wide variety of literary styles, behind which, given some perspective, one can detect clusters of related themes, worries and assumptions. In its blending of the realistic, mythic, linguistic and historical dimensions of experience, a mature literature imparts a vision of how it felt to be alive at that time and place. Anthony Burgess maintained that a country is remembered only for its literature: we remember Greece because of Homer, we remember Rome because of Virgil. Russia in the nineteenth century is a bleak, haunted shadow in my memory because at an impressionable age I read all the nineteenth-century Russian literature I could lay my hands on. If you read the work of Milan Kundera, Ivan Klíma, Bohumil Hrabal, Ludvík Vaculík and Josef Škvorecký, then, even in translation and in spite of these writers' differing sensibilities, a layering of impressions, images, recurring motifs and character types will sediment into a firm sandbar of recollection that *is* daily life in Czechoslovakia during the years of Nazi and

Soviet domination. Even if you do not speak Czech or have never been to Czechoslovakia, a certain refracted legacy of Czech cultural memory has become yours. A reader who had never been to Canada but read the better novels of, say, Mordecai Richler, Margaret Laurence, Robertson Davies and Margaret Atwood would acquire an impression of what living in English-speaking Canada felt like between the 1940s and the 1980s, as the country was shaking off its colonial lethargy and emerging into the modern world. The modernizing Canada of these years left behind a literary impression. In Burgess's terms, it is a country that can be remembered.

No one can remember the Canada of the 1990s.

No sooner had the Free Trade Agreement gone through than Canadian novelists lost the thread of contemporary Canadian experience. The majority of the widely discussed novels published in the 1990s were set in the eighteenth century (Douglas Glover's *The Life and Times of Captain N.*), the nineteenth century (Atwood's *Alias Grace*, Jane Urquhart's *Away*, Rudy Wiebe's *A Discovery of Strangers*, Guy Vanderhaeghe's *The Englishman's Boy*), the early twentieth century (Jack Hodgins's *Broken Ground*, Ann-Marie MacDonald's *Fall on Your Knees*) or the 1940s (Gail Anderson-Dargatz's *The Cure for Death by Lightning*), or in exotic foreign settings (*The English Patient, Fugitive Pieces*, Barbara Gowdy's *The White Bone*, the novels of Rohinton Mistry and Shyam Selvadurai, the two more popular volumes of Nino Ricci's trilogy, and a host of less successful works). In many of the novels that were set in Canada, the setting remained deliberately suppressed (as in Cordelia Strube's *Alex & Zee*), assiduously unevoked (Gowdy's *Falling Angels*), obstinately anachronistic (Mordecai Richler's *Barney's Version*), or assimilated into the free trader's homogenized 'North America' (Carol Shields's *The Stone Diaries*). The pungency of the best writing of the 1960s and 1970s with Canadian settings, its evocation of people, place and language, had disappeared. By the late 1990s it seemed that only writers from Atlantic Canada – Wayne Johnston, Alistair MacLeod, David Adams Richards – still wrote Canadian novels; this may help explain the surge in these writers' popularity.

After *The English Patient* and *Fugitive Pieces*, the most commercially and critically successful Canadian novel of the 1990s was Carol Shields's *The Stone Diaries*, the only novel ever to win both the Governor

General's Award for English Fiction in Canada and the Pulitzer Prize in the United States. The Pulitzer is reserved for books that warm middle America's heart. The key term here is 'life-affirming'. Books that are 'life-affirming', of course, are also supportive of the social status quo, since to criticize society would be to imply that for some people life falls below the bar of glorious affirmation. (Gail Anderson-Dargatz made this bias explicit when she praised David Bergen's *See the Child* as a 'life-affirming novel that celebrates the world just as it is'.)

Shields's fiction has acquired a glib pseudo-postmodern veneer in recent decades but her contentedly family-values vision of existence, cut by the sting of a certain school-marmish reproval, has altered little since she began publishing fiction in Ottawa in the 1970s. Back in those residually hippie times her domestic vision was ridiculed; but with the advent of the neo-conservative 1990s, society caught up with Carol Shields. In reviewing *A Celibate Season,* the novel Shields wrote in collaboration with Blanche Howard, I denounced the book as 'a reactionary fable'. Shields's publishers were so delighted by my comment that they slapped the quote onto the cover of the paperback edition. I had failed to realize that in the climate of the 1990s, 'reactionary' had become a compliment!

The Stone Diaries is mediocre fiction but brilliant calculation. It plays to two mutually hostile constituencies, charming the 'just folks' market with its tale of a nice, simple, rich woman, complete with family photographs and easy-to-read letters, recipes and lists; these same photographs and lists thrill the academics and avant-garde critics, who see in them a postmodern questioning of traditional narrative techniques. Shields is taking both groups for a ride. The folksy readers aren't getting the full, fleshed-out story they deserve and the academics, if they are honest about it, will recognize that Shields's forays into postmodernism are facile and desultory. Planting a recipe in the middle of a chapter does not an Italo Calvino make. Postmodernism is not simply structurelessness; it has its own rigour and discipline, none of which is on view in *The Stone Diaries* (though the offhand elegance of Shields's phrasemaking is undeniable).

Yet the offence against traditional storytelling may be graver than that against the avant-garde. Readers often notice that the first quarter of the novel is more readable than the remaining three hundred pages.

The reason for this is simple: in the opening scenes, the big events take place on stage. Daisy's father Cuyler Goodwill's decision to leave his family, the numbed happiness of his early married life and the scene describing Daisy's birth in the presence of the Jewish travelling salesman are all clearly *evoked*. Once Daisy has been born, Shields's puritanical upper-middle-class Wasp sensibility clamps down on what can be decently told about a woman's life. From this point on, all the big moments – Daisy's childhood, her courtship and marriage, her husband's suicide during their honeymoon – take place off-stage. The accounts we receive of these events are all second-hand and ironically knowing: Wasp prudery passing itself off as postmodern ellipsis. Drama, passion, complicated feelings – all the stuff of life – are shielded from the reader's view. The scene where Daisy meets her former guardian Barker Flett at the Ottawa train station after not having seen him for nearly twenty years illustrates the problem:

He has forgotten all his resolve; his blood is on fire.

Her knees are shaky after so many hours on the train. The sudden light of the station unbalances her, and she can think of nothing to say.

'Daisy?' he murmurs across the combed crown of her hair, making a question of it. Almost a sob. He forgets what he said next.

*

At his age they could not face the fret and fuss and jitters of a full-scale wedding, and so they were married quickly, quietly, in a judge's chambers. August 17th, 1936. The telegram dispatched to Cuyler and Maria Goodwill in Bloomington minutes before the ceremony was framed in the past tense: 'We have just been married. Letter to follow.'

The lurching of the narrative point of view from Barker ('He has forgotten ...') to Daisy ('she can think of nothing to say') and back again ('He forgets what he said next') demonstrates Shield's inability to handle either the modernist rigour of a consistent point of view or a creative postmodern melding of multiple voices. The voice of *The Stone Diaries* is simply the clumsy omniscient third person of commercial fiction. More seriously, perhaps, the black hole of that asterisk in the middle of the scene sucks away everything the reader really wants to know about these characters. What happens when they meet again after twenty years? What are the first words they speak to each other? (It seems incredible that Barker should forget such crucial utterances.) What illusions have they built up about one another, and how do these illusions fare in the light of a woman in her thirties and a man in his fifties whose lives have gone in different directions? How do they talk to each other? Do they sleep together before they get married?

In the prim and proper world of Carol Shields, such questions are inappropriate and will be deflected with narrative irony.

The scene is a cheat. It is typical of the novel's narrative procedures. The scrappy, perfunctory prose of the later sections combines evasiveness with a reductive wit that ensures that part of the reason that readers view Daisy as a heart-warming ('life-affirming') creation is that we know that we, the readers, know more about life than she does. As members of the middle class, we find it easier to champion as lovable those creatures – Lassie, for example, or E.T. – to whom we feel superior. Daisy is Lassie on two legs, E.T. as a full-stature apostle of family values. When she dies, Shields provides the following summation of her existence: 'Flett, Daisy (née Goodwill), who, due to historical accident, due to carelessness, due to ignorance, due to lack of opportunity and courage, never once in her many years of life experienced the excitement and challenge of oil painting, skiing, sailing, nude bathing, emerald jewelry, cigarettes, oral sex, pierced ears, Swedish clogs –' The list goes on to intersperse 1970s fads such as water beds, group therapy and yoga with suffering such as hunger or being 'struck on the face or body by another being'. Some of the experiences Daisy has missed, obviously, are better avoided; in this way, her life becomes a hymn to the pleasures of sheltered upper-middle-class existence in a simpler time. But, at the same time that she praises Daisy's simplicity, Shields sneers at it. A cruel, disparaging voice inserts that reference to oral sex into the list, along with references to good food, European travel and hearing the words 'I love you' spoken aloud. Again, Shields walks a clever line. If the reader is a fairly conservative upper-middle-class woman – legions of whom have read *The Stone Diaries* – she will find a novel that both reinforces her bedrock family values and makes her feel sophisticated for having enjoyed experiences that Daisy is too timid to sample. Praised for its celebration of ordinary lives, *The Stone Diaries* owes much of its success to its denigration of its protagonist's ordinariness.

The novel's central metaphor is stone. Stone is Daisy's mother's maiden name, and limestone is her father's business. Cuyler Goodwill quarries limestone in Manitoba, builds a limestone tower as a memorial to his first wife, then moves to Bloomington, Indiana, where he prospers in the limestone business. Like Anne Michaels (and Margaret Atwood before her), Shields employs geological metaphors to deflect the claims of human history. *The Stone Diaries,* published in 1993, is the flagship novel of Free Trade Fiction. At the beginning of the novel the Goodwill-Flett family is Canadian; by the novel's close they are American, with only great-niece Victoria Louise still resident in Canada. By depicting the family's initial move from Manitoba to Indiana in terms of a geological similarity (the presence in both places of limestone), Shields suppresses historical and cultural differences. Other writers, both Canadian (Mavis Gallant, Clark Blaise, Keith Maillard, Elizabeth Hay) and American (Joyce Carol Oates, Annie Proulx), have written fiction about characters who move between Canada and the United States. But all these writers have defined their characters' moves as a transit between different histories and cultures: as an ordeal of disorientation ('unhousement' is Clark Blaise's word) or an opportunity to escape one mythology and replace it with another. Shields is unique in preaching an untroubled, ahistorical North Americanism in which Canadians placidly assimilate into continental (i.e., U.S.) norms. It can hardly be a coincidence that this book was one of the most popular works of fiction in both Canada and the U.S., particularly among wealthy professionals, during the months in which NAFTA was implemented. The novel's allegiance to the abstraction of the continentalist ideal helps to illuminate its hasty, imprecise narrative tone, emotional evasions, glib generalizations and inability to do its characters justice within specific, carefully rendered cultural contexts. Benedict Anderson, noting the persistence of local or national culture as the backdrop for European novels during the onset of European integration, has argued that, just as as no one is willing to 'die for the EU' (as they might, for example, die for France), writing a successful novel grounded in citizenship in a supranational, anti-historical entity such as the European Union is both lacking in emotional appeal and unlikely to be successful. There are French and Dutch and Basque novels; there is no 'EU novel'. *The Stone Diaries* demonstrates that, propaganda purposes aside, the prospects for the 'NAFTA novel' are equally sickly.

Shields is not alone in working this vein of limestone. Emphasizing the commercial entertainment and high tech cultures that unite Canada and the U.S. (along with much of the rest of the planet), rather than the discrepancies in history, culture, outlook, landscape, climate, language and institutions that differentiate them, Douglas Coupland has turned himself into a sort of poet of the ephemera of movies, coffee bars and e-mail conversations. Yet, at bottom, his sweet, soppy West Coast vision could not be more different from Shields's hard-nosed Midwestern irony. And, though critics who have pinned their hopes on the merging of 'Canadian literature' into 'North American literature' have praised him highly, Coupland remains a peculiarly Canadian writer, romanticizing Hollywood and Microsoft as only a foreigner can. His work often reads like the sort of 'glamorous America' novel that writers from France published in the 1960s and 1970s, on the heels of their first visits to the United States. (Or, to take one Canadian and one pseudo-Canadian example, like the novels of Jacques Poulin and Jack Kerouac.) Significantly, Coupland's most substantial work, *Girlfriend in a Coma* – his only novel to receive heavyweight critical consideration outside Canada and the United States – is set in Vancouver. By acknowledging his position on the margins of the U.S. moviemaking hub and returning to the myths of his teenage years, Coupland – in spite of a ridiculous plot that involves killing off the entire planet – creates a dark elegy to lives wasted consuming foreign visions. His most frankly Canadian book is also his most emotional, perceptive and successful work. U.S. critics, in contrast to those nearly everywhere else, hated this novel. But then, for the first time, Coupland had failed to pretend to be one of them. How could they help but be offended?

The fourth enormous Canadian best-seller of the 1990s, and the book which, far more profoundly than *The English Patient, Fugitive Pieces* or *The Stone Diaries,* blurred the distinction between the two words in the expression 'literary best-seller', was Jane Urquhart's *Away.* Urquhart's novel, which occupied the *Globe and Mail*'s best-seller list for more than two years, is a romantic potboiler. Only in Canada could such a novel be classified as 'literary'. Urquhart's cliché-strewn prose style, essentially flatfooted in spite of its adjectival melodrama and adverbial nudging, recalls the prose of pulp fiction such as Jean M. Auel's *The Clan of Cave Bear* rather than anything challenging. Urquhart's use of metaphor often verges on the laughable: 'Their first argument broke into Eileen the way she'd seen a panicked moose crash into the forest in Elzivir Township, totally unmindful of bushes and trees in its path, damaging everything around it.' What makes this sentence misfire so grievously is less the lazy metaphorical excess of the panicked moose than Urquhart's over-explaining. The two extra clauses ('totally unmindful of bushes and trees in its path, damaging everything around it') that Urquhart tacks on to make sure that the reader understands how much damage a moose can do, sink the sentence.

One struggles to find analogies to this sort of writing. The U.S. novelist Anita Shreve, author of *The Pilot's Wife* and *Fortune's Rocks*, writes infinitely more fluidly than Urquhart and creates more intellectually complex situations. Yet in the United States Anita Shreve is a middlebrow popular novelist, while in Canada Jane Urquhart is regarded as high literature. Originating anywhere else, *Away* would be recognized for the pulp best-seller that it is. In Canada, where the weakness of the overall national culture has forced fiction to bear the burden of middle-class self-definition in a way that is potentially stimulating in its opportunities but too often deadening in its results, *Away* is elevated to the status of 'literary fiction' simply because it tries to bolster national identity at a time when national cohesion is under threat. Like *The Stone Diaries*, *Away* was published in 1993, on the eve of NAFTA. Urquhart's novel preaches resistance to the NAFTA mentality, but ultimately the two novels are not that far apart.

Urquhart's seventeen-year-old heroine Eileen falls in love with a man named Lanighan whom she believes to be a Fenian freedom fighter. The figure of Thomas D'Arcy McGee recurs throughout the novel; Eileen decides to follow Lanighan to Montreal and Ottawa to hear McGee speak. At this point, any reader who graduated from a Canadian high school knows that McGee's assassination will form the novel's climax. A fiery Fenian who became a visionary Canadian nationalist and Father of Confederation, McGee was shot dead on Sparks Street in Ottawa in 1868, almost certainly by Fenians who saw him as having betrayed Irish ethnic nationalism for Canadian federal nationalism. (He had just made a speech against Nova Scotian separatism.) In the novel's allegorical scheme, the Fenians, based largely in Montreal, stand in for Quebec nationalists trying to break up the country, but also for American expansionism (most Fenian raids were mounted from the U.S.) and for all those troublesome uppity ethnics who harangued the Canadian public with their complaints in the early 1990s. This is federalism as seen from deepest traditional Ontario. Eileen's romanticism leads her to hand the gun that Lanighan has left in her care to the Fenian who assassinates McGee, under the impression that this is Lanighan's wish. In fact, Lanighan turns out to be a double agent working for the federal government who has entrusted Eileen with the gun in the hope of preventing the assassination. Eileen, in other words, is a silly young girl led astray by romantic visions and a desire to participate in a great struggle. 'You killed him,' one of Lanighan's friends says, going on to argue that she has also damaged Canada. Eileen, the novel's conclusion tells us, should have listened to her man.

By handing the gun to the assassin, Eileen loses her lover, Lanighan, and nearly destroys her country. The pattern helps to explain Urquhart's enormous popularity among the doctors' and lawyers' wives who form the core of the women's novel-reading groups that sprang up during the 1990s. Idealism is all very well, the novel tells these readers, but women will do more to preserve the country by curbing their activism and obeying their alpha-male husbands (most of whom support N A F T A). As Eileen walks away from Parliament Hill into a life of dutiful solitude, she is confronted by a vision of Canadian unity: 'Looking above the heads of the spectators she saw the whole city light up, like a fragmented nation coming alive, coming to its senses.' The message, though inconsistent, could hardly be clearer: accept your limitations, accept the status quo, within the family as within the nation, and you can save the country. *Away* unites a deeply middle-class fear of activism and instability with a nostalgic Canadian nationalism. Carol Shields is at least consistent in linking conservative social values to a neo-conservative vision of Canada's destiny; Urquhart insists, that quiescence – women's quiescence, at least – will preserve the country's independence. Like the middle-class voters who supported Jean Chrétien in 1993 in the hope that he would bring back the pre–Free Trade, pre-globalization Canada of the 1970s, enthusiastic readers of *Away* are indulging in antiquated delusions. The book taps into the *Zeitgeist* of an essentially passive middle class that yearns to get its country back, though it is unwilling – unlike nation-building middle classes elsewhere in the world – to make any sustained effort or sacrifices to achieve this goal.

While Urquhart's solemn novels take themselves absolutely seriously, Ann-Marie MacDonald's blockbuster, *Fall on Your Knees,* offers much of the same appeal as Urquhart's work – romantic Celtic history, family mysteries, young women discovering their emotional, cultural and sexual identities – interrupted by incessant nudges and winks to tell the reader it's all a joke. The tale goes on far too long and some of the improbabilities in the final sections make you want to throw the book out the window, yet it is almost impossible to abandon the story. A self-consciously trashy novel conceived by a highly intelligent writer, *Fall on Your Knees* enfolds within its pages both halves of the 'literary best-seller' paradigm. The book is deviously calculated so as to appear neither too literary nor too best-sellerish. Bursts of compelling writing jar the formulaic rituals of the blockbuster-family-saga genre. MacDonald's descriptions of the tensions of a mixed-race upbringing muster more emotional force in any given chapter than Urquhart can accumulate in hundreds of pages. Yet even the harshest passages are soon glimmering with a haze of romantic Cape Breton dew. Like so many popular Canadian novels of the 1990s, *Fall on Your Knees* is a tale of traditional Atlantic Canada written from the heart of Toronto, a nostalgic glimpse back at the disappearing heritage of eccentric, marginalized Canadianism elaborated in the context of a globalized market. Sections set in New York entice the American reader. The opening page provides the implicitly foreign reader with a helpful guide to locating Cape Breton Island on the map. After describing the family home where most of the novel's action will transpire, MacDonald writes: 'So that's the house at 191 Water Street, New Waterford, Cape Breton Island, in the far eastern province of Nova Scotia, Canada.'

William Faulkner never felt he had to explain where Mississippi was. In *One Hundred Years of Solitude* Gabriel García Márquez mentions towns in his native region, such as Riohacha, without needing to situate these towns in a nation called Colombia. The Icelandic Nobel laureate Halldór Laxness took for granted in his fiction that Iceland was the centre of the world. But the Canadian, colonized once again in the aftermath of 1989, must nervously explain the location of Nova Scotia.

This pattern, alas, is all too pervasive. One of the strongest novels of the early 1990s was Carole Corbeil's *Voice-Over,* which meshed past and present in innovative and suggestive ways to create an intimate family portrait that was also a telling reading of Montreal and Toronto, French Canada and English Canada, the 1950s and the 1980s. Few other Canadian novels have fused personal and societal destinies so deftly. Yet, on the foreign rights front, *Voice-Over* ran into the 'too Canadian' problem. The presence of dialogue in untranslated (also, unfortunately, uncolloquial and occasionally incorrect) French was not conducive to sales in the U.S. market. Corbeil's less successful second novel, *In the Wings,* opens, all too predictably, at the edge of a swimming pool in California.

Keeping one eye cocked on the foreign market unravels meaningful engagement with Canadian life and history. An engagement with history is different from a historical novel: the phrase refers to the artistic enhancement of experience by radiating it through the prism of the novel's cultural context. Most historically engaged novels have been set in the here and now, or at least in the near past. Historical fiction, when it is drenched in the didactic nostalgia of *Away* or draped in the flashy narrative garb of *Fall on Your Knees,* is more often an escape from historical engagement – the conversion of history into entertaining spectacle – than a coming-to-grips with the persistence of the patterns and legacies of the past. Some historical novels manage to do both; but with a few genius-level exceptions – Marguerite Yourcenar's *Memoirs of Hadrian,* Robert Graves's novels about the ancient world, Sigrid Undset's *Kristin Lavransdatter* – the historical novel is usually a genre piece, hobbled by the difficulty of achieving free-flowing, persuasive characterization amid the painstaking reconstruction of another era. Yet it is remarkable that one consequence of the Canadian novel's inability during the 1990s to inhabit the Canadian present was a burst of historical fiction, much of it by older writers who renewed their artistic vision by dipping into the past. Jack Hodgins produced arguably his best novel in *Broken Ground.* Rudy Wiebe, most of whose previous work had also employed historical settings, portrayed the past with greater complexity than before, and in a prose of far greater clarity (some of his earlier work having read like asthmatic translations from Low German), in his powerfully imagined Governor General's Award–winning novel *A Discovery of Strangers.* One of the most underrated Canadian novels of the 1990s, John Steffler's *The Afterlife of George Cartwright*, recreates the European exploration of the Labrador coast during the 1770s. Steffler's novel opens uneasily, with an account of Cartwright's early military career in India that displays some of the too-careful reconstruction typical of many historical novels. Once Cartwright returns to London and prepares to set out for Labrador, Steffler's writing takes wing, becoming effortlessly at home with Cartwright's language and perceptions, the grim far North Atlantic setting and the tangled interactions between Cartwright and the Inuit people. The novel has no particular historical axe to grind and refuses to belabour its ironies (Cartwright, for example, regards the Inuit as 'savages' for believing herbal remedies a more effective cure for fever than bleeding the patient). Cartwright's parading of the Inuit through London, through a mixture of personal pride, friendship and sheer publicity-stunt avarice, is one of the novel's high points. His intense, unfaithful relationship with the independent, proto-feminist widow Mrs Selby is expertly caught. The story's outcome, which is tragic for Cartwright and even more so for the Inuit, gains in power by the restraint with which it is conveyed. Steffler weaves together diary entries, straight historical narration and impulsive peregrinations on the part of Cartwright's ghost, into a resourceful blend of different narrative modes. In a decade when so much mediocre fiction hopped aboard the foreign-rights gravy train, it seems unfair that a novel as good as this one missed the journey. But then Steffler, who divided his time during the 1990s between Corner Brook, Newfoundland and Montreal, lived beyond the range of the TorLit media.

Douglas Glover also slipped off the radar during the 1990s. Regarded as an important writer of short fiction during the 1980s, Glover has been less at home in the form of the novel. Nor did his difficult, often cerebral fiction fare well in the more commercial post-1989 environment. Settling in upstate New York, where neither the Canadian nor the U.S. media viewed him as significant, seems to have sealed Glover in obscurity. Yet his novel *The Life and Times of Captain N.*, published in 1993, may outlive much fiction that has been more highly praised. The novel does not strike me as entirely successful; its juxtaposition of high philosophical seriousness and sophomoric clowning can become irritating in the extreme. It is as though a brooding German philosopher had collaborated with an insouciant 1960s undergraduate. Like John Barth's *The Sot-Weed Factor*, which it in some ways resembles, *The Life and Times of Captain N.* is a postmodern quest for national origins. The contradiction enfolded in this goal is never satisfactorily resolved. Glover uses the historical novel to delineate the formation of the Canadian personality – a nation built 'against the future' – in the defeat of the British forces during the final months of the American Revolutionary War and the migration of the wretched Loyalists into the Niagara Peninsula: 'not a gambler or a risk taker among them. Thin piety is the state religion. And they have acquired a pernicious snobbery from the English half-pay officers and remittance men who come here to be gentlemen on the cheap.' Yet, as a postmodernist, Glover believes that all identities are literary constructs. 'The words used me', one of his incessantly scribbling characters confesses. The novel's dedication – 'For my son Jacob that he might know the people who went before' – comes on with the zeal of a maker of national mythologies. Yet Glover can no sooner begin to elaborate a myth than he feels the urge to deconstruct it by inducing his eighteenth-century characters to speak about the interstate highways of the future or blurring the boundaries between the identities of his various narrators. The result is a novel turned against itself, unable to resolve whether it wishes to create great Canadian myths or unmask them. The book is intellectually impressive, often witty, yet its characters seem to be more ideas in flux than flesh-and-blood human beings. Glover lacks the headlong storytelling impulse that enables Barth to leaven and more fully dramatize his deep thoughts about the Virginia colonies; no scene in *The Life and Times of Captain N.* attains the gasping immediacy of Glover's superb short story, 'Swain Corliss, Hero of Malcolm's Mills (now Oakland, Ontario), November 6, 1814', which deals with a later military confrontation between Canada and the United States.

Glover's sovereign indifference to the commercial dimension of his writing career – 'Writing and career aren't the same thing,' he stated in an essay, 'I will always write' – is not attainable for all writers. The trajectory of Guy Vanderhaeghe's career illustrates the obstacles posed by the environment of the 1990s to a writer from outside Toronto struggling to retain his national readership. The genesis of Vanderhaeghe's first book, *Man Descending*, could have occurred only within the short-lived CanLit world: a manuscript of short stories by a young, unheralded prairie author, it was accepted off the slush pile by a major Toronto publisher and went on to win the 1982 Governor General's Award for English Fiction. Though his first novel, *My Present Age*, was less successful than the stories, Vanderhaeghe began to carve out a significant niche for himself as a kind of male Alice Munro, writing technically accomplished, humorous, earthy stories about rural Canada. But with the sinking of CanLit and the rise of TorLit, Vanderhaeghe's career went into a tailspin. *Homesick*, a substantially stronger novel than *My Present Age*, was a commercial flop. Vanderhaeghe's career (as opposed to his writing) reached its nadir with the short story collection *Things as They Are?* Line by line, this collection of stories is as well written as any Canadian book of the first half of the 1990s. But Vanderhaeghe's subject matter – prairie life, male violence, the troubled insights of sensitive children in a hard-nosed rural world – had become deeply unfashionable. TorLit critics slammed the book for being everything they no longer wished Canadian writing to be: white, male, rural. In this environment even a sympathetic (white, male) Toronto reviewer such as Keith Nickson could find Vanderhaeghe's work troublingly out of tune with globalized literary taste:

I remember attending a reading in the fall of 1989.... The British novelist Kazuo Ishiguro was also on the bill.... Most of the audience had clearly come to revel in Ishiguro's refined, understated style. Vanderhaeghe's prose was more like a prairie hailstorm, hard, stinging, and very funny. A small group of us giggled hysterically ... it appeared that his profile was shrinking: he seemed to be in danger of becoming a regional writer with only regional appeal.

Embodying an aspect of Canadian reality that the increasingly Toronto-centred media now perceived as embarrassing, Vanderhaeghe had to choose between retreating from McClelland and Stewart to a regional publisher and loosening his tight narrative focus on present-day Canadian life. The faltering of Vanderhaeghe's career during the years prior to the publication of his internationally successful historical novel *The Englishman's Boy* (the title demonstrates that he had learned from Michael Ondaatje the trick of labelling his book with a reference to a stronger culture) provides an exceptionally graphic chronicle of how one significant Canadian writer began to write more commercial 'literary blockbuster' fiction for the international market. Had Vanderhaeghe persisted in creating bracing literature about present-day Saskatchewan, his next book would have been published by Coteau, Thistledown or Turnstone, not McClelland and Stewart. As the national market shrivelled, the choice between a regional career and an international career loomed ever more starkly. Anyone who doubts that this is a peculiarly Canadian problem need only read 'Jealous', the middle novella in Richard Ford's collection, *Women with Men*. Ford presents rural Montana realities in a straightforward, enviably detailed, unapologetic way that would no longer be possible for a Canadian writing about nearby Saskatchewan who hoped to be published in Toronto, and through Toronto, in the world beyond. Ford's centrality as an American protects him against becoming peripheral, no matter how marginalized the realities he depicts. The Canadian writer enjoys no similar protection.

Vanderhaeghe, too, takes Montana as his primary setting, though the action of *The Englishman's Boy* eventually gallops north into Saskatchewan. The influence of Cormac McCarthy is pervasive: stuck with his identity as a certain kind of male writer, Vanderhaeghe has rendered his career viable by joining the stable of Western U.S. literate cowboy writers pioneered by Larry McMurtry in *Lonesome Dove*. His protagonist, Harry Vincent, has made the same choice. Anxiety about U.S. cultural influence and how to respond to it racks *The Englishman's Boy*. A Saskatchewan scriptwriter who has moved to Hollywood of the Golden Age, Vincent justifies himself to his infirm, patriotic mother, who wants to know why he is writing movies about U.S. history (just as Vanderhaeghe himself is writing a novel about a history that belongs largely to the United States), by saying:

Canada isn't a country at all, it's simply geography. There's no emotion there.... There are no Whitmans, no Twains, no Cranes. Half the English Canadians wish they were *really* English, and the other half wish they were Americans. If you're going to be anything, you have to choose. Even Catholics don't regard Limbo as something permanent.

By the novel's conclusion Hollywood's nastiness has changed

Vincent's mind, dispatching him and his mother back to Saskatoon. Vincent chooses decent Canadian compromise over vulgar American success. Yet the novel makes the case for American dynamism more strongly than that for cautious Canadian adherence to tradition. Vincent is all too aware that he has chosen to remain a 'loser'. The sole, perfunctory expression of a positive vision of Canadian life comes from Vincent's mother, who croaks, 'Home, home', as she lies in her hospital bed. The novel's inability to elaborate upon this appeal in a meaningful way illustrates its conformity to international commercial values. In the final pages Vincent discovers that Canadian histories of the Cypress Hills Massacre are also distorted; Canada simply lacks the cultural clout to convert its version of the truth into celluloid mythology. The real subject of *The Englishman's Boy* is Vanderhaeghe's own painful ambivalence about his decision to salvage his career by writing the literary equivalent of a wide-screen epic. Though a readable and literate novel, *The Englishman's Boy* feels calculated by contrast with Vanderhaeghe's earlier fiction. The novel has some small flaws, such as the excessive melodrama of the conclusion, but what is missing most is the gritty immediacy and brutal humour of Vanderhaeghe's best prose.

The kind of proximity to lived experience that Vanderhaeghe achieves in his best work is increasingly difficult to muster in the globalized ether which, to a greater or lesser degree, we all now inhabit. The difficulty of the position occupied by a writer such as Vanderhaeghe – a writer whose regionalism used to be the source of his centrality – should not be underestimated. Yet the historical novel is an uncertain refuge from the vaporous present. Our era's detachment from chronological time, which seems to have dissolved into an eternal present during the years after 1989, converts the historical novel into spectacle, usually at the service of contemporary illusions. It is unsurprising, though depressing, that no recent Canadian novel has succeeded in encapsulating our present. What may be more surprising is that a few of the historical novels of the 1990s attained a significant degree of artistic success. The two Canadian novels published during the 1990s which, from the fragile, transient, hopelessly subjective perspective of the present, seem most likely to continue being read in future years – Wayne Johnston's *The Colony of Unrequited Dreams* and Margaret Atwood's *Alias Grace* – both employ historical settings.

Johnston's novel achieves for Newfoundland what the Canadian novel in its aggregate failed to achieve during the 1990s: it blends the historical and the personal into a seamless mythology. Newfoundland and Joey Smallwood become nearly inseparable, neither complete or imaginable without the other. The novel's most dazzling set-piece scenes – the panorama of the sealers from the *S.S. Newfoundland* frozen to death on the ice, the migration of the caribou through a remote area of southern Newfoundland, the various confrontations at Government House – take root in the reader's imagination as they are perceived by Johnston's fictionalized version of Joey Smallwood. Character, the great stumbling-block of most historical novels, becomes the central strength of *The Colony of Unrequited Dreams*. It is Johnston's creation of a convincing psychology, family life, sexuality and personal mythology for Smallwood that rends the book with deeply earned pangs of loss. Johnston's fictional Smallwood, who would be incomplete without his perversely believable lifelong foil, the limping, alcoholic, entirely fictional journalist Sheila Fielding, seems destined to replace the historical Smallwood in the Canadian imagination. (If the novel's conclusion feels rushed, it is partly because, at the last moment, Johnston's hammerlock on Smallwood's character appears to slip. His understanding of the powerful Smallwood is arguably less complete than his grasp of the man perpetually on the fringes of power.)

Johnston's suggestive shuffling of diary entries, first-person narrative, letters and excerpts from 'Fielding's Condensed History of Newfoundland' exemplifies the unbreakable bond between narrative innovation and the mythologization of a marginalized place. If English-speaking Canada has failed to match the novelistic achievements of some other peripheral or formerly colonial societies over the last sixty years, if we have failed to produce a novel quite as totalizing and 'God-destroying' (to use Mario Vargas Llosa's term) as *One Hundred Years of Solitude* or *Midnight's Children*, then *The Colony of Unrequited Dreams* is at least a respectable delegate to the global literary feast. Part of the book's appeal to Canadians from other regions – and arguably also to readers elsewhere – derives from the resemblances between the cultural particularity that Newfoundland yielded by joining Canada in 1949, and the cultural distinctness that all Canadians (along with people from other countries) lost by joining the globalized world forty to fifty years later. The fictional Smallwood's lament for the Newfoundland he destroyed by trying to save it has an almost archetypal force in a world where we are all busily sacrificing our cultures in an effort to keep up with our competitive neighbours in the global village. There is little doubt that the nostalgia of suburbanites from Toronto to Los Angeles to London for the cultures they or their ancestors put behind them explains much of this novel's international success. But, unlike many other works whose appeal is nostalgic, Johnston's novel displays an imaginative density and a literary daring that should enable it to continue feeling contemporary for many years to come.

Margaret Atwood's *Alias Grace*, by contrast, is a more conventional historical novel. Like Hodgins and Wiebe, Atwood shook off rusty literary mechanism by escaping into the past; like these writers, and in contrast to Vanderhaeghe, she broadened her engagement with the novelist's essential material of the reality of her society by adopting an historical setting. The greatest compliment a reader can pay *Alias Grace* is that one could easily read the first three hundred pages without suspecting that they had been written by Margaret Atwood. The withering irony that reduced characters to little more than projections of ephemeral social trends, the often bitingly amusing but ultimately limiting love-hate relationship with the authority of fashion, the high-Wasp, Upper Canadian disparagement of outsiders, failures and nonconformists – all the most rankling of the traditional Atwood traits dissolve in her evident passion for this novel's Victorian setting. Atwood's vast reading in Victorian literature enables her to deploy detail with far more subtlety, detachment and concern for literary effect than she does in the contemporary settings of novels such as *The Robber Bride* or *Life Before Man*, where she seems to be amassing inventories of fresh fads. As a result, character, a traditional weak point of Atwood's fiction, becomes a strength in *Alias Grace*. If Grace Marks remains an enigma, she is at least an enigma the reader learns to know intimately. The most intriguingly contradictory character, Simon Jordan, is, surprisingly, both a man and an American; but even minor characters such as Jordan's landlady Mrs Humphrey develop in unexpected, satisfying ways. The social interactions at the dinners and transcendentalist sessions of the stout colonials of Kingston read more naturally and persuasively than the often travestied accounts of social interaction in contemporary Toronto in Atwood's earlier novels. It is true that as the book approaches its conclusion some irritatingly Atwoodian ticks obtrude. Grace's self-consciously rendered 'dementia', leading to her blackout during the crucial murder scene, recalls the phoniest moments of *Surfacing*. And Atwood's refusal at the novel's close to choose between her protagonist's two possible destinies, here as in *The Handmaid's Tale*, is less cliff-hanging than stuffily fence-sitting. But there is no denying the novel's quality. By turning her back on the present, Atwood has created a novel readers may still wish to read in the future.

But if the best novels of the 1990s are about the past, what happened to our present?

. . .

In his book *Ripostes: Reflections on Canadian Literature*, Philip Marchand wrote:

The first wave of Canadian writers to win respect abroad – Davies, Atwood, Richler, Munro – has pretty well made its mark. Unfortunately, newer writers who have had international success – Ondaatje and Shields and Mistry – are gallingly prone to be mistaken for non-Canadians outside Canada, partly because they were born and raised outside Canada, and partly because they tend to set their fiction outside Canada. The nation cries out for indubitably Canadian successors to Munro, et al.

Marchand goes on to suggest that Barbara Gowdy is 'a candidate' for this successor role. The curious choice of the word 'candidate' highlights Gowdy's nebulous position. Young Canadian women who know little else about Canadian writing have heard of Barbara Gowdy: they have seen her on television, perhaps even read one of her books. If you ask them which Canadian writers they know, Gowdy's name will be mentioned, much in the way that young women of an earlier generation brandished the frosty mien of Margaret Atwood as a banner of identity. Yet Atwood, in the early 1970s, stood for something: she symbolized the existence of a distinct Canadian culture and, for at least some women, the quest for a literary language more attuned to female experience. Gowdy, by contrast, is famous mainly for being famous. And though she is Atwood's anointed successor, her career vigorously promoted by

Atwood in the United States, Great Britain and Germany, sharing her mentor's penchant for perpetual fashionableness and reductive parody, she remains trapped in a subordinate position. The young women who know about Barbara Gowdy also know about Margaret Atwood: they know that Atwood is the senior writer, the undisputed mistress of taste and trend.

Whether her peculiar position within the Canadian literary firmament is the cause or the effect of the enduring girlishness of Barbara Gowdy's public image is difficult to determine. The fact that Gowdy, who has set only two of her four novels in Canada, can be considered the leading contender in the writing of 'indubitably Canadian' novels only emphasizes the drastic disappearance of Canadian reality from our fiction.

Gowdy's first novel, *Through the Green Valley*, is a genre novel, a historical romance about Ireland. It is commercial fiction, pure and simple. Her second and best novel, *Falling Angels*, is set in a kind of suburban never-never land. The rites of passage of the three sisters who share the secret of their baby brother's death are narrated with verve. As they grow up and move out into the wider world, and as the early 1960s evolve into the late 1960s, the sisters' lives are channelled by global fashion: first Frank Sinatra and sex at drive-ins, then drugs, Bob Dylan and *The Tibetan Book of the Dead. Falling Angels* is readable and involving. The book has an appealing freshness; yet, paradoxically, it also suffers from a static, familiar quality. Events are dictated by social trends. At each stage, the reader knows what is coming next. Though it probably contributed to the novel's success, this dependence on mass cultural fads for narrative momentum creates a problem for the subsequent development of Gowdy's fiction. The social context into which Lou, Sandy and Norma move as they reach adulthood is defined not by place but by fashion; character, which always takes shape in part out of a reaction to a culture, dwindles to mass-media stereotypes: the fat lesbian, the skinny party girl. The 'downtown' – presumably Toronto – to which the sisters travel as they grow up has no existence beyond being a place of larger buildings. Gowdy's inability to imagine Canadian society breeds her repetition in three consecutive novels – *Falling Angels, Mister Sandman* and *The White Bone* – of the story of squabbling young females growing up together. Lacking a social context in which to move as adults,

Gowdy's characters are condemned to the repeated re-enactment of adolescence.

Gowdy's most 'Canadian' novel, *Mister Sandman,* is also her weakest. Here the names of Canadian cities, such as Toronto and Vancouver, and recognizable institutions, such as *Maclean's* magazine and York University, are allowed to blot the page. Yet these places are not evoked or engaged with: pop culture – U.S. pop culture – furnishes the novel with its reference points, including its title. Even the descriptions presume a prior familiarity on the reader's part with these U.S. pop icons: 'He folds his Paul Bunyan arms over his chest.' (Here one assumes Gowdy is alluding to the 1960s Paul Bunyan cartoons, rather than to the traditional figure of New England folklore.) Though this is Canada in the 1960s, there is no Diefenbaker, no flag debate, no Expo 67, no Trudeaumania, no Quebec separatism. The combination of U.S. pop culture with a few Torontonian references (Rosedale, Glenn Gould) incarnates the TorLit view of the world, illuminating the foundations of our increasingly Toronto-centred literature's inability to come to grips with a palpable, national reality. (It may also explain Gowdy's popularity among younger readers for whom global pop culture references are often the *only* cultural references.) Atwood's nationalism, for all the simple-mindedness of its exposition in *Survival,* enabled her to provide minimal grounding for her novels beyond the ebb and flow of trend; the characters, though hardly memorable, are projected against Canadian backgrounds sufficiently fully realized to endow them with a basic certitude of existence. And Atwood's rendering of the inseparable strands of place and character is feeble by comparison with that of some of her contemporaries. Reading Gowdy, the pungently particular worlds of Alice Munro, Mavis Gallant, Mordecai Richler or Margaret Laurence feel impossibly distant. The result is that Gowdy's familiar archetypes – fat lesbian sisters, thin nymphomaniac sisters, assorted freaks – act out a plot which, as a number of critics have noted, reads like a more awkward, sensationalistic rerun of *Falling Angels. Mister Sandman* ends where a good novel should begin, with the revelation of the skeletons in the family closet. The characters react to these revelations by walking out of the house and playing ball together. At this point, when the reader finally wishes to know what happens next, the book ends. The kind of complex human interaction that would be necessary to render the next stage in this family's life lies far beyond the scope of the kind of quick-sketch characterization in which Gowdy specializes.

Like *Falling Angels, Mister Sandman* is full of freaks. Philip Marchand has argued in detail that Gowdy's freaks, like those of Atwood, are people with whom Gowdy does not feel 'any kinship at all'. This failure of novelistic compassion – playing the outsider for laughs – is symptomatic of southern Ontario Wasp primness, with its famously double-edged, Atwoodian attitude towards the authority of fashion. Outsiders, in this view, are mad, bad and dangerous to know, hence portraying freaks invests a writer like Atwood or Gowdy with 'cutting edge' credentials. At the same time, people who step outside the bounds are showing that they do not understand how to follow the rules, and for this lapse in propriety they are to be spurned with chilly parody or tight-lipped irony. The writer makes hay from her proximity to freaks, but she does not, in a novel aspiring to portray social reality, actually adopt their point of view. Yet the flimsiness of Gowdy's engagement with Canadian society – the point at which her work diverges from that of Atwood – means that she needs to develop a context where her personal archetypal patterns – mainly revolving around sisters and coming-of-age rites – can acquire sufficient density to sustain a novel. It was only a matter of time before her work veered into fantasy of a sort that permitted her to denounce human society in its totality as freakish.

In *The White Bone,* narrated from the perspective of African elephants being hunted to the verge of extinction, Gowdy adopts the people-are-animals-and-animals-are-people formula that has made Timothy Findley's work so popular. No one can dislike an animal; if animals denounce society as awful, it *must* be true. The origin of this stance lies in Atwood's statement in *Survival* that if *Moby-Dick* had been written by a Canadian it would have been told by the whale. In the 1970s this assertion was interpreted as suggesting an inherent Canadian affinity with the natural world; in light of the careers of Findley and Gowdy, one needs to consider whether it does not in fact stem from a post-colonial élite's legacy of disdain for its unwashed fellow subjects that continues to this day to infect Wasp Toronto. Drafting animals to sneer at your fellow citizens muffles the moral repercussions of sneering at them yourself.

The White Bone, though overly long, excessively worthy in the way only a middlebrow Canadian novel can be and ultimately rather dull, is written in a controlled, disciplined prose style. The novel contains moments of authentic power, such as the slaughter of Mud's family by the ivory hunters. The depiction of men hacking off the elephants' faces to get their tusks succeeds as an inversion that elucidates human brutality. But as the novel progresses, the identity of these elephants grows increasingly ambiguous. *The White Bone* opens with eleven pages of maps, genealogies and elephant vocabulary that would put the most diligent fantasy writer to shame. In the novel's first hundred pages Gowdy's approach, like Jack London's approach in *White Fang* or *The Call of the Wild*, seems to be to employ the scientific theories of her time to describe the instinctual activities of animal protagonists. Mud, the adolescent heroine, is initially a believable elephant. But, after the massacre, all this changes. The elephants become Victims. As such, they must be humanized. The interactions of the young female elephants begin to mimic the psychological tensions between the sisters in *Falling Angels* and *Mister Sandman*:

She-Snorts and She-Screams, when they start in on each other, are no less irritating, She-Screams especially, but shouldn't She-Snorts know better? Much as Mud resents She-Screams for resenting her, she doesn't gloat when She-Snorts mocks or otherwise offends the ridiculous cow. Had Mud any authority she would ask She-Snorts to *pretend* to indulge She-Screams, as She-Sees used to.

This is Tolkien infused with the tangled rivalries of adolescent girls. Gowdy's elephants are hobbits afflicted by dyspepsia. The problem here is that even highly intelligent mammals such as elephants act according to instinct rather than moral choice; this makes them poor subjects for drama. By the novel's closing sections the elephants are, out of dramatic necessity, thinking like people: 'It occurs to her [i.e. Mud] that it is madness for four cows and a calf to be risking themselves in an almost hopeless search for a single calf.' It *is* madness. It is not believable that animals programmed for group survival would commit such folly. While they would certainly notice a calf's disappearance and search for it, portraying them as risking group survival in the interests of an individual ushers in anthropomorphism. But failure to look for the lost calf would render the elephants inhuman, making them unworthy objects of sympathy and challenging the reader to identify with creatures whose morality is severely different from that of a middle-class Toronto reader – and this identification with difference, in Gowdy's fiction as in Atwood's, is the line that cannot be crossed. One must remain within the bounds of decent society, even while mocking society's assumptions. By the novel's close, the elephants are no longer elephants, but a kind of intermediate creation: lovably intrepid Disneyesque cuties, distant cousins of Timothy Findley's Mottyl the Cat. Like teddy bears, these elephants can be sold all over the world. *The White Bone*'s retreat into fantasy fuels its global commercial success. But do not look here for 'indubitably Canadian' fiction.

Is it still possible to write a novel about Canada? Russell Smith's *Noise* grapples with the problem more directly than any other Canadian novel of the 1990s. The plot, insofar as one exists, deals with the attempts of James Willing, a Toronto freelance journalist, to sell to a New York magazine called *Glitter* a profile of Ludwig Boben, a CanLit writer bearing a suspicious resemblance to Rudy Wiebe. (Born in the prairies of Germanic roots, Boben, like Wiebe, has written novels about the Riel rebellion, and has won the 'Responsible Fiction Award' for work about the Arctic, as Wiebe won the 1994 GG for his Arctic novel, *A Discovery of Strangers* – beating out Smith's novel *How Insensitive*, which was also shortlisted that year.)

Willing, as his name suggests, is a slave of fleeting fashions. Smith's ambivalence about the decline of CanLit and the rise of TorLit permeates the novel. The CanLit writer Boben is satirized as an incoherent drunk and denounced as a 'fucking asshole'; a famous 'prairie recluse', he turns out to be secretly living in the Toronto commuter-belt, confirming the dictum that 'most writers live in Toronto'. Yet at the same time that Smith insists on Toronto's centrality and cultural superiority to the rest of the country, he launches a despairing assault on the mindless din of big-city vacuity and personality-based journalism. Willing is morosely aware of the impact on literature of the globalized entertainment industry which he himself exemplifies. Explaining Boben's significance to his dippy photographer Nicola, Willing says: 'It used to be that you could get a lot of recognition by writing about Canada, as long as it was about small towns and nature.' He points out that this has changed. In an apparent allusion to the international success of Rohinton Mistry and Anne Michaels, Willing says: 'Nowadays you can win big contracts and even awards and prize money if you write big fat books about starving people in other parts of the world, or the Holocaust or something.' In response to Nicola's incomprehension, Willing sums up: 'Novels are like movies now. They can't be about things here.'

The recognition comes wrapped in bitterness. As Smith's obsession with the local minutiae of Toronto artistic life has so far blocked his own entry to the foreign-rights bonanza, it is not surprising that the novel's conclusion pivots on the unacceptability of intransigently Canadian detail to the international market. Willing sells his Boben article to *Glitter*, but the magazine performs a radical edit, eliminating all references to Boben's Canadian citizenship and residence and substituting 'Alaska' for all references to the Canadian Arctic. Publication in the United States, even in this butchered form, consolidates Willing's reputation in culturally subservient Toronto, where his newly exalted status as a writer who has published in New York enables him to bully an editor into giving him a classical music column that will preserve both his solvency and his intellectual integrity.

The wish-fulfilment conclusion fails to nullify *Noise*'s harsh insights. If Smith portrayed Toronto in wavering, grandiose images like Anne Michaels or the Michael Ondaatje of *In the Skin of a Lion*, or if, like Barbara Gowdy, he defined his characters against an otherwise unevoked background of U.S. pop culture references, his fiction might overleap the 'too Canadian' hurdle. It is his adherence to local detail – the detail crucial to bringing his characters to life – that maroons him without foreign rights. Yet Smith's identification with downtown Toronto places him at a disadvantage when the few remaining crumbs in the CanLit larder are being distributed. The rural and the regional seem to maintain their edge in the allocation of the Governor General's Awards. Smith's lament may be plaintive, and out of tune with *Noise*'s viciously knowing surface, but no other Canadian novelist has confronted more directly the tensions between the local and the global currently hobbling our longer fiction.

The local can be merely local colour, but keen observation of such detail is also the vital first step on the road to literary universality. It is not always evident during an author's lifetime which is which. The subject has been hotly debated in a number of literary cultures. Argentine literature during the 1920s and 1930s, for example, was marked by a rupture between writers who piled on local detail in an indiscriminate, naturalistic way and writers who selected these details more carefully, in the search for avant-garde forms capable of generating universal mythologies out of local history. The leading exponent of this latter wing of Argentine literature was Jorge Luis Borges, whose short stories continue to be read around the world. The contemporary Argentine writer Beatriz Sarlo points out that in his essays and book reviews of the 1920s and 1930s, 'Borges discusses many times which is the acceptable localism and which the unacceptable, in what way one, leaning towards local colour, is a vestige of the past, while the other, rejecting the well-worn tracks of the old localism, is a formal aesthetic invention ushering in "the new".'

To make the work new, the writer must ransack his own mythologies. Without a commitment to local detail, there can be no artistic innovation. (Nadine Gordimer has argued that to achieve 'artistic truth' the writer must be implicated in the world she is describing). Fleeing North York for the Holocaust or Cabbagetown for Tuscany will engender art only if you carry your local detail with you and deploy it in a pattern no one has thought of before; but the odds are that art is more likely to ambush the writer in the town where she has lived for most of her dreary life. The equation of foreign settings with 'sophistication' is merely the latest chapter in the Canadian epic of perpetually forestalled literary innovation. 'Newness' in Canadian fiction over the last forty years has been expressed in terms of new subject matter rather than new literary approaches. Every time innovation threatens, Canadian writing skirts artistic engagement by setting out on a detour into material previously marginalized. Where other literatures have capitalized on this integration of new material to force fresh contours on literary art, Canadian writing has turned to new subject matter in order to repeat and conserve the same old narrative techniques. During the 1990s the trend for immigrant writing merged seamlessly into the trend for foreign settings without leaving a ripple of fresh invention on the surface of Canadian prose.

The decade closed with a curious return to traditional Canadian material. Alistair MacLeod's surprise best-seller *No Great Mischief,* Bonnie Burnard's Giller-winning *A Good House* and Matt Cohen's *Elizabeth and After,* which won the Governor General's Award for English Fiction – the major works of 1999 – all mark a return to Canada. But in what guise? MacLeod's novel owes much of its success to its nostalgic evocation of a vanishing Celtic traditional culture from which many Canadians claim descent. A fine short story writer, MacLeod is a less accomplished novelist, and certainly not an innovative one. Burnard's *A Good House,* written in a brusque, almost point-form version of narrative summary containing few dramatized scenes, seems to me to render the past appealing by actively falsifying it. The novel's relentless wholesomeness, in which every parent is sensitive, every accident brings a family together, every girlfriend helps wash the dishes and hard-bitten, religious rural Ontarians of the 1950s speak openly and honestly of their sexuality, romanticizes and distorts the family and community of a bygone era. The traditional cultures of the past – in any country – provided a stronger sense of identity at the cost of limiting the individual's freedom and self-expression. Rural Ontario, even in the 1970s when I was growing up there, was notable for puritanical uncommunicativeness. Burnard's novel portrays the rural past as enjoying both the cultural security of intact traditions *and* the relatively painless interpersonal communication of the 1990s. The book is a mushy, odious lie. It softens reality's edges, obviating the hard choice between identity-at-the-cost-of-individual-freedom   and   freedom-at-the-cost-of-cultural-security that abides at the core of our era. The novel's flat prose and paint-by-numbers characterization are the outcome of this central hypocrisy. Matt Cohen's *Elizabeth and After* commits no such distortion. A relentless account of the decay of traditional eastern Ontario life before the onslaught of globalized commerce and right-wing populism, this book sparked my admiration when I returned to Canada after a long absence and could find no other Canadian fiction that brought to life the dramatic changes I saw around me. Cohen's ambition in tackling such a large subject as the alteration of Canadian society at a time when it was profoundly unfashionable to do so still strikes me as exemplary. My initial enthusiasm for the book has waned, however, as I have become more impatient with its melodrama and often clichéd writing. What remains is a temporal structure more intricate than those to be found in most other Canadian novels and an unfulfilled gesture in the direction of a route combining local detail, historical engagement and structural inventiveness that the Canadian novel might follow towards greater achievement – if it is able to do so.

· · ·

In the weeks following the publication of Gustave Flaubert's *The Sentimental Education*, that divine bridge between the nineteenth- and the twentieth-century novel, the author sent copies to his friends. Most of them did not reply: they found the novel embarrassing. Discussion in the French press was paltry and negative. The book sank into obscurity. Years passed before *The Sentimental Education* was recognized as a major work of literature.

Literary history abounds with *Sentimental Education*s. Each such case is a warning against extrapolating excessively from John Irving's observations about the literariness of the 'book business in Canada'. It is the 'book business' and not *literature* that Irving was discussing. Rarely in history have the most striking literary works been a country's best-sellers; it would be folly to assume that this is the case in contemporary Canada. Leonard Woolf made this point when he wrote:

Novels by serious writers of genius often eventually become best-sellers, but most contemporary best-sellers are written by second-class writers whose psychological brew contains a touch of naïvety, a touch of sentimentality, the story-telling gift, and a mysterious sympathy with the day-dreams of ordinary people.

It would be equally destructive, though, to lapse into the Romantic myth of the author as misunderstood genius, replete with visions of the tortured artist dying of starvation-consumption-AIDS in a garret-squat-rooming house and leaving behind an unappreciated manuscript of soaring genius. This does not happen. Significant writers may not be best-sellers, but they usually have a profile during their own lifetimes. It is possible for a writer to alienate his audience by opting for a particularly forbidding viewpoint or aesthetic. Herman Melville, who with the publication of *Typee* established himself as a popular writer of South Seas adventures, chiselled away at his Manifest Destiny–besotted

American audience with the pessimistic fables of *Moby-Dick* and *The Confidence Man* until the overwhelming negative reaction reduced him to silence. Melville is remembered today for a part of his *oeuvre* that was unpopular during his lifetime. Even so, he had his readers. The Romantic myth ('artists are neglected in their own lifetimes'), like the conformist myth ('in Canada the literary writers are the best-sellers'), conspires to hide the disturbing truth that the market-driven elimination of the mid-list writer and the marginalization of the literary presses have done away with the zones where many good but not highly commercial writers linger for much of their careers. Our future classics may be among these writers. The destruction of the traditional refuges for less-commercial fiction threatens the foundations of our future literary canon.

But to have a canon we will have to write good books. The crucial obstacle to the extension of a significant novelistic tradition in Canada today lies in our inability to pull our own society into focus. In the absence of a firm engagement with our history, language, realities and myths, we cannot set sail on the tides of the globalized planet. One must first be independent before being able to probe the pleasures of interdependence. The rift dividing the self-confident approach to foreign settings demonstrated by *St. Urbain's Horseman*, *The Diviners* and the Deptford Trilogy from the no-name self-effacement of *Fugitive Pieces*, *The English Patient* and *The White Bone* reflects the shocks dealt to our sense of being, as individuals within a nation, between the 1970s and the 1990s. By covering up much of the old Canada, globalization has rendered our national realities more difficult to discern, articulate and dramatize. In his seminal essay 'Writing Canadian Fiction', Clark Blaise observes that among the Canadian writers of the generation preceding his who left Canada, those who went to Great Britain or Europe (Richler, Gallant, Laurence) sustained their writing careers, while those who went to the United States (Blaise gives the examples of Jack Ludwig and various scriptwriters) subsided into silence. Historically, almost no Canadian prose writer has continued to write literary fiction during a prolonged residence in the United States. The two semi-exceptions to this rule, Robert Kroetsch and Douglas Glover, both resided in upstate New York, close to the Canadian border, and made frequent trips back; both are exceptionally cerebral writers whose fiction derives more from theories and other fiction than from the details of lived experience; and Glover, at least, has been noticeably less prolific since settling in the U.S. (As has Blaise himself, who has lived most of his life in the U.S., but whose writing blossomed during his years in Canada.) My own experience confirms Blaise's suggestion: the only period of my life when I have not written fiction was when I was living in Pennsylvania. The power of U.S. mythology, with its insistence on both the distinctness and the 'normality' of U.S. life, makes a belief in the slightly askew reality of Canada exceptionally difficult to maintain, let alone embellish and reimagine in fictional form. The writer struggles against the predominant U.S. notion that Canada does not really exist, that it is 'just like us, only boring'. He comes to doubt the authenticity, and even the legitimacy, of his own private storehouse of eccentric Canadian experiences, memories and details – precisely the details necessary to bring to life a work of fiction. The advent of Free Trade, NAFTA and globalization, sanding down the rough-edged differences between the two countries' surface realities, has to some extent immersed all Canadian writers in the dilemma of the Canadian writer living in the United States. Our Americanization has made our own reality more remote to us, more difficult to evoke. This change, and our ineffectual artistic responses to it, must share with brute commercial pressures the responsibility for our current fondness for vague foreign settings.

A second important factor in our failure to feast fictionally on our own reality can be traced to the debilitation of the urban novel. Rural and regional realities currently being admissible primarily in antiquated, highly romanticized form – *No Great Mischief, A Good House* – literature has lost touch with the *contemporary* life of areas of the country that continue to hoard the residue of our history and traditional culture. Meanwhile, the new Canada is being forged in our multi-racial, multi-ethnic, multi-linguistic cities. But where are these big, synthesizing cities' big, synthesizing fictions? We have an immigrant novel, a minority novel, but, as yet, little in the way of Montreal, Toronto or Vancouver novels. The urban novels of the 1990s are self-consciously partial and limited in scope. M. G. Vassanji's *No New Land* deals with a specific immigrant community, Margaret Atwood's *The Robber Bride* focuses on prosperous, middle-aged, liberal-minded women of Wasp or Jewish heritage, the protagonists of Russell Smith's *Noise* have ultra-English names like James, Julian and Nicola, with the ethnic characters being relegated to bit parts as taxi drivers and uncouth peasant neighbours, Mordecai Richler's *Barney's Version*, bereft of francophone characters but for two subservient women, is defiantly out of touch with contemporary Montreal – defined, as Charles Foran wrote of Richler's earlier work, by a 'refusal to acknowledge a city's genuine make-up'. Some would argue that in an era of postmodern fragmentation the days when Charles Dickens could take a five-hour walk through London, inhale the sights, sounds and idiosyncrasies of the street and return to his writing desk to spill them out on the page are unrecoverable. Perhaps; a contemporary Dickens would require fluency in sixty languages to understand all the conversations he might overhear in downtown Montreal or Toronto. Yet each city retains an energy, a characteristic torturing of language, a manic linguistic flow that the writer could tap into in order to evoke evoke evoke – But such writing would require daring, and our infantile interdictions about representation and 'voice appropriation' have curtailed our willingness to venture out on imaginative limbs, to create characters rather than ideological stereotypes. (Here it is worth pointing out that even Gayatri Spivak, the founder of academic 'subaltern studies', once wrote: 'The intellectual's solution is not to abstain from representation.' If only some Canadians who imagined themselves to be her followers had heeded her advice!)

The representation furore, though largely over, haunts us still. Reading a novel as uninhibited as James Baldwin's *Another Country*, where black and white characters grapple in a welter of uncomfortable emotions and contradictory revelations, is a disconcerting experience for a contemporary Canadian reader. *Another Country*, published in 1962, contains a dozen passages whose gruelling honesty about the intersection of race and sex would make them unpublishable in contemporary Canada: the characters' experiences, on the street and in bed, annihilate every known liberal piety. The furious waves of feeling generated by Baldwin's refusal to recoil from his own thorny insights generate a wrenching work of literature unimaginable in our time and place.

In Canada the prohibitions against describing others or creating morally dubious characters from disadvantaged or minority backgrounds have not been dispatched so much as assimilated into our collective literary unconscious, where they continue to straitjacket our imaginations. This remains a major obstacle to the creation of a vital urban novel in Canada. There are some words Canadian readers of English simply are not allowed to read – these words, for example:

J'avais ce jour-là ma canne écossaise, qui est en chêne avec un pommeau en ivoire et un bout ferré. J'ai pris mon élan et j'ai frappé, de toutes mes forces! ...A la troisième tentative, le bout ferré l'a atteinte à la bouche. Ça a fait ploc! [That day I had my Scottish cane, which is made of oak, with an iron-tipped ivory pommel. I took a bound and I struck with all my strength.... On the third attempt, the iron tip hit her on the mouth. It made a plocking sound.]

The quote is from *L'Écureil noir*, by the Franco-Ontarian novelist Daniel Poliquin, translated into English by Wayne Grady as *The Black Squirrel*. The translation above is mine. Douglas & McIntyre, Poliquin's English-Canadian publisher, refused to print this scene, in which a blind narrator beats his girlfriend across the face with his cane. In English-speaking Canada, Poliquin was informed, the sight-challenged do not abuse the gender-challenged.

If only it were so! Until English-Canadian writers and editors feel comfortable with frank portrayals of the competition, enmity, resentment and even violence characterizing relations among different disadvantaged or minority groups in our cities there can be no synthesizing urban novel in Canada. Until frenetic commercialization, and the nostalgic reactions bred by it, relax their grip, there can be no rural or regional novel which surpasses dewy romanticization.

Can there be a Canadian novel?

It is possible that we are living in what is simply a bad time for literature (however lucrative it may be for commercial publishing). Canada, one might argue, was a dreary colonial country until the 1960s, when it finally began to find its way out from under a stifling second-hand Englishness. Literary light flickered, at varying degrees of intensity, for three decades before being extinguished by our economic assimilation into the United States, which has made us once again a dreary, colonized country whose culture of second-hand trends stymies artistic originality. Even writers of genius fight an uphill battle against an unfavourable environment: being born at the wrong time is all it takes to wreck an artistic career. It is probable that future readers, if they exist, will look back upon the trite commercial novels of our era with disdain. (It is also possible that within a few years a galaxy of palmpilots and PDF files will have transformed literary culture into something fleeting, flashy and Web-friendly, making any essay dealing with that long-winded linear dinosaur the *novel* about as relevant as a treatise on stained-glass technique in baroque cathedrals.)

There may be ways out. A country that no longer exists in spirit may still exist in literature: this is one of the lessons of German-language literatures. Robert Musil, Joseph Roth and Stefan Zweig were Austro-Hungarian novelists long after Austria-Hungary disintegrated; today Christa Wolf and Monika Maron remain East German novelists, though there is no longer any East Germany. Meanwhile, the English-language tradition is in upheaval, with Anglo-Indian and African writers shaking up many of the strictures that continue to swaddle most Canadian fiction. In Europe the emergence of major figures such as José Saramago and Harry Mulisch has revived in a more playful, approachable vein the novel of ideas, moribund since the death of Thomas Mann; this appears to have braked the advancing 'Updikeization' (as some had called it) of European fiction. Or we can cast our eyes back to the 1960s, when Latin American novels blended the social and historical sweep of the nineteenth century with the avant-garde ambitions of the twentieth through a ferocious, mythologizing commitment to local history – a process which is continuing, or being recapitulated, today in the work of novelists as varied as the Martinican Patrick Chamoiseau, the Mozambican Mia Couto, the Angolan Pepetela, the Turk Orhan Pamuk. Globalization should enable us to broaden our palette of artistic options, not force us to narrow it; by providing multiple perspectives against which to contrast our own experience, closer contact with other cultures can bring out unsuspected hues, crannies, eccentricities in our own lives. These, in turn, make artistic innovation inevitable.

Always must we honour the world with our attention and listen to the sound of the words.

Acknowledgements

I would like to thank the editors and conference organizers who invited, commissioned, assigned or pruned these pieces or their prototypes: Scott Anderson, Katherine Ashenburg, Terence Byrnes, Barbara Carey, Bryan Demchinsky, Lindsay Duguid, Kim Jernigan, Julie Mason, Judit Molnár, Elizabeth Renzetti, Tim Struthers, Glenda Turner, Dennis Walder. I am grateful to Tom Henighan, Marilyn Carson Henighan, Diana MacDonald and Robin MacDonald for sharing with me their ideas and impressions. I would like to thank Lisa Dalrymple for research assistance. I wish to thank my colleagues Daniel Chouinard, Dorothy Odartey-Wellington and Gordana Yovanovich for helping me to arrange my teaching schedule in a way that has enabled me to continue writing, and my colleague François Paré for introducing me to Jacques Ferron's *L'Amélanchier*. I am also indebted to a number of Canadian readers and writers who provided me with insights and information but preferred not to be mentioned in these acknowledgements. I am grateful to Doris Cowan for her excellent editing. My greatest debt is to John Metcalf, whose commitment to literary debate extends to the encouragement of writers with whom he may not agree. Without John's enthusiasm for writing, and writing about writing, this book would not exist.

Stephen Henighan is the author of four books of fiction, including the novel *The Places Where Names Vanish* (Thistledown, 1998) and the short story collection *North of Tourism* (Cormorant, 1999), which was selected as a 'What's New What's Hot' title by indigo.ca. His short fiction has been published in more than thirty journals and anthologies in Canada, Great Britain, Europe and the United States, and has been taught in university courses in Canada, the U.S. and France.

Henighan's literary journalism has appeared in *The Times Literary Supplement,* the *Globe and Mail,* the *Montreal Gazette,* the *Ottawa Citizen* and many other publications. He has published scholarly articles on literature in major international journals such as *The Modern Language Review, Comparative Literature Studies* and the *Bulletin of Hispanic Studies.*

Lecturer in Spanish at University College, Oxford and Lecturer in Hispanic Studies at Queen Mary and Westfield College, University of London, Stephen Henighan has also taught English as a Second Language in Colombia and Moldova, and Creative Writing at Concordia University, the Maritime Writers' Workshop and the University of Guelph. He currently teaches Spanish-American literature and culture in the School of Languages and Literatures, University of Guelph.